GH00982656

Goforth of CHINA

JONATHAN GOFORTH
1925

Goforth of CHINA

by
Rosalind
Goforth

DIMENSION BOOKS
Bethany Fellowship, Inc.
Minneapolis, Minnesota

This edition contains the full text of
the original edition, first published in 1937
COPYRIGHT 1937
ZONDERVAN PUBLISHING HOUSE
PRINTED BY SPECIAL ARRANGEMENT

DIMENSION BOOKS are published by
Bethany Fellowship, Inc., 6820 Auto Club Road
Minneapolis, Minnesota 55438
Printed in the United States of America

ISBN-0-87123-181-6

INTRODUCTION

DR. GOFORTH was one of the most radiant, dynamic personalities that ever enriched my life. God's missionary program of the past half-century would not have been complete without him; the literature of missionary biography would be sadly lacking without this story of his life and work. He towers as a spiritual giant among God's missionary heroes of his generation.

He was an electric, radiant personality, flooding his immediate environment—wherever he might be—with the sunlight that was deep in his heart and shone on his face because his life was "hid with Christ in God." For some twenty years I had the privilege of knowing this man of God intimately—at conferences in America, in the mission field in China, in his home in Toronto, and in my home in Philadelphia. In all these places the rare sunshine of his presence abides as an undying memory.

With the sunshine of God's love in his heart there was an irresistible enthusiasm and a tireless energy. Nothing could stop his dynamic drive in that to which God had commissioned him. It was the same when he was seventy-seven as when he was fifty-seven. The loss of his eyesight during the last three years of his life did not halt the energy—it seemed only to heighten it. When this providence of God was permitted, after forty-eight years of missionary service, the undaunted apostle of the Gospel said to a newspaper reporter: "Bless you my boy, I'd go back for another forty-eight years if my sight were only good."

But Dr. Goforth's radiant smile and brilliant spirit did not mean indifference to the dark side of life, its

stern realities and the sinister attacks of the Adversary
With his warmth and love there was also keenest dis
cernment of the falsehood of Modernism, and an un
swerving, undying intolerance of all that sets itsel
against the Word of God. The sharply defined issu
between Modernism and Fundamentalism in the for
eign mission field was coming to the front in the sum
mer of 1920, when Mrs. Trumbull and I had an un
forgettable visit with Dr. and Mrs. Goforth in thei
home at Kikungshan. Dr. Goforth told me, with fir
in his eye and his heart, of the inroads on missionar
testimony being made by missionaries who were betray
ing the faith and substituting eternally fatal poison fc
the Gospel and the Word. Always he stood like Gibra
tar, steadfast and uncompromising for the old fait
which is ever new; and that is another reason wh
God so abundantly blessed his ministry to the ver
hour of his death.

First, last, and always Dr. Goforth was an eva
gelist, a soul-winner. That is what he went to the fo
eign mission field for; no other interest, no other a
tivity, no other ministry appealed to him. The Scri
ture that comes to one, in thinking of Jonathan Gofort
is that other great missionary's inspired word: "No
then we are ambassadors for Christ, as though God d
beseech you by us: we pray you in Christ's stead, be
reconciled to God" (II Cor. 5:20).

His life-long, unflagging, persistent and import
nate zeal in giving the Gospel to the unsaved was a r
buke to the many missionaries who turn aside from t'
only missionary call God ever gives to take up sid
issues and who thus drop out of God's great progra
for evangelizing a lost world. Being "not ashamed
the Gospel of Christ," and knowing that "it is the pow

of God unto salvation to every one that believeth," Dr. Goforth believed in God's revival power. God used him in mighty revivals over and over again through his long life; and there would be more revivals among God's children who have lost their first love if there were more witnesses like Dr. Goforth.

Dr. and Mrs. Goforth were given of God to each other. It was a marriage of rare beauty, fellowship, and unity in faith and work. They were a rich blessing to all who entered their home in China, in Manchuria, or in Canada, and they brought a rich blessing into every home they entered. When Mrs. Goforth's hearing was impaired, Dr. Goforth was ears for her; and she, in his blindness, was eyes for him. But no physical weaknesses or limitations ever stopped their enthusiastic labors in winning souls for their Lord. May He bless this life-story to the raising up of many to walk in their footsteps, till the Lord come.

CHARLES G. TRUMBULL

Philadelphia, Pa.

FOREWORD

NINE MONTHS ago, a few days after my husband had passed "beyond the veil," the conviction came to me that I had survived him for the writing of his life-story. In the days that followed, the Lord undertook for me in such a remarkable way as to leave no room for doubt but that "the good hand of my God" was leading me to undertake the work. A Christian lady, Mrs. S. H. Blake, gave me a quiet, ideal refuge in her home while engaged in the work: her fellowship and encouragement contributed in no small measure to the accomplishment of the task. My son Frederic rendered invaluable aid in collecting data.

A second imperative need was for someone to help in the clerical work. But before this need was actually felt, a Christian young woman, Mrs. F. O. Maddock, daughter of China Inland missionaries, offered her services as stenographer. On my asking her charges, she opened her eyes a little wider as she smilingly said, "I am undertaking this as a ministry for the Lord, not for pay." So all through the months following, her work was as unto the Lord. She has been indeed a God-given companion and helper over many hard places.

But that which gave courage and lasting inspiration for the writing of these memoirs was the following:

One evening I sat in front of the trunk containing my husband's diaries, letters, and other private papers. I had unlocked the trunk and then gave myself up to a feeling of utter despair at the magnitude of what I was facing. My advanced age alone seemed to make it impossible. I came almost to the point of giving up all thought of attempting the work when on opening the trunk I found on top of a pile of old Christmas cards a card of which the following is an exact duplicate—

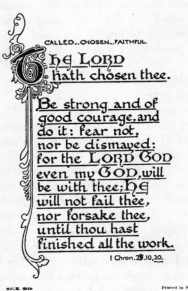

CALLED...CHOSEN...FAITHFUL

The LORD hath chosen thee.

Be strong and of good courage, and do it: fear not, nor be dismayed: for the LORD GOD even my GOD, will be with thee; He will not fail thee, nor forsake thee, until thou hast finished all the work.

I Chron. 28.10,20.

Printed in England

What could I do in face of such a timely and wonderful message, but just go forward in faith believing for the Divine strength and wisdom and power needed and promised?

It is with a heart filled with deepest gratitude and thankfulness to my faithful Almighty LORD for His continued grace and strength throughout the writing of the story that I now commit it unto Him to be used for His glory.

ROSALIND GOFORTH

CONTENTS

I.
1859 - 1887

II.
1888 - 1900

III.
1901 - 1925

IV.
1926 - 1936

ILLUSTRATIONS

I.
1859 - 1887

. . . Behold your calling, brethren, how that not many wise . . . not many mighty, not many noble, are called: But God chose the foolish things of the world . . . and the things that are despised did God choose . . . THAT NO FLESH SHOULD GLORY BEFORE GOD.

THE APOSTLE PAUL

1.

· EARLY LEADINGS

Even a child is known by his doings.

PROVERBS 20:11

IT IS the sincere desire of the writer of these memoirs that they be both written and read with the lesson of Jonathan Goforth's favorite story in mind. The story is as follows: While the Goforths were attending a summer conference, south of Chicago, it was announced that a "brilliant speaker" was to come on a certain day for just one address. A very large expectant audience awaited him. The chairman introduced the speaker with such fulsome praise there seemed no room for the glory of God in what was to follow. The stranger had been sitting with bowed head and face hidden. As he stepped forward he stood a moment as if in prayer, then said:

"Friends, when I listen to such words as we have just been hearing I have to remind myself of the woodpecker story: A certain woodpecker flew up to the top of a high pine tree and gave three hard pecks on the side of the tree as woodpeckers are wont to do. At that instant a bolt of lightning struck the tree leaving it on the ground, a heap of splinters. The woodpecker had flown to a tree near by where it clung in terror and amazement at what had taken place. There it hung expecting more to follow, but as all remained quiet it began to chuckle to itself saying, 'Well, well,

well! who would have imagined that just three peck
of my beak could have such power as that!'"

When the laughter this story caused ceased th
speaker went on, "Yes, friends, I too laughed whe
I first heard this story. But remember, if you or
take glory to ourselves which belongs only to Almight
God, we are not only as foolish as this woodpecke
but we commit a very grievous sin for the LORD hat
said, 'My glory will I not give to another.'"

Many times Jonathan Goforth on returning fror
a meeting would greet his wife with, "Well I've ha
to remind myself of the woodpecker tonight," or, "I'v
needed half a dozen woodpeckers to keep me in place.
Early in life he chose as his motto, "Not by might no
by power, but by my spirit" (Zech. 4:6). It was re
marked that of the many wonderful tributes paid t
the memory of Jonathan Goforth at that last triumphar
service following his translation, there was not one bu
could be traced back to the abounding grace of God i
him.

Dr. Andrew Bonar wrote of Murray M'Cheyne
"All who knew him not only saw in him a burning an
a shining light but felt also the breathing of the hidde
life of God; *and there is no narrative that can full*
express this peculiarity of the living man." Thes
words might truly have been written of Jonathan G
forth. He was God's radiant servant always. Of a
the messages which reached his wife after he had er
tered the gloryland, none touched her as the followin
A poor Roman Catholic servant girl in the home whe
the Goforths had often visited, on hearing of his pas
ing said to her master, "When Dr. Goforth has bee

here I have often watched his face and have wondered *if God looked like him!*" That dear girl saw in his face, sightless though he was, what she hoped for in her Heavenly Father!

————o————

John Goforth came to western Ontario, Canada, from Yorkshire, England, as one of the early pioneers in 1840. His wife was dead. He brought with him his three sons, John, Simeon, and Francis. Francis married a young woman, named Jane Bates, from the north of Ireland. They settled on a farm near London, Ontario. Of their family of ten boys and one girl, Jonathan was the seventh child. He was born on his father's farm, near Thorndale, February 10, 1859.

Those were hard, grinding times for both father and mother, and for the boys, as one by one they were able to help by working out at odd jobs with neighboring farmers. There are those still living who remember how "the Goforth boys were diligent, hard working lads." The hardships endured by the Goforth family, and indeed other pioneers of those early years, may be glimpsed by the following told in later years by Jonathan himself: "I remember my father telling of his having tramped through the bush all the way from Hamilton to our home near London, a distance of seventy miles, with a sack of flour on his back."

When Jonathan was but five years of age, he had a miraculous escape from death. We quote from his diary:

"My uncle was driving a load of grain to market. I was to be taken to my father's farm some miles distant. The bags were piled high on the wagon, and a place was made for me just behind my uncle in a hole which was deemed perfectly safe. Suddenly, while driving down a hill, a front wheel sank deep into a rut, causing the wagon to lurch to one side. I was thrown out of my hole and started to slide down. Before my uncle could reach me I had dropped between the front and back wheels. The back wheel had just reached me, and I felt it crushing against my hip. At that same instant my uncle also reached me, but I was so pinned under the wheel he had difficulty in getting me free. A fraction of an inch farther and my hip would have been crushed."

The above was but the first of many remarkable deliverances from imminent death in Jonathan Goforth's life. In writing of those early years he says:

"My mother was careful in the early years to teach us the Scriptures, and to pray with us. One thing I look back to as a great blessing in my later life, was mother's habit of getting me to read the Psalms to her. I was only five years of age when I began this but could read easily. From reading the Psalms aloud came the desire to memorize the Scriptures which I continued to do with great profit. There were times when I could not find anyone with time or patience to hear me recite all I had memorized.

"From those earliest years I wanted to be a Christian. When I was seven years of age a lady gave me a fine Bible with brass clasps and marginal references. This was another impetus to search the Scriptures. One Sunday, when ten years old, I was attending church with my mother. It was Communion

Sunday, and while she was partaking of the Lord's Supper, I sat alone on one of the side seats. Suddenly it came over me with great force that if God called me away I would not go to heaven. How I wanted to be a Christian! I am sure if someone had spoken to me about my soul's salvation I would have yielded my heart to Christ then."

For almost ten "school" years Jonathan was under the great handicap of being obliged to work on the farm, from April till October or even November. We are told, however, "though naturally behind his schoolmates when returning to school in the autumn, by spring he could compete with the brightest."

The following striking picture of Jonathan as a schoolboy comes from the pen of Dr. Andrew Vining, a Canadian Baptist leader and one of Jonathan's early schoolmates:

"I remember Jonathan as cheerful, modest, courageous and honest, and I recall his constant sense of fairness, because my friendship with him began one day when he challenged and very effectively trounced a schoolhouse bully who had been making life unhappy for me, a younger and smaller boy. The years of his matchless service have given significance to one clear recollection I have of him. He had a habit of standing during recess in front of the maps which hung in the schoolroom. I clearly remember seeing him, day after day, studying these maps: the World, Asia, Africa. Many times since I have wondered if even as a boy there stirred within him a realization that his work was to lie in far-away places of the earth."

His father put Jonathan at the age of fifteen in charge of their second farm, called "The Thamesford Farm," some twenty miles distant from the home farm. His younger brother Joseph was to assist him. Of this responsible commission for a lad of his age, Jonathan wrote:

"I was ambitious to run my farm scientifically, and I was well rewarded for my pains for my butter always sold for the highest price in the London market. In farming and cultivating I consistently endeavoured to apply scientific methods and with gratifying results. In handing over the farm, Father had called special attention to one very large field which had become choked with weeds. Father said, 'Get that field clear and ready for seeding. At harvest time I'll return and inspect.'"

Jonathan, in later years, kept many an audience spellbound as he described the labour he put into that field. Ploughing and reploughing, the sunning of the deadly roots and again the ploughing till the whole field was ready for seeding; then how he procured the very best seed for sowing, and finally, he would tell of that summer morning, when just at harvest-time, his father arrived, and how his heart thrilled with joy as he led his father to a high place from which the whole field of beautiful waving grain could be seen. He spoke not a word—only waited for the coveted "well done." His father stood for several moments silently examining the field for a sign of a weed but there was none. Turning to his son he just smiled. "That smile was all the reward I wanted," Goforth would say. "I knew my father was pleased. So will it be if we are faithful to the trust our Heavenly Father gives us."

About this time an incident occurred which might well have ended fatally for the young lad. He was assisting at a neighbour's barn-raising, an affair sufficiently dangerous, at that time, to keep the women folk in suspense till all was over. Operations had reached the dangerous point when the heavy beams had one by one been hauled up and laid on the cross "bent." Jonathan was standing below these beams in the centre of the barn when a sudden cry rang out, "Take care, the bent is giving!" Looking up, he saw the beams had already started downward. There was no time to escape by running. There was but one thing to do—stand still and watch the beams as they fell and dodge between two. This he did, escaping unhurt.

While on the Thamesford Farm he became ambitious to study law and become a politician. After the evening chores were done he would walk miles to attend a political meeting. At the back of the home was a swamp. Here he would get out alone and practice speaking. Travellers on the highway some distance away could hear the voice. Being well versed on both sides of political situations, he was often the centre of heated discussions both at school and at home. "Mother would often say I should be a teacher," he has said, "but I argued the country needed *good* politicians!"

Jonathan Goforth was now getting well on in his eighteenth year. He was known as a "good lad, diligent, always ready to help others, eager to get an education (though this seemed, at times, hopeless), and he was liked by all for his happy, friendly ways"— but he was still an unawakened soul.

After taking a short commercial course in London, Ontario, Goforth returned to the old country school near his home, hoping to struggle through his high school there. The Rev. Lachlan Cameron, Presbyterian minister at Thamesford, visited the school regularly, holding Bible-study services with the pupils. Mr. Cameron was "a godly man, of strong convictions, tireless energy, and deeply concerned about the salvation of his flock."

Jonathan's marked proficiency in art penmanship, much in vogue at that time, attracted Mr. Cameron's attention. The lad, always responsive to kindness, took a great liking for the minister and determined to hear him in his own pulpit. One who was present at that first Sunday gives the following:

"Almost sixty years have passed since then but I can still see the young stranger sitting immediately in front of the minister with an eager, glowing look on his face and listening with great intentness to every word of the sermon."

It was Mr. Cameron's unvarying custom to close each sermon with a direct appeal for decisions. We give in Jonathan's own words what took place the third Sunday under Mr. Cameron:

"That Sunday, Mr. Cameron seemed to look right at me as he pled, during his sermon, for all who had not, to accept the Lord Jesus Christ. His words cut me deeply and I said to myself, 'I must decide before he is through.' But contrary to his usual custom, he suddenly stopped and began to pray. During the prayer the devil whispered, 'Put off your decision for another week.' Then immediately after the prayer, Mr. Cameron leaned over the pulpit and with great intensity and fervour again pled for decisions. As I sat there, without any outward sign except to simply bow my head, I yielded myself up to Christ."

How complete was that yielding can be seen by his after life, and also from the following dictated to a daughter on his seventy-fifth birthday:

"My conversion at eighteen was simple but so complete that ever onward I could say with Paul, 'I am crucified with Christ; nevertheless I live; yet not I but Christ liveth in me; and the life which I now live in the flesh I live by the faith of the Son of God who loved me and gave Himself for me' (Gal. 2:20). Henceforth my life belonged to Him who had given His life for me."

At the next Communion, Jonathan joined the church and at once began to seek avenues of service for his new-found Master. He was given a Sunday-school class but this did not satisfy him. He sent off for tracts and became an object of wonder to the staid old elders, something akin to bewilderment to others, and amusement to the young, as he stood Sunday after Sunday at the church door giving to each one a tract! Very soon he started a Sunday evening service in the old schoolhouse a mile or more from his home.

We give in his own words two incidents of this time:

"At the time of my conversion I was living with my brother Will. Our parents came on a visit, and stayed a month or so. For some time I felt the Lord would have me lead family worship. So one night I said, 'We will have worship tonight, so please don't scatter after supper.' I was afraid of what my father would say for we had not been accustomed to saying 'grace' before meals much less having family worship.

"I read a chapter in Isaiah and after a few comments we all knelt in prayer. Much to my relief, father never said a word. Family worship continued as long as I was home. Some months later my father took a stand for Jesus Christ."

The following occurred while he was attending high school in Ingersoll, twelve miles from the home farm:

"My teacher was an ardent follower of Tom Paine. He persuaded all the boys in our class to his way of thinking. The jeers and arguments of my classmates proved too much for me. Suddenly all the foundations slipped. I was confounded! Instead of going to my minister or any other human aid, I felt constrained to take the Word of God alone as my guide. Night and day for a considerable period of time, I did little else than search the Scriptures until, finally, I was so solidly grounded I have never had a shadow of a doubt since. All my classmates, as well as our teacher, were brought back from infidelity, the teacher becoming one of my lifelong friends."

Thus the Lord began to use him from the time of his conversion. But for one year he still retained his ambition of becoming a lawyer and a *good* politician, believing he could serve the Lord thus. His Master, however, had other plans for this servant of His.

One Saturday afternoon Jonathan had occasion to go with horse and buggy to see his brother Will, whose farm lay some fifteen miles distant. He remained over night, and early Sunday morning started homeward. As he was leaving, Will Goforth's father-in-law, Mr. Bennett, a saintly old Scot, handed Jonathan a well-worn copy of *The Memoirs of Robert Murray M'Cheyne,* saying, "Read this, my boy, it'll do you good." Laying the book on the seat beside him the young man drove off.

The day was one of those balmy, Indian Summer days in October. Jonathan had not gone far when remembering the book he opened it and began to read as he drove slowly on. From the first page the message of the book gripped him. Coming to a clump of trees by the roadside, he stopped the horse, and tethering it to a tree made a comfortable seat of dried leaves and gave himself up to the *Memoirs.* Hour after hour passed unnoticed, so great was his absorption in what he was reading. Not till the shadows had lengthened did he awake to how time had passed. He rose and continued his journey, but in those quiet hours by the roadside, Jonathan Goforth had caught the vision and had made the decision which changed the whole course of his life.

The thrilling story of M'Cheyne's spiritual struggles and victories, and his life-sacrifices for the salvation of God's chosen people, the Jews, sank deep into his very soul. All the petty, selfish ambitions in which he had indulged vanished for ever, and in their place came the solemn and definite resolve to give his life to the ministry, which to him meant the sacred, holy calling of leading unsaved souls to his Saviour.

That good man, Rev. Lachlan Cameron, greatly rejoiced on hearing of Jonathan's decision. At once arrangements were made for the young man to come regularly to the Manse for lessons in Latin and Greek in preparation for his entering Knox College. I have before me a list of the books which Goforth says himself he "devoured" at that time. Here it is: Spurgeon's *Lectures to His Students*; Spurgeon's *Best Sermons*; Boston's *Fourfold State*; Bagster's *Call to the Unconverted*; Bunyan's *Grace Abounding*, and Baxter's *Saint's Rest*.

The Bible was, however, even then, the *great* Book with him for he has left this record that for two years previously to his entering Knox College, Toronto, he rose two hours earlier each morning in order to get time for unbroken Bible study, before getting to work or off to school.

The story of Jonathan Goforth's call to foreign service we now give in his own words:

"Although I was clearly led to be a minister of the gospel, I rejected all thought of being a foreign missionary. All my thoughts and plans were for work in Canada. While attending high school in Ingersoll, studying Greek and Latin especially with a view to entering Knox College, I heard that Dr. G. L. Mackay, of Formosa, was to speak in Knox Church, Ingersoll. A schoolmate persuaded me to go with him to the meeting. Dr Mackay, in his vivid manner, pressed home the needs and claims of

Formosa upon us. Among other things, he said, 'For two years I have been going up and down Canada trying to persuade some young man to come over to Formosa and help me, but in vain. It seems that no one has caught the vision. I am therefore going back alone. It will not be long before my bones will be lying on some Formosan hillside. To me the heartbreak is that no young man has heard the call to come and carry on the work that I have begun.'

"As I listened to these words, I was overwhelmed with shame. Had the floor opened up and swallowed me out of sight, it would have been a relief. There was I, bought with the precious blood of Jesus Christ, daring to dispose of my life as I pleased. I heard the Lord's voice saying, 'Who will go for us and whom shall we send?' And I answered, 'Here am I; send me.' From that hour I became a foreign missionary. I eagerly read everything I could find on foreign missions and set to work to get others to catch the vision I had caught of the claims of the unreached, unevangelized millions on earth."

At last the time drew near for Jonathan Goforth to leave the old farm home for the new, untried city life at Knox College. His mother, noted among the neighbours for her fine needlecraft, worked far into the night putting her best effort on the finishing touches to shirt or collar for the dear boy who was to be the scholar of the family. Little did she dream how the cut of the clothes or the fineness of the stitches would be regarded later!

During the last days at home, Jonathan's heart was

thrilled as he thought how soon he was to live and work with other young men who, like himself, had given themselves to the most sacred, holy calling of winning men to Christ. He had visions on reaching Knox of prayer-meetings and Bible study-groups where, in company with kindred spirits, he could dig deeper into his beloved Bible. So his joyous, optimistic spirit had reached fever heat when he arrived in Toronto and entered Knox College.

II.

BEGINNING AT JERUSALEM

When he found his own soul needed Jesus Christ, it became a passion with him to take Jesus Christ to every soul.

SAID OF JONATHAN GOFORTH

ON ENTERING Knox College, Jonathan Goforth quite unconsciously carried upon him in an unmistakable manner, the then (over fifty years ago) city-despised earmarks of the country—the farm. He was unconventional to a degree, and utterly unacquainted with city habits and ways.

He had been but a very few days in his new environment when he became keenly conscious that his home-made garments would not pass muster in the college. He was very poor, depending entirely on his own resources, for he would not look to his father for help. Probably with a desire to economize as much as possible, he bought a quantity of material, intending to take it to a city seamstress to make into a new outfit. But before he could do so, the students got wind of it. Late that night a number came into his room, secured their victim, then cutting a hole at one end of the material (which was white), they put his head through and forcing him out into the corridor, made him run the full length up and down through a barrage of hilarious students.

The reader will say, "Just a harmless prank." Yes, perhaps so—let it pass at that. The story is included in this record because of the effect it had upon Jonathan Goforth's character. That night he knelt with Bible before him and struggled through the greatest humiliation and the first great disappointment of his life. The dreams he had been indulging in but a few days before had vanished, and before him, for a time at least, lay *a lone road*. Henceforth he was to break an independent trail. It is not hard to see God's hand in this, forcing him out as it did into an independence of action which so characterized his whole after life.

We feel deeply grateful for the following noble and illuminating letter of those early days at Knox from Dr. Charles W. Gordon, (Ralph Connor), a classmate of Jonathan Goforth's. The letter speaks for itself.

"Toronto, October 30, 1936.

"MY DEAR MRS. GOFORTH:

"Very recently came to me the tidings of your husband's death. The news stirs in me many memories . . . of my old and dear friend, Jonathan Goforth. It was during my college days, of course, that I first came to know him. He was then working in a downtown mission and many were the strange stories told by him. My first impression of him was that he was a queer chap—a good fellow—pious—an earnest Christian, but simple-minded and *quite peculiar*. I was then a student in the University of Toronto, and though a member of St. James Square Church, a regular attendant upon Dr. King's ministry, and a member of his very fine

Bible class. Yet Jonathan's earnest devotion to his work—mission work down in the slums of St. John's Ward—seemed to me as rather quaint. I was rather prominent in the athletic and literary circles of the college, and not personally or deeply interested in the saving of fallen women in St. John's Ward. Theoretically? Yes! Personally? No. But to Jonathan Goforth, the denizens of St. John's Ward were of those "poor and broken-hearted" to whom the young enthusiast of Nazareth felt Himself pledged.

"Jonathan Goforth in his enthusiastic innocence, aroused the amusement of his tablemates at dinner with his naive stories of his experiences in the Ward. His labors carried him into strange surroundings. He was too innocent to recognize a harlot when he saw her, or too pitiful to avoid her. His dinner-table tales sometimes amused, at other times annoyed, his fellow-students. His activities in the saving of the lost aroused in some a contempt for his simplicity. He became a subject for an 'Initiation Ceremony'; hailed at midnight before his judges, students of Knox College, he was subjected, I learned, to indignities, and warned against further breaches of good form by his tales of his 'experiences with sinners.' Goforth was deeply hurt, not so much for himself, but that such a thing should happen in a Christian college. He felt that so grievous a thing should be reported. He went to Principal Caven. The wise old saint soothed his hurt feelings, treated the 'Initiation Ceremony' as a silly prank of foolish boys, but took no official action. Jonathan, saddened and hurt, went on his way but learned his lesson that it avails little to 'cast pearls before swine.'

"The day came when honored by the whole body of students, he went forth to his mission to China, their representative supported by their contributions, and backed by their prayers, the first Canadian missionary to be supported in his work by his fellow-students. Twenty-five years later, in the great Missionary Convention in Massey Hall, gathered from all parts of Canada, cleric and lay, men and women, some thousands, acclaimed with grateful hearts, touched with the Divine fire that burned in the heart of their great champion among the hundred millions of Chinese, the services of Jonathan Goforth. The slogan of that meeting was "China for Christ, in this generation." It was my privilege and honour to speak that night for China to that great assemblage of enthusiastic Presbyterians. I remember saying that night *that it had taken twenty-five years to prove that Jonathan Goforth in his method and spirit as a missionary, was right, and that we who made light of him, were wrong.* . . .

"The characteristic features of Goforth were the utter simplicity of his spirit, the selfless character of his devotion, and the completeness of his faith in God. As I came to know him better, I came more and more to honour his manliness, his humility, his courage, his loyalty to his Lord, and his passion to save the lost. As I think of him today, my heart grows humble with the thought of his selfless devotion, and warm with love for him as one of my most honoured friends.

"I know well that the grief and loneliness will be swallowed up in your humble pride in him, in your glad thankfulness for *the grace of God in him that made him the great man, the great missionary, the great servant of Jesus Christ that he was.*

"Twenty-two, I think, were members of our graduating class; the great majority of them volunteered for service in the mission field at home or abroad. Not one of them, I am quite sure but would greatly love Jonathan Goforth and thank God for his influence on their characters and lives. . . .

"Very truly yours,
"CHARLES W. GORDON (Ralph Connor)"

We have glimpsed enough to understand something of what Jonathan Goforth went through during that first period at Knox. Suffice it now to add that without one exception, every student who had taken part in what had hurt and humiliated him during those early days at Knox, had, before he left the College, come to him expressing their regret.

On his very first day in Toronto, Jonathan Goforth walked down through the slum-ward, south of the college, praying that God would open the way for him to enter those needy homes with the gospel of Jesus Christ. The first Sunday morning was spent in visiting the Don jail, a practice he kept up throughout his whole college course. Until the warden came to know him, he was allowed only into the assembly hall. Then, when he had won the official's confidence, he was given liberty to go into the corridors.

One Sunday morning, as he was standing in the centre of the corridor, about to begin his address, a man burst out in a bombastic manner, "I don't believe there is a God." There was tense silence for a moment.

Then Jonathan walked over to the man's cell, and said in a very friendly way, "Why, my good friend, this Book I have here speaks about you." The man laughed incredulously. What could any book have to say about him? Goforth turned up Psalm 14, and read the first verse: "The fool hath said in his heart, There is no God." At that the whole corridor burst out laughing. Although he had intended to speak on another subject, he went ahead and spoke from the text just quoted. The men gave him close attention, and when he was through, all seemed to be under deep conviction and some were in tears. He then went from cell to cell, making a personal appeal to each man. Several came out definitely for Christ that morning.

For two years his work in the slums was in connection with the William Street Mission. Then he became city missionary for the Toronto Mission Union, a faith mission which guaranteed him no stated salary. His income therefore was very uncertain. Sometimes he had not sufficient to buy even a postage stamp. The four years of Goforth's life as city missionary of the Toronto Mission Union, gave him many opportunities to prove God's faithfulness in answering prayer for temporal needs. We give just two definite instances along this line.

The first was when one Saturday morning, as the hour drew near to settle with the housekeeper for his board, Jonathan felt greatly troubled, for he was then two weeks behind and had nothing with which to meet this debt. He then prayed definitely that the Lord might undertake for him, for he felt that it was not right to be in debt to anyone. As he prayed, a call came for him to preach in a certain place out of the city. He was obliged to leave at once, as there was barely time to catch the train. That Sunday something over seventeen dollars was given him, over and above his expenses—to him, an unheard-of thing. So, on his return to Toronto, he was able to pay his board up to date, with sufficient money over to meet some very pressing needs.

The second instance was when graduation time drew near. Goforth began to feel the urgent need for a good suit. He again prayed very definitely for this. One day, while walking down Yonge Street, the head of a well-known tailoring establishment, Mr. Berkinshaw, was standing in front of his shop and on seeing Goforth, he hailed him with, "Say, Goforth, you're the very man I'm looking for! Come in." A black suit of the finest quality was brought out. Goforth expostulated, saying, "I do need a suit, but this is too much for my pocket." Mr. Berkinshaw, however, insisted upon his trying on the suit. It fitted perfectly. "Now," said the tailor, "are you too proud to accept it as a gift? For it's yours for the taking. A customer of mine had the suit made but it didn't please him, so it was left on my hands." Then Jonathan told him of his felt need and prayer for a suit. The blessing that followed was two-fold—to the giver, that God had used him as His channel—and to the receiver, the strengthening of faith for this fresh token of God's faithfulness in answering prayer.

On each furlough, Goforth always dealt with that firm "as a debt of honour." Fifty years later, one of the first letters to reach Mrs. Goforth after her husband's

translation, was the following from Mr. Collier, the
then head of the same firm.

"One of 'God's gentlemen' has gone home to his
reward and what a reward it must be! If ever a
Christian gentleman trod this earth, Dr. Goforth was
one of the best. His religion and his love for helping others shone in his face!

"His true and simple faith in God was passed on
to others. As his Master, he went about doing good.
Jonathan Goforth is dead so far as this world is
concerned, but he is not dead, his spirit lives on not
only in the 'better world' but in the lives of those
whom he has touched here. We will never know
how far-reaching his ministry has gone—it will go
on and on, forever. You have lost a loving husband
and father and I and others have lost a wonderful
friend. I loved to have him come in and always
felt that I had met a good man who influenced my
life."

As I write, an interesting word-picture of those
student days at Knox College comes from an old elder
in Toronto who, for many years, has been Jonathan
Goforth's prayer-helper:

"On one occasion, Goforth was scheduled to speak
at a certain place on Sunday. When about to leave
for the station he found he had only sufficient money
to buy a ticket one station short of where he was to
speak. At once he decided to get his ticket to that
station and walk the rest of the way, a distance of
ten miles. This he did. When about eight miles
of his foot-journey had been covered he came upon
a group of road-menders sitting by the roadside.

Glad to rest he sat down among them. One offered him a "pull" from his whiskey flask! It was not long before he had the ears and hearts of his audience. On leaving he gave all a hearty invitation to his meeting the following day. To his great joy several of the men turned up. And at least one of these men decided for Christ that day."

Of Sunday-school work in the slums, Goforth writes:

"Sunday-school was a nerve-racking ordeal for the mission workers. Try as he might, the superintendent simply could not keep order. When he started to pray some of the boys would begin pitching their caps around in all directions. Groans and mocking 'amens' almost drowned out the superintendent's voice. One of the worst offenders among the boys was a little stunted Roman Catholic lad, named 'Tim.' One day Tim went over to a trough nearby and filled his mouth with dirty water. Creeping up behind me, he spued the contents of the water into the faces of the boys. In an instant the room was in an uproar, and only after great difficulty were the teachers able to get some kind of order again. And then Tim was in another part of the room, knocking the girls' hats on the floor. He went thus from one thing to another keeping the school in almost continuous turmoil. For more than a year we could do nothing with him.

"One winter afternoon, when the snow lay deep on the ground, I was walking along Queen Street when I spied Tim dragging a sleighful of coal across the street-car tracks. Deep trenches had been dug in the snow to enable the cars to run on the tracks. Tim's sleigh had got stuck in one of these trenches. A car was approaching and Tim, seeing it, tugged frantically this way and that, but to no avail. I ran forward to his assistance, and in a moment, the sleigh and Tim were safely out of the trench. He looked up into my face with a smile that spoke louder than words and in the next instant was gone. I never had any more trouble with Tim. He was on my side ever afterwards."

On weekdays, Jonathan spent much of his time visiting in the slum district. His strategy was to knock at a door, and when it opened a few inches, he would put his foot in the crack. He would then tell them his business and if, as was usually the case, they said they were not interested and went to close the door, his foot prevented the proceedings from being brought to an abrupt end. As he persisted, the people of the house almost invariably gave way and let him in. Of all the many hundreds of homes that he visited during his years of slum-work, there were only two where he definitely failed to gain an entrance.

While visiting in slum homes, Goforth would sometimes lead as many as three people to Christ in a single afternoon. Dr. Shearer, who accompanied him on his visits one day said, as they parted, "Goforth, *if only this personal contact could have been made with every human soul, the Gospel would have reached every soul long ago.*" He carried his message into all kinds of places, even brothels. He visited seventeen of these places on one street. It was his joy to be able to lead a number of the young women to Christ. Only once, during all his years of work, among this class of people, did he meet with flippancy and contempt.

One night as he was coming out from a street that had a particularly evil reputation, a policeman, a friend of his, met him. "How have you the courage to go into those places?" he asked. "*We* never go except in twos or threes." "Well, *I* never go alone, either," Goforth answered. "There is always Someone with me." "I understand," said the policeman. He was a Christian.

Goforth was returning to the college late one other night, from some ministry in the slum ward, when he noticed a light in a basement window. Always keen, not only to take advantage of opportunities but to make them, he tried the door beside the window and finding it unlocked walked in to face a group of gamblers. One of them asked his name. "Goforth," he replied. This so amused the men, they broke into hearty laughter. Cards were pushed aside and Jonathan was given a chance to preach Christ from his ever ready Bible.

At the beginning of a fall session at Knox College, Principal Caven asked Goforth how many families he had visited in Toronto that summer. "Nine hundred and sixty," was the reply. "Well, Goforth," said the Principal, "if you don't take any scholarships in Greek and Hebrew, at least there is *one* book that you're going to be well up in, and that is the book of Canadian human nature."

The experience which he had had in the slums of Toronto proved invaluable to Jonathan Goforth in after years, for he found Chinese human nature very much the same as Canadian human nature.

Goforth's first Home Mission field lay in the Muskoka district. He had four preaching points, Allensville, Port Sydney, Brunel, and Huntsville. The field was twenty-two miles long and twelve miles wide. He set out at once to visit every home in the whole area, regardless of denomination or creed, and this, so far as he knew, he succeeded in doing.

At Allensville, Port Sydney, and Brunel, Goforth's work soon began to show most encouraging results. The little frame buildings in which the services were held became too small to hold the people, many of whom had to walk miles to get to church. The people would be crowded in everywhere, even on the pulpit steps. Once, in his excitement, he flung his hand back and hit several people behind him, thus causing convulsions in the audience. A number of people, notably Tom Howard, one of the most notorious characters in the countryside, were led to Christ. This man broke right down in the middle of a service and confessed his sins. When Goforth discovered Howard had a fine voice, he appointed him to lead the singing. He would almost "raise the roof" with his intensity, the tears streaming down his cheeks.

How to reach the boys of Huntsville was from the beginning a problem with the young missionary. He could not persuade them to come to church, though he asked them often enough. One afternoon as the boys were playing baseball on the common across the river from the church, Goforth joined them. After a while the profanity became so bad, he dropped his bat and excused himself from the game. The boys were thereupon most apologetic and promised they would not offend again. After the game, the boys accompanied Goforth to the church where they spent an hour studying the Bible together. This continued almost every evening throughout the summer.

On one occasion while following the trail through a thick bush, when turning a sharp bend in the path he came face to face with a great bear just to one side of the path. The bear rose, sat back on its haunches, and stared. For brief moments, Goforth stood still and stared back at the bear. Then the thought came, "I'm on my Master's business and He can keep me." Going steadily but slowly forward, he had to almost touch the bear to pass him but the great beast made no sign of moving. When some distance on, he looked back and saw the bear walking slowly off into the bush.

The following letter gives a very "human" picture of Goforth on his first mission field.

"The year 1882 was a delight to the Presbyterians at Allensville. Father and mother, who were living in Huntsville, told me so much about the Spirit-filled young student they had, Mr. Jonathan Goforth. I was sitting with my baby on my knee one day when a young man came to the door and announced himself as Jonathan Goforth, Presbyterian student for Huntsville and Allensville. I invited him in and we talked over many things. He told me he was walking from Aspidin to Huntsville, a distance of some ten miles, and calling at every house, reading the Word of God and offering prayer if no objection was made. . . . Mr. Goforth read and then prayed for the baby and me and I think I sometimes feel the influence of that prayer even yet. After leaving us, he went on his way, carrying his friendliness and God's message to each home. . . . All through the years, here and there, I have met with kind remembrances of these evangelistic ministries. . . . I know his influence is still abiding in the lonely places of that pleasant country. . . . Oh, he came in the Spirit and power of the Holy Ghost."

Another writes of the same time: "The evangelist, Goforth, was young and slightly built, attracting everyone by his gentle humility and intense earnestness and Christlikeness." Mr. Alexander Proudfoot one of the Huntsville Church leaders reckoned that Goforth must have walked from sixteen to eighteen miles each Sunday, besides speaking three times.

III.

"MY LORD FIRST"

That in ALL *things He might have the pre-eminence.*
THE APOSTLE PAUL

IT SEEMS fitting, and as Jonathan Goforth himself would wish, that a loving tribute should here be paid to the memory of one whom he ever remembered and spoke of as "his guardian angel of the early years."

In the old log schoolhouse of West Nissouri, and later, for seven years in the building which took its place, Charlotte McLeod, leader among the girls, and Jonathan Goforth, the recognized leader among the boys, attended school together. It was but natural that between these two there should come to be an abiding friendship, which, as the years passed, ripened into something deeper. Miss McLeod was devoted to her church, the Baptist denomination, and always this, since Jonathan Goforth was a Presbyterian, seemed to her the one insurmountable barrier that kept her from joining her life with his. Soon after the Goforths sailed for China, Charlotte McLeod sailed for India, where for twenty-eight years, she gave devoted and loving service among the Telegus. She died in India, remembered by the natives as "the star-eyed missionary."

We come, now, to a very intimate story. The writer has pondered and prayed long before summoning the courage to give it, but many details later on in this record, can be better understood after knowing something of one, who for forty-nine years, was Jonathan Goforth's closest companion and the mother of his eleven children.

I was born near Kensington Gardens, London, England, on May 6th, 1864, coming to Montreal, Canada, with my parents three years later. From my earliest childhood, much time was spent beside the easel of my artist-father, who thought that I should be an artist. My education, apart from art, was received chiefly in private schools or from my own mother.

In May, 1885, I graduated from the Toronto School of Art and began preparations to leave in the autumn for London to complete my art studies at the Kensington School of Art. I was an Episcopalian. Those of you who have read thus far may wonder how I could have been the one of God's choice for such a man as Jonathan Goforth. The foregoing, however, is but half the picture. Here is the other side.

When twelve years of age, I heard Mr. Alfred Sandham speak at a revival meeting, on John 3:16. As he presented with great intensity and fervour, the picture of the love of God, I yielded myself absolutely to the Lord Jesus Christ and stood up among others, publicly confessing Him as my Master. On the way home from that meeting, I was told again and again how foolish it was for me to think I could possibly be sure that Christ had received me. So early the next morning, I got my Bible, given me by my godmother in England, and turning the pages over and over, I prayed that I might get some word which would assure

me Christ had really received me. At last I came to
John 6:37, "Him that cometh to me I will in no wise
cast out." These words settled that difficulty for I saw
clearly that this included all, even me.

Then another difficulty arose. I was told I was too
young to be received, and again I went to my Bible
and turned the pages to see if there was any message
to meet that problem, and I came, after searching a
long time to these words, "Those that seek me early
shall find me" (Prov. 8:17). On these two texts I
took my stand and have never doubted since then that
I was the Lord's child.

From that time, and increasingly as the years
passed, there seemed to be two elements contesting
within me, one for art, the other—an intense longing
to serve the Master to whom I had given myself.

In the early part of 1885, when still in my twentieth
year, I began to pray that if the Lord wanted me to live
the married life, he would lead to me one *wholly given
up to Him and to His service*. I wanted no other. One
Sunday in June, of that year, a stranger took the place
of the Hon. S. H. Blake, our Bible-class teacher. This
stranger, Mr. Henry O'Brien, came to me about the
hymns, as I was organist. Three days later, two large
parties were crossing the lake on the same boat, one,
an artists' picnic, bound for the Niagara Falls, the
other, bound for the Niagara-on-the-Lake Bible Conference. I was with the former group, but my heart was
right with the others who were evidently having a wonderful time of spiritual conference. That evening, all
returned on the same boat with the addition of a conference group who had crossed on the mid-day boat.

I was sitting in the artist circle, beside my brother, F. M. Bell-Smith, when Mr. Henry O'Brien touched me, saying, "Why, you are my organist of Sunday last! You are the very one I want to join us in the Mission next Saturday. We are to have a Workers' meeting and tea, and I would like you to meet them all." I was on the point of saying this was impossible, when my brother whispered, "You have no time. You are going to England." Partly to show him I could do as I pleased—what a trifle can turn the course of a life—I said to Mr. O'Brien, "Very well; expect me on Saturday."

As Mr. O'Brien turned to leave, he spied, and called to one who looked to me to be a very shabby fellow, whom he introduced as "Jonathan Goforth, our City Missionary." I forgot the shabbiness of his clothes however, for the wonderful challenge in his eyes!

The following Saturday found me in the large, square, workers' room of the Toronto Mission Union. Chairs were set all around the walls, but the centre was empty. Just as the meeting was about to begin, Jonathan Goforth was called out. He had been sitting across the corner from me with several people between. As he rose, he placed his Bible on the chair. Then something happened which I could never explain, nor try to excuse. Suddenly, I felt literally impelled to step across, past four or five people, take up the Bible and return to my seat. Rapidly I turned the leaves and found the Book worn almost to shreds in parts and marked from cover to cover. Closing the Book, I quickly returned it to the chair, and returning to my seat, I tried to look very innocent. It had all happened within a few moments, but as I sat there, I said to myself, *"That is the man I would like to marry!"*

That very day, I was chosen as one of a committee to open a new mission in the east end of Toronto, Jonathan Goforth being also on the same committee. In the weeks that followed, I had many opportunities to glimpse the greatness of the man which even a shabby exterior could not hide. So when, in that autumn he said, "Will you join your life with mine for China?" my answer was, "Yes," without a moment's hesitation. But a few days later when he said, "Will you give me your promise that *always* you will allow me to *put my Lord and His work first*, even before you?" I gave an inward gasp before replying, "Yes, I will, *always*," for was not this the very kind of man I had prayed for? (Oh, kind Master, to hide from Thy servant what that promise would cost!)

A few days after my promise was given, the first test in keeping it came. I had been (woman-like) indulging in dreams of the beautiful engagement ring that was soon to be mine. Then Jonathan came to me and said, "You will not mind, will you, if I do not get an engagement ring?" He then went on to tell with great enthusiasm of the distributing of books and pamphlets on China from his room in Knox. Every cent was needed for this important work. As I listened and watched his glowing face, the visions I had indulged in of the beautiful engagement ring vanished. This was my first lesson in *real values*.

The two years given to work in the East End slums, was of the greatest possible value in gaining experience which gave me a realization of my own personal responsibility towards my unsaved sisters. Of course, by this time, art had practically dropped out of my life, and in its place had come a deep desire to be a worthy life-partner of one so wholly yielded to his Divine Master, as I knew Jonathan Goforth to be.

IV.

THE VISION GLORIOUS!

OBEDIENCE *is the one qualification for* FURTHER VISION.

G. CAMPBELL MORGAN

EVER SINCE the night in Ingersoll when George Leslie Mackay's appeal for recruits for the foreign field touched him so deeply, Jonathan Goforth's heart was on fire for foreign missions. He lost no opportunity to press home the claims of the unevangelized masses of the earth. He compelled a hearing by the intensity of his enthusiasm. The following incident will show what persuasiveness he had in pleading the cause that was so dear to his heart.

He was sent out one Sunday to fill a pulpit, and as usual, spoke on missions. On the Monday morning, as the train was pulling out of the station, a man asked if he might share his seat. "I heard you preach on missions in our church yesterday," said this man. "When I heard that you were coming to speak on missions, I prepared myself with five cents for the collection. I usually give coppers on Sunday, but seeing that this particular collection was to go for missions, I decided that I couldn't think of giving less than five cents. Well, I went to church with my five cents. After you commenced speaking, I began to wish it were ten cents. A little later, and I thought a quarter too little. You were not half-way through till I wished I had a dollar bill, and by the time you finished, I would gladly have given a five-dollar bill."

Some months later, Goforth received a letter from this man's pastor in which he said, "I suppose you will remember having had a conversation with a certain member of my congregation on the train. Well, that man has since sold a piece of property and has given several hundred dollars of the proceeds to foreign missions."

The time came when Jonathan Goforth faced the problem of how he was to get to China, the field upon which his heart was set. His own church had no work in that country, and there seemed little prospect of her being induced to open a mission field there. So, although he would much have preferred to go out under his own Board, he began to look elsewhere for an appointment. Dr. Randal, of the China Inland Mission, when passing through Canada in 1885, had given Goforth a copy of Hudson Taylor's *China's Spiritual Need and Claims*. The book made a profound impression upon him and awakened in him a deep regard for the great Mission of which Hudson Taylor was the founder, a regard which grew stronger with the years. It was only natural, therefore, since there seemed to be no possibility of an opening, as far as his own church was concerned, that he should approach the China Inland Mission. This he did, sending in his application to the headquarters of the Mission in London. Thus, Goforth was the first one on the American Continent to offer for the China Inland Mission, his friend, Alexander

JONATHAN GOFORTH
1887

Saunders, being the second, sending as he did, his application some months later.

A month and more went by, and no answer came. (He found out, later, that his letter had gone astray). Nothing daunted, he wrote again. In a short time he received word that his application had been favourably received. In the meantime, however, his own fellow-students at Knox College learning of his plans, had started a movement which was to decide the question of the Board under which Goforth should work.

When Jonathan Goforth first entered Knox College, brimming over with missionary enthusiasm and anxious to tell everyone about it, his fellow-students set him down as a crank. But this did not cool his ardour, and his enthusiasm proved contagious. Gradually there developed among the student body a remarkable interest in the cause of foreign missions.

The movement at Knox was coincident with a revival of missionary interest throughout a large part of the Christian world. At the East Northfield Conference in 1886, the Student Volunteer Movement was set in motion. On the last day at Northfield one hundred young men and women announced their willingness to become missionaries. The movement spread in a truly amazing fashion through the universities and theological schools of the continent. President McCosh of Princeton said that "not since Pentecost had there been such an offering of young lives."

At Knox and in other Canadian Colleges, daily prayer-meetings for missions were started. In the winter of 1886-87, among the students of Knox and Queen's alone, there were thirty-three volunteers for the foreign field. It was the Knox students who, when they heard that Goforth had applied to the China Inland Mission, as his own church could not send him, decided to raise the necessary funds and start a mission in China with Jonathan Goforth as their missionary.

In order to ensure the success of the venture, it was felt necessary to secure the cooperation of the College Alumni. The matter was brought up at the annual meeting of the Alumni Association, in the fall of 1886. Many of the Alumni were strongly set against the scheme, arguing that the Presbyterian Church had too many fields already. It was also urged that her Home Mission work came first, and was all that she could handle. One man after another spoke with such telling force against the scheme, that its promoters feared the battle was lost. Then Jonathan Goforth was called upon. He spoke with unusual power as the result of the meeting indicated. For him the issue was crystal clear, and his ringing challenge went home to the hearts of ministers and students alike. He reminded them of Joshua going down to the rim of the swollen floods of Jordan in obedience to God's command. He did not wait for a bridge to be thrown across, but went forward by faith and the way opened up. "As soon as we are prepared to go forward and preach the Gospel at God's command," he went on, "then the Lord of the harvest will surely supply the need." When he had finished speaking the Alumni Association, without any further discussion, voted unanimously to support the venture.

Some years later, Jonathan Goforth when home on furlough, was speaking in a Presbyterian Church in Vancouver. The minister introducing him said:

"This fellow took an overcoat from me once. It happened this way. I was going up to the Alumni meeting in Knox College, Toronto, determined to do everything in my power to frustrate the crazy scheme which the students of the college were talking about, i.e., starting a mission field of their own in Central China. I also felt that I needed a new overcoat; my old one was looking rather shabby. So I thought I would go to Toronto and kill two birds with one stone. I would help side-track the scheme and buy an overcoat. But this fellow here upset my plans completely. He swept me off my feet with an enthusiasm for missions which I had never experienced before, and my precious overcoat money went into the fund!"

The Alumni of Knox College had been won over. The next step was to win the official sanction of the Church. Jonathan Goforth had already done not a little on his own account to turn the mind of the Church towards China. Not content with the opportunity which Sunday supply work afforded him, he bought hundreds of copies of Hudson Taylor's *China's Spiritual Need and Claims,* and other books on China, mailing them chiefly to ministers of the Church. The expense of this undertaking was at first shouldered by himself. (Money that might have gone for personal needs such as clothes, doubtless going into this work). Then, later, gifts came in which enabled him to carry it on. One who knew him at this time tells of frequently going to his room to help in the work of mailing out the books. In the room were piles of books and pamphlets on China ready to be sent out. Sometimes, three or four students were helping. A regular routine was observed, Goforth first reading aloud letters received containing donations for the work, many of these being small gifts from Sunday-school children who had heard him speak. Then all knelt in prayer for blessing on the books sent out, and thanksgiving for gifts received.

We cannot doubt but this work was an important agency in forwarding and feeding the remarkable tide of interest in foreign missions of this period and also that it paved the way for the visit of Dr. Hudson Taylor to Canada in 1888. Dr. Henry W. Frost, for many years Home Director of the China Inland Mission for Canada and the United States, writes the following striking tribute which will be read with deep interest, especially so by members and friends of that great Mission:

"In the year 1885, I attended for the first time, the Believers' Conference held at Niagara-on-the-Lake, Ontario. The spiritual pressure in the direction of foreign missions came in the year 1885 from the fact that there were present in the audience two persons whose lives were committed to foreign missions. These were Wm. E. Blackstone and Mr. Jonathan Goforth. The first friend was well known throughout the States and Canada as a great preacher and a notable advocate of the evangelization of the world, and the second was scarcely known at all, being but a student in Knox College, Toronto, yet recognized as one who was on fire in respect to work in the foreign field. A missionary afternoon was given to Mr. Blackstone and Mr. Goforth for addresses upon foreign missions. I was old enough to be in business at that time, and yet, I had never heard anyone speak on work amongst the heathen. It was largely curiosity, therefore, that took me to the afternoon meeting.

"The first speaker was Mr. Wm. E. Blackstone, who gave us a pyrotechnic display, intellectually speaking, which was illuminating and thrilling and which left us exhilarated as touching divine possibilities. The second speaker was the unknown Jonathan Goforth. The first thing that I discovered about this young man was that he had the face of an angel, and the second thing was—I am tempted to say it—that he had the tongue of an archangel. Never had I been so stirred by an address. And, besides, the speaker was not content to depend alone upon his utterances; he had hung on every side back of the platform, charts which appealed to the eye and of these he spoke one by one and with great exactness.

"The chart which impressed me most was the one in the centre, and which showed the religious condition of the world's inhabitants. In the lower half of this chart, were nine hundred black squares representing the nine hundred millions of heathendom. In the midst of these black squares was a white dot which set forth the Christian Church in heathendom.

"As Mr. Goforth described these black squares and this one tiny white dot, a great conviction took hold upon me. I felt that the church at home was guilty of a great crime, to leave these nine hundred millions of people in such midnight spiritual darkness when Christ was the light that lighteneth every man that cometh into the world. Sitting there, looking and listening, I cried in my inmost soul, "O God, what can I—what shall I do?" Mr. Goforth little knew what the Spirit was doing there that day in the soul of one of his hearers. It was not necessary that he *should* know. But it is a fact that he wrought with God in that meeting and that he left one of his hearers prostrate at the feet of Christ, surrendered unto Him for the fulfilment of His compassionate will toward those who knew Him not.

"This was the beginning of my interest in foreign missions. It was not long afterwards that I offered to the China Inland Mission for service in China. I could not go; but God gave me a work to do for China while at home and out of it has come the China Inland Mission in North America. I am constrained to say, therefore, that Mr., afterwards Dr., Goforth, was the originator of what is now a large enterprise in behalf of the Christless Chinese. This then is another jewel in a crown which has many gems, all of which now sparkle in the glory which excelleth, to the praise of Christ our Lord."

The doctrine of the Lord's premillennial return was much emphasized at those Niagara-on-the-Lake Conferences. Goforth came to accept fully this teaching which was also believed in by all his associates of the Toronto Mission Union. His belief in the possible return of Our Lord, at any time, was ever a most blessed and inspiring element in his religious life.

Of the children's response to his message, Goforth himself wrote:

"I spent a Sabbath talking on missions at a certain place. The Sunday-school boys and girls were greatly interested. How did I know? Well, when I got through speaking, a number of them came forward, some with pennies, some with five-cent pieces and even twenty-five cent pieces. But the interest didn't end there, for next day as I was staying at the manse, they came in ones and twos and even in groups of eight or ten with their offerings for missions. On Monday forenoon, as I was going down the street, I met a crowd of sunny faces on the way to school and they said, 'We are going to China too when we grow big.' "

Among Jonathan Goforth's papers we found the following story for children which will speak for itself:

"I remember once, when I was but a little boy, someone gave me five cents. I never had so much money before. I felt rich. I thought, 'Why, these five cents will buy six sticks of candy!' I raced into the house to ask my mother if I might not go to the store at once and buy that candy. My mother said, 'No, you may not go for it is Saturday evening and the sun will soon be setting. You must wait until Monday. I never felt so impatient about Sunday before. It came between me and the candy. Just then something seemed to say to me, 'Well, little boy, do you not think that you ought to give your five cents to the heathen?' At that time I didn't know who put that thought into my heart, but I had heard about a collection for missions announced to be taken on the morrow and I know now that God's Spirit spoke to me then. He wanted to make me a missionary but I wasn't willing. The heathen were far away. I didn't know much about them and didn't care. But I knew all about candy and it was only two miles away at the store. I was very fond of it and decided I must have it. But that didn't end the struggle.

It was candy and the heathen and heathen and the candy contending for that five cents. Finally I went to bed, but couldn't sleep. Usually as soon as my head touched the pillow I was off to sleep, but that night I couldn't get to sleep because of the war going on between the heathen and candy, or between love and selfishness. At last the heathen got the better of it and I decided to go up to Sunday-school next day and put my five cents into the collection. I felt very happy then and in a moment was asleep. But when I awoke the sun had arisen and my selfishness had returned. I wanted the candy and the fight went on, but before Sunday-school time, love had gained a final victory and I went to Sunday-school and when the plate was passed around for the mission collection, I dropped my five cents in. And would you believe me, I felt more happy than if I had got a whole store full of candy! And so will any boy or girl who acts unselfishly for Jesus' sake."

We are grateful to Dr. McNichol of the Toronto Bible College for the following sidelight on Jonathan Goforth at this period:

"I remember the first time I saw Dr. Goforth. It was in the dining-room of old Knox College in the morning after my arrival in Toronto as a raw, green student. At breakfast I was seated close to the head of the table, where were grouped some of the graduates of the previous spring. Two of them were specially pointed out to me,—J. A. Macdonald, at the end of the table, and Jonathan Goforth next him at the corner.

"I have never forgotten the sight of Mr. Goforth's

radiant and animated face as the talk went on about the new mission which the Presbyterian Church was establishing in China that fall. That incident was the beginning of my own interest in foreign missions, and it has been continually fed since then by the radiant enthusiasm of his life."

We are also indebted to Miss Mabeth Standen for the following letter. She was one of the most honoured and loved among the many "Hidden Heroines" of the China Inland Mission. It was my great privilege to have known Miss Standen's saintly parents who were among the early pioneers of Canada:

"How well I remember the farewell meeting in our old church at Minesing just before Dr. and Mrs. Goforth left for China in 1888. I was much impressed by the large missionary map, the white spot indicating where the gospel was known, while the large remaining black surface spoke impressively of the millions who had never yet heard.

"As Dr. Goforth closed his address he used an illustration that I never forgot. Referring to the miracle of the feeding of the five thousand, he pictured the disciples taking the bread and fish to the first few rows of the waiting and hungry multitude. Then he imagined these same disciples, instead of going on to the back rows, returning to those who had been already fed and offering them bread and fish until they turned away from it, while the back rows were still starving.

"Said Dr. Goforth, 'What would Christ have thought of His disciples had they acted in this way, and what does He think of us today as we continue to spend most of our time and money in giving the Bread of Life to those who have heard so often while millions in China are still starving?' God spoke to me that night about *my* responsibility regarding China and I promised Him then that if He opened my way, I would when old enough go to the "back rows." Later on when other claims seemed insistent and one was tempted to care for the front rows only, the vision of China's need as I had seen it that night always came before my eyes. I could not get away from it and finally said, 'Lord, here am I, send me— to the back rows.'"

In the spring of 1887, the Knox College students sent a deputation which included Jonathan Goforth, to plead their cause before the Synod of Hamilton and London, which was meeting that year in Chatham. On the Tuesday afternoon a member of the Synod suggested that a representative of the students be invited to address the meeting.

His fellow-students said to Jonathan, "It's up to you, Goforth; you do the preaching, we'll do the praying." When he commenced his address that evening, Dr. ———— who had been the chief opponent, was writing vigorously as though he were too busy to listen. But after several futile attempts to keep his mind on his writing he laid his pen down and from then on showed as keen interest in what was being said as the rest of the audience.

Dr. John Buchanan, of India, sends the following vivid and somewhat amusing, but characteristic, picture of Jonathan Goforth at this period:

"Jonathan Goforth, though young, was even then,

in 1887, a fearless prophet of Jehovah. I well remember when he and I were sent to Zion Church,
Brantford. The Convenor for Home Missions, was
pastor. Zion Church at that time gave almost ex-
clusively to Home Missions. . . . At the very beginning of our service, Heber's missionary hymn was announced and read in part, perhaps as a sort of con-
cession to the visitors,—

> *"From Greenland's icy mountains,*
> *From India's coral strand. . . .*
> *Waft, waft ye winds His story,*
> *And you ye waters roll,*
> *Till like a sea of glory*
> *It spreads from pole to pole."*

but before the organ could sound, Jonathan Goforth,
in his short homespun, much used brown coat, the
sleeves wrinkled up till too short for his Elijah arms,
was on his feet. In his left hand was the Church
Blue Book, opened at the point where the Zion Church
statistics were revealed; his prophetic eyes flashed; his
right condemning forefinger pointed at the givings for
foreign missions by Zion Church for the previous year.

"'No!' he demanded, 'a congregation strong as
Zion Church giving only seventy-eight cents per member a year for foreign missions, cannot sing such a
hymn as that. *We must sing a penitential Psalm—*
the 51st.' The Psalm was sung with deep emotion.
The stage was set!

"But what was I, the first speaker to do? I began
with fear and trembling on the great call that had
come to us students. After speaking some time, I

started on wasteful expenditures, when Goforth, always sure and never backward, from his seat behind the pulpit, pulled my (also short) coat tail. As I took no heed, again he pulled and whispered, 'Leave that to me, I am to speak on that.' He was quite right! He had a lash prepared for those at ease in Zion.

"Like his Master, Goforth had a great compassion for the needy and helpless and a two-edged flashing sword for the self-satisfied Christian Pharisee. It was probably this searching penetrating method of preaching to bodies of even Christian workers that caused opposition to his being sent, as was urged years later, on a Mission tour in India as he had in China."

Thus all opposition melted away before the enthusiasm of these missionary-minded students. The missionary vision captured the Presbyterian Church of Canada as it never had before. Churches, which formerly had hardly given a thought to the foreign field, made themselves responsible for the support of missionaries. At the General Assembly in June of 1887, Jonathan Goforth and Dr. J. Fraser Smith of Queen's were appointed to China. In the following October, Goforth was ordained, and on the twenty-fifth of the same month, was married to Florence Rosalind Bell-Smith in Knox Church, Toronto, the beloved pastor, Rev. H. M. Parsons, D.D., conducting the ceremony.

After Goforth's ordination, the Foreign Mission Board planned for him to go through the churches giving his addresses on foreign missions until Dr. Smith was through his course, that the two might go together for the finding and founding of the new mission in China. But early in January of 1888, reports of a great famine raging in China decided the Board to hasten Goforth's departure so that he might carry with him considerable funds which had been raised for famine relief and might even engage in famine relief himself.

Of that wonderful farewell meeting, words fail one to describe. On January 19, 1888, the old, historic Knox Church was filled to capacity. The gallery was crowded with students from Knox and other Colleges. Among those on the platform were the Hon. W. H. Howland, then Mayor of Toronto, one of the most honoured and loved Christian workers Toronto has ever known, Principal Caven and Professor McLaren of Knox, Rev. Dr. H. M. Parsons, and Goforth's closest friend, Rev. William Patterson.

One story was told at that farewell meeting which made a deep impression on all present and touched a note which sounded through the Goforths' whole after career! The story was of a young couple, when bidding farewell to their home country church as they were about to leave for an African field, known as The White Man's Grave. The husband said, "My wife and I have a strange dread in going. We feel much as if we were going down into a pit. We are willing to take the risk and go if you, our home circle, will promise *to hold the ropes.*" One and all promised.

Less than two years passed when the wife and the little one God had given them, succumbed to the dreaded fever. Soon the husband realized his days too were numbered. Not waiting to send word home of his coming, he started back at once and arrived at the hour of the Wednesday prayer-meeting. He slipped in unnoticed, taking a back seat. At the close of the meeting he went forward. An awe came over the people, for death was written on his face. He said:

"I am your missionary. My wife and child are buried in Africa and I have come home to die. This evening I listened anxiously, as you prayed, for some mention of your missionary to see if you were keeping your promise, but in vain! You prayed for everything connected with yourselves and your home church, but you forgot your missionary. I see now why I am a failure as a missionary. It is because *you have failed to hold the ropes!*"

Each speaker at that meeting seemed eager to have a share in sending the Goforths off with joyful enthusiasm. At the close of the two-hour meeting practically all pressed forward in line to shake hands with Mr. and Mrs. Goforth—for days their right hands pained with the "grips" given them! Their train was to leave at midnight from the Old Market station half a mile distant. Soon after eleven o'clock, hundreds started for the station, among them, Principal Caven with his professors and students.

Toronto probably never witnessed such a scene as followed. The station platform became literally packed. Then hymn after hymn was sung. As the time drew near to start, Dr. Caven, standing under a light in the midst of the crowd, bared his head and led in prayer. A few moments later, as the train began to move, a great volume of voices joined in singing *Onward Christian Soldiers*—hands were stretched out for a last clasp, —then darkness. Jonathan Goforth's new life had begun, and, incidentally, his training of Rosalind!

II.
1888 - 1900.

A great "without" has been written on heathenism. Men and women are toiling without a Bible, without a Sunday, without prayer, without songs of praise. They have rulers without justice and without righteousness; homes without peace; marriage without sanctity, young men and girls without ideals and enthusiasm; little children without purity, without innocence; mothers without wisdom or self-control; poverty without relief or sympathy; sickness without skilful help or tender care; sorrow and crime without a remedy; and worst of all, death without hope.

MRS. WHITFIELD GUINNESS

V.

FOR CHRIST AND CHINA

*I gave up all for Christ, and what have I found?
I have found everything in Christ!*

JOHN CALVIN

As THE last glimpse of the waving friends vanished, Goforth turned to his wife and bowing his head prayed that they might live worthy of such confidence. Of that first journey to the coast but little need be said. The remembrance of their reception at Winnipeg and the warmth and courtesy shown them by Principal King, of Manitoba College, with whom they stayed, remained with them through the years. In her diary of January 25, 1888, Mrs. Goforth writes:

"Mrs. McLeod and a number of others met the train at Portage la Prairie. Each one was loaded down with all sorts of good things. There was a goose, a chicken, a roast of beef, pickles, preserves, apples, honey, etc., etc."

Jan. 29th: "Delayed so much by snow drifts and washouts, we are now thankful for the good things brought to us at Portage la Prairie. Though at the time the amount seemed burdensome, we have needed it all, sharing with others who like ourselves are travelling tourist. On Sunday, J. had two meetings on the train, both well attended."

On reaching Vancouver, they found the city, which but a short time before had been swept by a devastating fire, little more than a heap of charred ruins. No time was lost in seeking out their boat, the S. S. "Parthia." To their unsophisticated eyes, the vessel seemed "quite splendid," and it was with the utmost joy and hopefulness they began settling in their cabin.

The following is taken from a letter written by Goforth dated Vancouver, February 4, 1888:

"Just a few words before our pilot leaves us. . . . We went on deck at 7 o'clock this morning and watched the ship loosed from her moorings. We had not the slightest wish to stay though strong emotion filled us at thought of leaving "native land,"—more properly, those of you our friends who made Canada a dear spot to us. I never saw Mrs. Goforth more happy than now as we turn out into the ocean towards our future home. Let us leave no stone unturned in the effort to move God's people to spread the message to every creature. I know that many eyes are fixed on this movement. It rests with us either to inspire or discourage the host of God forming our church. We have the aid of many prayers. The means sufficient shall certainly not be wanting. Let us win ten thousand Chinese souls. It will please him, our Lord." (How fully was this fulfilled in the years to come!)

The first rather jolting surprise came when it was learned Mrs. Goforth was the only woman passenger! Then, just after they had passed through the straits and were facing out to sea, a strange hubbub was heard outside their cabin. It was found to be caused by several of the boatmen half hauling and half carrying the captain, a large man, down to a lower cabin, *dead drunk!*

The remembrance of the fourteen days that followed ever remained — to Mrs. Goforth, at least — a terrible nightmare! They tried to comfort themselves by the thought that they were only going through what all ocean travellers have to put up with, but the truth finally came out. — They discovered that for twenty-five years the "Parthia" had plied the Atlantic, but under another name. As the years passed, the vessel acquired such a notorious reputation for its rolling, pitching, and heaving that none would take passage on her. So the owners had the boat re-painted, re-named the "Parthia" and put on the Pacific run.

The shores of Canada were not long out of sight when the ship's carpenter, a fine old Christian, came to Goforth, asking him to pray for the safety of the ship. He seemed greatly worried about some very heavy machinery on board which was being taken over for the Mikado of Japan, one piece being so large it could not be lowered into the hold and had been fastened, as securely as possible, to the deck. The carpenter said there was grave danger of the sides of the vessel being pressed outward. During the fourteen sunless, stormy days that followed, Jonathan Goforth had abundance of time to accede to the carpenter's request. He lay on his bunk, his hearty, cheering laugh no longer heard; even his usually ready smile seemed depressed.

On the fifteenth day, everyone on board became galvanized into new life when word was passed around that they were nearing the shores of Japan. Quickly the passengers gathered on deck. Then a dense fog settled down. Whether the captain was intoxicated again or not they did not know, but the ship continued on its course only partially slackening speed. Passengers became alarmed. At least two on board did some hard praying. Then suddenly the fog lifted and revealed the bow of the vessel pointing directly towards the shore of Japan and dangerously near some jagged shoals. The vessel quickly turned about, but none too soon! Jonathan Goforth's own description of this first journey to China was contained in one sentence. "An ordinary winter voyage; bad enough; sick all the way!"

On reaching Shanghai, that great cosmopolitan metropolis of the Far East, Goforth was so wrapped up with his mission and the responsibility resting upon him, that the sights which drew many tourists held little attraction for him. As soon as accommodation had been secured in a modest boarding-house, he at once called on some of the leading missionaries and arranged for a meeting the following day. At this meeting it was decided Goforth should hand over to others the famine funds entrusted to him, for it was thought impossible for him, without the language, to take part himself in famine relief work. It was also decided that the triangular section of country north of the Yellow River, known as North Honan, be given to the Canadian Presbyterian Church as their field. The Goforths were strongly advised to make a temporary home at Chefoo on the northern coast of China, where they could study the language until such time as the next step was made clear. Goforth decided to follow the advice of these missionary veterans.

The venerable Dr. Williamson, who had lived many years in Chefoo, offered the Goforths the use of his small, furnished native house there at a modest rental. This offer was gladly accepted. Navigation along the coast had just opened but Goforth was so eager to get on he would not wait for a good boat but took passage on a very third-rate vessel called the "Newchwang."

On their way to the boat, and having some time to spare, one of the missionaries kindly volunteered to lead the Goforths through the great "opium palace" of Shanghai. Palace it truly was! Gorgeously decorated and brilliantly lighted,—men and women were stretched on their narrow beds fully dressed, with the opium paraphernalia beside them, none seeming the least ashamed as visitors passed by. Later, Goforth was told that the "far country" of the "Prodigal Son" meant Shanghai to the Chinese. The disgraceful fact that covered every missionary with shame was that these opium palaces and literally streets of brothels inside the International Settlement of Shanghai, were permitted because of the great financial gain derived from them. The governing board of the International Settlement was made up of representatives from so-called Christian countries.

Upon arriving at Chefoo at dusk, the Goforths at once set out for Dr. Hunter Corbett's house situated on Temple Hill which was above the native city and outside the walls. Mr. Paton, agent of the Scotch Bible Society, kindly offered to act as guide. After losing their way several times, the party arrived at Dr. Corbett's home well on to nine o'clock. Though they were not expected, the good doctor and his wife gave them just the hearty, loving welcome they needed.

The following day the Goforths settled in the house which Dr. Williamson had offered to them as their residence while at Chefoo. This home was situated on the outskirts of a village two miles to the east and on the plain below Temple Hill. The prospect of having their own home was so attractive, they, perhaps unwisely, declined the generous invitation of the Corbetts to make their home with them. Within a day or two, Goforth had engaged a teacher and was hard at work on the language and since he, from the first, insisted that the full time for language study must be uninterrupted, getting settled was necessarily slow work. Neither of the Goforths could, of course, speak a word of Chinese, so Mr. Paton took pity on them and arranged to stay and work with them a short time to give them a start.

They had been in their home about a week when Mr. Paton came to Mrs. Goforth with a grave face and very solemnly said, "I do not want to be a Job's comforter, but really you should be warned. Your husband takes everything so intensely, *he can never stand China.* Unless you can get him to go more slowly, in a year he will either be dead or have returned home!"

It is necessary here to make plain the plan of the Williamson's Chinese house. It consisted of a row of rooms, all with doors and windows facing on to an open court. The first of these rooms near the gate was the bedroom, next came the study, then two rooms filled with Dr. Williamson's things, and lastly, the small dining-room.

A day or two after Mr. Paton had left, while the Goforths sat at dinner, screams and shouts were heard. Running outside, they found the bedroom at the farther end of the house was on fire. The old, thatched roof, dry as tinder, was ablaze and already beginning to drop fire below. Again and again Goforth entered the burning rooms. The first things to be secured were his beloved Bible and a valise containing the money. As he returned for more things his panic-stricken wife grasped the valise and ran for the road, thinking it to be the safest place. In her agitated state she was unconscious of the hundreds of eyes watching eagerly for a chance to secure the valise. Fortunately, Goforth missed it before it was snatched from her. Running to his wife as she stood dazed by the roadside, he said sternly, "Pull yourself together and don't give way to panic! Do you not know the Chinese will steal?" It was the best thing for her for it brought her to her senses and from then on she was quite calm.

Returning to the court, where the fire could be seen through the open doors, it was not a pleasant sight to watch wedding presents, pictures (one of them of her father painted by himself from a mirror), and other precious *home* things being licked up by the flames, but so it was. Practically everything of real value to them was burnt. Later, Goforth tried to comfort his wife by saying, "My dear, do not grieve so. After all, they're *just things*."

The fire meant little more to Goforth than a temporary hindering of his language study, for his optimism remained as unshadowed and his radiant cheerfulness as helpful as if it had not occurred. To his wife, it meant the burning of the bridges behind her as far as art was concerned and it meant also the dawn of personal responsibility towards the souls of her Chinese sisters.

Just three weeks from the evening they had landed at Chefoo, the Goforths were settling in their second home, a two-story, semi-detached foreign built house near the landing place and within a minute's walk of the seashore.

About the end of April, Goforth gave his wife her first lesson in real giving. Coming to her with his open account book in hand, he said:

"I have been going carefully into our accounts and I find we have given a tithe of one year's salary already and we have been married just six months. What would you suggest about it?"

Now his wife had not been accustomed to tithing in her parent's home, and had thought it very generous of her husband to tithe their salary. She hesitated somewhat, however, before replying.

"If we have already given a tithe of our year's salary, I suppose we need not give any more till the end of the year."

"Do you really feel we should do so?" Jonathan replied gravely, rather taken aback. "To me it seems right when the Lord has done so much for us that we should just close the account to date, and begin again."

This he did. So that year a fifth was given. This was but the first lesson of a "progressive course" in giving, for as the years passed, his wife became accustomed to a half, and on till only sufficient of their income for pressing needs was kept.

Though very sacred to the writer, the following incident is given which occurred just a month before Jonathan Goforth passed beyond the need for earthly finances. He was resting on a couch, waiting for a call to a meeting. His wife saw he was thinking keenly about something. Stepping to his side she said laughingly: "Jonathan, I believe I can read your thoughts!"

"Nonsense," he answered. "But say on."

"You are planning how much of next month's salary you can safely give away without leaving us quite destitute!"

His hearty laugh rang out as he rose, "Well, my dearest, you are not far wrong!" he replied.

Jonathan Goforth always felt the nine months spent in Chefoo were of great value to him in his after life. About a mile along the seashore from their home, the China Inland Mission had established a large plant of three schools (boys', girls' and "prep."), a large hospital, and a sanitarium. The almost daily fellowship with these friends was a constant inspiration and help to the young missionaries. On Temple Hill were two great stalwarts of the faith, Dr. Nevius and Dr. Corbett, who were ever ready to give of their best to Mr. Goforth, and needless to say, he was ever keen to seek their advice and counsel. Every Sabbath morning found him at the native service on Temple Hill, with notebook and pencil, seeking to get accustomed to the strange sounds of the native language.

The months of July and August seemed constantly interwoven with joy and sorrow. Early in July, a fine young teacher in the C. I. M. Boys' School, named Norris, gave his life in saving his boys from a mad dog. He was bitten in the hand and died a month later. Then, on August 12, Gertrude Goforth arrived bringing with her great joy. For some time the dreaded cholera had been becoming more and more menacing in the native city. One afternoon, Mrs. ———— of the Baptist Mission called at the Goforths and while returning through the native city, contracted the dreaded cholera and died a few hours later. Late in August, Mrs. Hunter Corbett died suddenly. The Goforths felt keenly her death for she had been as a mother to them both.

By the middle of August, recruits began to arrive from Canada, among them Dr. and Mrs. J. F. Smith. A little later a cordial letter was received from that most famous of China's missionaries of his day, Rev. Dr. Arthur H. Smith, offering his services as escort on a tour of inspection of North Honan, their future field.

On Sept. 13, 1888, Mr. Goforth and Dr. J. F. Smith, started on their tour of exploration through North Honan.

Of this trip, Goforth records one incident as follows:

"We crossed the northern boundary into Honan province over the Chang River. The country before us lay rich and fertile with villages as thick as farmsteads in most parts of Ontario. To the west could

be seen the beautiful Shansi mountains. I was
thrilled with the thought of being at last inside our
'Promised Land.' Walking ahead of the carts, I
prayed the Lord to give me that section of North
Honan as my own field, and as I prayed, I opened
"Clark's Scripture Promises," my daily text-book,
and found the promise for that day read as follows:
*'For as the rain cometh down, and the snow from
heaven and watereth the earth and maketh it bring
forth and bud, that it may give seed to the sower, and
bread to the eater; so shall my word be that goeth
forth out of my mouth: it shall not return unto me
void, but shall accomplish that which I please, and
it shall prosper in the thing whereto I sent it.'* Isaiah
55: 10, 11.

"The promise seemed so wonderful, coming as it
did just at that juncture, and as I went on, I kept
praying that this promise might be fulfilled to that
region."

How wonderfully God fulfilled this promise to
Jonathan Goforth we shall see as his life unfolds.

VI.

"GO FORWARD ON YOUR KNEES!"

We are asked to do an impossible task, but we work with Him who can do the impossible.

HUDSON TAYLOR

A VERY warm invitation had come from the American Board missionaries living at Pangchwang, an inland country station, several days' journey by river house-boat nearer North Honan. Goforth, eager to get even one step nearer the field, had accepted the invitation.

The last Sunday morning in Chefoo, little Gertrude was taken to the Chinese service on Temple Hill and baptized by Dr. Hunter Corbett. Their journey took them first by coast steamer to Tientsin, where they found real interest among the missionaries in the new Canadian mission they represented: some of the oldest and most experienced, however, were none too optimistic regarding an early entrance into what was considered one of the most dangerous and anti-foreign sections of anti-foreign China.

It was about this time, Dr. Hudson Taylor's historic letter reached Goforth in which he said, "We as a Mission have sought for ten years to enter the Province of Honan from the south and have only just succeeded. . . . Brother, if you would enter that Province, you must *go forward on your knees*." These

80

latter words became the slogan of the North Honan
Mission.

Mr. Goforth realized, only too well, that the China
Inland Mission during those ten unsuccessful years of
seeking an entrance into South Honan, had at their
command what he and his comrades had not—experienced missionaries, with a knowledge of the language
and people, and what was of even greater importance
in pioneer work, trained, trusty Chinese evangelists.
But in spite of the humanly hopeless outlook, the Goforths embarked on their tiny houseboat with great joy
and hopefulness at the prospect of having a home, their
third, which brought them nearer the Province of
Honan.

Pangchwang, i.e., the village of the Pang family,
was a small village situated a mile or more from the
river bank, in the midst of a thickly populated farming region; the farmers living in villages, not in isolated
farmsteads, as in the homeland. The Goforths found
their new home greatly superior to what they had expected in an interior mission station. They were able
to purchase some much needed second-hand furniture
left for sale by a missionary then on furlough.

With some difficulty, a language teacher from North
Honan had been secured for Goforth, a Mr. Li, who,
however, showed great uneasiness from the moment of
his arrival at the mission station. Goforth treated him
in his usual, cordial, friendly fashion, indeed, went out
of his way to show him extra kindness, seeing him so
suspicious. The man would drink nothing except water
that he himself saw had actually been boiled. He ate
almost nothing, showing in his every action, distrust and

suspicion. Two mornings after his arrival, he disappeared, leaving no word behind.

Shortly after Goforth arrived in China, the Rev. Donald McGillivray, his closest friend in Knox College, had written him that he feared church finances would delay his coming. Goforth had at once written back, "Come and share with us." But by the time this word had reached McGillivray, he already was starting for China. Great was Jonathan's joy when at last his friend reached Pangchwang. It was truly the meeting of David and Jonathan for them. Their friendship was deep and true and for more than thirty-five years till Donald McGillivray passed away, not a shadow darkened their friendship.

McGillivray's progress in the language was phenomenal. In one month he memorized all the Chinese characters in John's gospel, being able to give the sound, tone, and meaning of each character, and this besides the regular language study. Jonathan Goforth worked just as hard and just as faithfully at the language as did McGillivray, but the contrast in progress was pitifully evident. We have a wonderful story to tell in this connection later on.

A letter from a fellow-student still in Knox College reached Goforth about this time. "Say, old boy," it read, "have you lost any of that flaming optimism you carried with you to China? Has getting down to brass tacks changed your view-point on foreign missions?" Goforth on reading this and much more, laughed heartily. Then turning to his wife he said with passionate earnestness: "Oh, that the eyes of Christians at home could be opened to their responsibility towards these neglected millions! Optimistic! How could I help but be when I believe with Carey that 'the prospects are as bright as the promises of God'?"

Some months after arriving in China, an old, experienced missionary came to Goforth with the following advice: "Do not attempt to speak of Jesus the first time when preaching to a heathen audience. The Chinese have a prejudice against the name of Jesus. Confine your efforts to demolishing the false gods and if you have a second opportunity you may bring in Jesus." Later, when telling his wife of the advice which had been given him, Mr. Goforth exclaimed with hot emphasis, "Never, *Never*, NEVER! The Gospel which saved the down and outs in the slums of Toronto, is the same Gospel which must save Chinese sinners." From the very first, when able to speak only in broken, imperfect sentences, he preached to the Chinese Jesus Christ and Him crucified, and from the first, sinners were saved from the lowest depths of depravity. He based his messages always on some passage in the Word of God. Never was he known to stand before a Chinese audience without the open Bible in hand, constantly referring to it as "The written Word of the One True God." In later years when asked by young missionaries as to the secret of his power in winning converts his reply was: "Because I just give God a chance to speak to souls through His own Word. My only secret in getting at the heart of big sinners is to show them their need and tell them of a Saviour abundantly able to save. Once a sinner is shown that no flesh can be justified in God's sight by the deeds of the law and that he can only attain unto the righteousness of God through faith in the Lord Jesus Christ, he readily yields. That was Luther's secret, it was John Wesley's and never did man make more of that secret than D. L. Moody." To be able to use "the sword of the Spirit" effectively, he realized the necessity of keeping it ever sharp through constant daily study of the Word.

In the spring of 1889, a native compound had been secured in Linching, an important city on the Wei River some fifty miles still nearer North Honan, our final objective. The place was in bad condition; Mr. McGillivray, therefore, left for Linching to superintend repairs. Word came about the end of June that, though much had still to be done, a place had been made ready for the Goforths.

The weather had begun to get exceedingly hot. Mrs. A. H. Smith, the one experienced woman at the station, who could, and probably would, have advised waiting till the heat broke, was away. Their first summer had been in Chefoo by the sea so the Goforths had really no experience of the great summer heat of inland China. They started on this journey July 4 with their precious little Gertrude, unconscious of any danger to her on that short—only two days'—but intensely hot, journey by small river houseboat to Linching. The heat on the boat was so overwhelming from early morning till sundown, they were scarcely able to breathe unless sheets dipped from the river were hung around and above them.

On reaching the compound at Linching, McGillivray's welcome was so cheery, it relieved for the moment, anxiety that was beginning to be felt for little Gertrude. The heat continued well over the hundred mark. There

were no wire screens to protect from flies which literally swarmed everywhere, the compound being in closest
proximity to Chinese neighbors. But what from the
first was most trying and nauseating, was a strange
smell that pervaded the air. At first it was thought
this came from the neighbor's courts, but the odour became worse. Then, it was discovered the coolies, carrying water for mortar, to save themselves a few steps,
had been filling their pails from an indescribably filthy
pool nearby, though comparatively clean water was not
far distant!

Dysentery broke out among the workmen. Mr. Mc
Gillivray's teacher contracted it, succumbing in a few
days. McGillivray himself became ill with the disease,
but quickly recovered. Then little Gertrude, that
precious first gift of God to the Goforths, was taken ill.
Mr. and Mrs. Perkins (a woman doctor), had the Goforths bring the child to their home about a half mile
distant. Everything was done to save the child's life,
but about noon on July 24, she passed away. The following letter, written by the father to friends in the
homeland, speaks for itself:

"Gertrude Madeline is dead. Ours is an awful
loss. Less than two weeks ago she was well, but on
July 24, she died, only six days after she was taken
ill with dysentery. There is no burying place here
for foreigners, so I took her body in a cart to Pangchwang. It is fifty miles away. I left here at eleven
o'clock at night and reached there at five the next
day. We had only left Pangchwang three weeks
before. Little Gertrude was the only baby in the
mission there and had won the love of all, old and

young. They were all sorry to see her go away and
when she came back so soon dead, everyone felt it
so very much. A Chinese service was conducted by
the missionary. Then the rude coffin, covered with
flowers, was borne by four Chinese outside the village
wall. There, in the dusk of evening, with scores
of curious heathen looking on, we laid our darling
to rest beside two other dear little foreigners who
were laid to sleep there before her.

"Later on in the evening, sixteen foreigners met in
one of the parlours, and the missionary, Rev. A. H.
Smith, spoke from the Scripture, 'Suffer little children to come unto me for of such is the kingdom
of Heaven.' He told the children who had cried so
because baby was dead, that it was only her body
that was resting in the grave outside the wall, for her
soul was now in heaven at rest in the arms of Jesus,—
that she could not come back to us, but that we could
go where she is. Then he urged each of the children
to give their hearts to Jesus now, for they knew not
when death would come to call them away.

"Next morning I went out early to see the grave,
but two of the little girls, Flora and Carrie Sheffield,
were there before me and had had the grave all decorated with wild flowers; besides, they had traced with
their fingers in the soft clay of the grave, 'G. G.', the
initials of our darling. The two dear girls told me
that their mother had consented to their coming out
every morning to place fresh flowers on the grave.

"None but those who have lost a precious treasure
can understand our feelings, but the loss seems to be
greater because we are far away in a strange land.

. . . 'All things work together for good.' The Lord
has a purpose in taking our loved one away. We
pray that this loss will fit us more fully to tell these
dying millions of Him who has gained the victory
over death."

Mr. McGillivray insisted on accompanying Goforth
to Pangchwang with the little body. As they left, the
broken-hearted mother—herself stricken with the same
disease—took up her *Daily Light* and found among the
verses for that day the following: *"It is the Lord. Let
Him do what seemeth Him good.* (I Sam. 3:18). *The
Lord gave and the Lord hath taken away. Blessed be
the name of the Lord.* (Job 1:21)."

On their return, Goforth and McGillivray at once
settled down to hard language-study. Languages had
always been McGillivray's best and Goforth's worst subject throughout their years of schooling. McGillivray
was Gold Medalist in Classics in Toronto University
and later became one of the most brilliant of Chinese
scholars and translators. The Chinese language written
and spoken was to Mr. Goforth exceedingly difficult.
Had he been of a less optimistic and hopeful disposi-
tion, he would have become utterly discouraged, for
although he had had almost a year at the languge study
ahead of McGillivray, his friend could speak better and
understand the people as Jonathan could not. When
Mr. Goforth was preaching in the chapel, the men often
pointed to Mr. McGillivray, saying, "You speak, we
don't understand him," pointing to Goforth.

Then, in God's own mysterious way, He performed
one of His wonders in answer to *others'* prayers. One
day as Jonathan was about to leave for the chapel, he

said to his wife, "If the Lord does not work a miracle for me with this language, I fear I will be an utter failure as a missionary!"

For a moment only he looked the heartbreak that that would mean. Then picking up his Chinese Bible, he started off. Two hours later, he returned.

"Oh Rose!" he cried. "It was just wonderful! When I began to speak, those phrases and idioms that would always elude me came readily and I could make myself understood so well that the men actually asked me to go on though Donald had risen to speak. I *know* the backbone of the language is broken! Praise the Lord!" Mr. Goforth then made a full note of this in his diary. About two months later, a letter came from Mr. Talling, (his former college room-mate, still in Knox,) saying that on a certain evening after supper, a number of students decided to meet in one of the class-rooms for prayer, "just for Goforth." The letter stated that the presence and power of God was so manifestly felt by all at that meeting, they were convinced Goforth must surely have been helped in some way. On looking up his diary, Mr. Goforth found the meeting for prayer by the students in Knox coincided with the experience recorded above.

To complete this testimony, it should be added that some years later, Dr. Arthur H. Smith, one of the best speakers and keenest critics of the spoken language, said to Mr. Goforth, "Wherever did you get your style of speaking? For any sakes don't change it! You can be understood over a wider area than anyone I know!"

"If radio's slim fingers can pluck a melody
from night,

And toss it o'er a continent or sea;
If the soft petalled notes of a violin
Are blown o'er a mountain or city's din;
If songs like fragrant roses are culled from
    thin blue air—
Then how can mortals wonder THAT GOD
    ANSWERS PRAYER!"

On December 5, 1889, eight recruits arrived from Canada, three married couples and two single women. That same evening by the authority of the Canadian General Assembly, Jonathan Goforth convened and formed the first Presbytery of North Honan, though as yet no permanent foothold had been secured in that field. A second Presbytery meeting was held February 20, 1890, at which two extended tours into Honan were arranged for, Mr. Goforth and Dr. Smith taking one route, Dr. McClure and Mr. McGillivray another.

One of the snares in the path of a young missionary is the temptation to put other than first things first—in other words, to "potter" or "fritter" precious time away on non-essentials, instead of bravely facing the inevitable hard task of regular language study. Many a missionary has gone through his or her missionary career with the great handicap of insufficient knowledge of either the written or spoken language because of having fallen into this trap. The following story illustrates Goforth's stand in this connection.

Among the young recruits arriving from the homeland were a Mr. and Mrs. X. Mr. X was a man with a college record equal to that of Donald McGillivray—a gold medalist, a fluent speaker, but also a clever mechanic, especially along the line of carpentry. When

visiting Mrs. X., Goforth's wife often looked with en-
vious eyes at the many clever conveniences X had made
for his wife. One day she determined to coax her husband into making similar things for her. Going to him
she said, "Now, Jonathan, don't you think you could
leave your work for a little and do some carpentry for
me like Mr. X does for his wife?"

"My dear Rose," he replied, "don't ask this of me.
There are fine Chinese carpenters who could do all you
want far better than I and would be thankful for the
job. Besides, I have determined never to spend my
time on what Chinese can do, for my work is to preach
or prepare to preach the Gospel that will save souls.
You know 'This one thing I do' is my motto. So, my
dear, get the best carpenter going. Have him do all
you require and I will foot the bill." She went away
only almost persuaded, but years later, she acknowledged how that many times she had thanked God for
giving her a husband always consistent in putting "first
things first." This trait in him many times helped her
to bear more bravely her share of life's burdens.

On Goforth's first preaching tour into Honan the
mystery of Mr. Li's strange behaviour and sudden dis-
appearance was solved. As their boat touched the landing place at a certain town, Mr. Li jumped aboard. He
seemed greatly excited and most eager to explain and
apologize for his conduct. It appeared the women folk
of his family had been in a state of panic when he left
them to become a teacher to the "foreign devil." The
terrible stories being circulated were wholly believed
by them and partly believed by himself. On arriving
at Pangchwang, he was seized with what he could only

describe as panic, so—fled. Now he begged Goforth to take him back, which he did. Later, Mr. Li said, "It is impossible to look into the face of "Ku Mushih" [Pastor Goforth], and not love and believe in him."

For two years, the Goforths' headquarters remained in Linching. During this time tours were made by the men into North Honan, seeking by every means to gain a foothold there. So full of danger were these journeys, the women left behind ever had the fear lest they might never see them return.

Returning from one of these tours, Goforth told of many narrow escapes from wild mobs. On one occasion, he with his colleague and an evangelist, came suddenly, by a sharp turn of the road, into a great crowd of thousands surrounding a village theatrical, combining a sort of fair. Though both foreigners were in Chinese dress, it was impossible to hide their identity, one having a queue, but *red*, the other being without a queue! In a few moments the crowd was upon them, hooting, yelling, and throwing clods of earth They tried to reach a solid wall, but could not, for again and again the crowd endeavoured and almost succeeded in getting them tripped underfoot. Just when things seemed hopeless, a sudden violent gust of wind blew a tent completely over. In a moment, the foreigners were forgotten and the mob turning, made a rush for the tent with hilarious eagerness to see the fun. Thus, the Lord delivered them, not once, but many times during those hard pioneering days.

On December 19, following little Gertrude's death, a beautiful wee boy arrived in the Goforth home. He was named Donald, after Mr. McGillivray, and during his brief life-span of nineteen months, gave joy to all. He was always called "wee Donald" to designate him from Donald McGillivray, and often spoken of as the "flower of the flock" as he played with the other foreign children.

The Goforths were moving into a foreign house, vacated by a missionary's family who had gone on furlough. The front of the house had a veranda with no railing. While things were being moved in, and everyone busy, wee Donald began racing on the veranda and around the posts. Before he could be caught, he fell over on to the ground below, his head striking a flower pot. Though at first no apparent injury could be discovered, gradually he began to lose the use of his limbs. His parents were hoping to take the child to Shanghai as soon as the intense heat passed, but on July 25, when nineteen months old, he went to join the great band of other little ones in the Glory Land.

For the second time, Mr. Goforth made the journey to Pangchwang with the remains of a precious child, and there wee Donald was laid beside the grave of his sister in the little cemetery just outside the Mission compound. Immediately on his return home Goforth and his wife began preparations for moving into Honan. Dr. McClure and his wife had been for some months in Chuwang, a small town just inside the border, but *inside* North Honan. As soon as the great heat had broken, the latter part of August the Goforths with their five-month-old Paul, left Linching for their sixth home. What a joy it was to both just to realize that at last they were, as a family, about to live and work together in their own field.

VII.

WITHIN THE PROMISED LAND

Many men owe the grandeur of their lives to their tremendous difficulties.

C. H. SPURGEON

THE TOWN of Chuwang was in every way as undesirable a place to locate a mission as one could well imagine. The town itself was little more than a collection of broken-down mud huts. The surrounding country was poor and had been swept by floods or burnt dry by drought till the people were, as Dr. Arthur H. Smith put it, "on the ragged edge of ruin." It was, however, a foothold, and the first foothold to be secured at this time inside North Honan. Little wonder then, that Mr. Goforth looked upon this place as but a stepping-stone to the important prefectural city of Changte, about thirty miles to the west. His friend, Donald McGillivray, was heartily with him in this.

These early years at Chuwang were hard pioneer seed-sowing days. The vile placards which for a time could be seen everywhere depicting the hated foreigners in ways that only an utterly depraved heathen mind could imagine, were still bearing the fruit of bitter hatred and distrust. At this time China seemed to be becoming more and more anti-foreign. To the south along the Yangtse River, missionaries were being driven from their stations,—some failing to escape were brutally murdered. Thus clouds of uncertainty and impending danger seemed to ever enclose our missionaries on all sides. In the midst of such conditions, Mr. Goforth and his colleagues went forward faithfully preaching and healing. During the good touring season, Goforth and McGillivray often travelled far afield, sometimes going as far west as the foothills beyond the city of Changte.

Could the Goforths' life at Chuwang be painted in actual colours, it would be a picture of deep shadows and bright lights. There were the weeks of anxiety when Goforth lay low with typhoid fever and again when he returned ill from one of his long tours. For at least one day, his life hung in the balance. On January 3, 1893, beautiful, golden-haired Florence Evangeline arrived. The following summer was an intensely hot one, unusually so. One unbroken spell lasted twelve days beginning with 100 degrees in the shade and rising one degree higher each day till 112 degrees was reached, when the break came only in time to save the life of little Paul, lying at death's door from heatstroke.

Goforth writes of one notable conversion of this period, that of Wang Fengao, as follows:*

"I rejoiced with trembling! Could it be that God had used me to lead this proud scholar into the kingdom? I have been leading him day by day since his conversion in the essential truths and am surprised at his rapid advance. I have had him witnessing in

---

*Miracle Lives of China. By Jonathan and Rosalind Goforth.

the chapel for about a month. I also have him expound tracts to the people. In this way I can detect any point on which he is not clear and afterwards instruct him.

"His testimony has this effect upon the people. They think, that since this scholar after investigation of this doctrine, comes out boldly in its defense as the only possible way of life, there must be something in it. The increasing interest dates from his giving witness to the truth. It was just today in reply to a man who said, 'Of course we scholars can all understand this doctrine as soon as we look into it,' Mr. Wang said, 'Not so. Before I was converted I too thought so but now the more I read the Bible the more profound it grows and the less I think I understand it.' Today he made request for baptism. It will be brought before the Presbytery.

"He now wants to be set free to go about everywhere as an evangelist to preach the gospel to his fellow-countrymen. To a man of fifty this itinerating means much hardship. The Chinese inns without fires are cheerless places in winter-time. One winter's night, Mr. Wang and three other Chinese and myself were put into a very small room for the night. One end was for the donkeys and pigs. Besides, we had to contend against other living things *not so big* as donkeys but a thousand times more troublesome. It also meant his accepting the smaller salary of an evangelist."

The following are a few extracts from Goforth's letters at this time. They will be read with interest, giving as they do, vivid pictures of what "touring" meant in those days.

"It may be interesting for you to know how I go about the country. I dread laziness in the Chinese helpers. I have already seen some of it. If the foreigner rides, his Chinese brother will also expect to ride. A Chinese may never have been able to afford a ride before he comes to you, but as soon as he enters upon the Mission work he thinks it does not look well for him to walk. To meet this innate pride and to crucify it, I determined to walk. I bought a barrow for $4.00 and hired a man to wheel it for about 15 cents a day. I shall not allow myself a ride on this barrow nor shall I allow a Chinese the luxury. The barrow conveys books and baggage, not missionaries. My expenditure which includes barrow-man's hire, amounts to 24 cents a day for the thirty-three days I have toured during the past autumn. As long as I keep to the wheelbarrow my average daily expense will never exceed 35 cents."

"I am now convinced that I can do better work by walking. The helpers hinted that there was a more excellent way, namely, for us each to ride a donkey, but I replied that our Master seldom enjoyed that luxury, so they fell in with the inevitable."

"In all the surrounding villages recently visited, with but one exception, I have been well received. On entering a certain village, I heard the people saying that the teacher of the Jesus doctrine had come. They then chose us a place for preaching and brought us a table and chairs. At another village a man brought me a seat

and a pot of tea. At still another, a wealthy man before whose house I was preaching, brought me out a
chair, and when I had been speaking some time, brought
me a drink of water. I was thirsty at the time and it
called to mind the cup of water our Saviour speaks of."

"On another occasion, in company with two Evangelists, I entered a village and started to preach. From
the outset they mocked me and would not listen. I tried
every device, but in vain; I could not hold them. I
then called upon Mr. Su to speak, but he fared worse
than I did and soon gave in. Finally, I called upon
Mr. Li. He was earnest and well up in years. I hoped
they would respect age; but no, they seemed determined
not to have us there. After about ten minutes of a vain
struggle, Mr. Li stopped and turning to me said, 'Let
us go. It is no use trying to speak. They will not
listen.' I was pretty well aroused by this time. I felt
it would never do to give the devil the victory, so I
opened up the Bible at Matthew 10:14, 15 and read
out the riot act recorded there. *"Whosoever shall not
receive you, nor hear your words, when ye depart out
of that house or city, shake off the dust of your feet.
Verily I say unto you, It shall be more tolerable for the
land of Sodom and Gomorrah in the day of judgment
than for that city."* While I proceded to explain it
a great fear seemed to come over the crowd and several
said, 'Forgive us. We have been rude. If you want
to speak we will listen.' I went on speaking and found
them most attentive. When we were leaving they invited us warmly to return.

"In due time we made a second visit to that village.
They received us most kindly and brought us out seats

and a stand for my Bible and some of the old ladies said I must be thirsty after talking so much and asked if we would not like them to make some tea."

Of the false reports hindering the work and how they were crushed, Goforth writes as follows:

"In the early part of 1893 evil stories were scattered around us like a plague. The chief of these stories was the old one of the children's hearts and eyes. The Chinese admit that the foreign physician works marvellous cures with his medicines. Their theory is that such efficacious medicine must have something very precious in its make-up. And what so precious as the hearts and eyes of children! They say that we kidnap these little ones and scoop out their eyes and cut out their hearts to manufacture our medicines. It is not only the more ignorant who give credence to these tales. All either believe or profess to believe them. Even a mandarin, who rules over at least 800,000 people, went so far as to post a proclamation throughout his district warning parents to keep a sharp watch on their children and never allow them far out of sight, for, said he, 'there are villains in our midst kidnapping children, and I can't be responsible for your little ones.' Men have actually been overheard saying that they saw whole boatloads of the children unloaded at the foreigners' compounds. They said that Mr. Chou, our chief convert, was the ringleader and that he managed all the beggars for us. Each beggar was paid ten cents a day and five dollars a head for every child brought in. They advocated killing Mr. Chou and razing his house to the ground.

"These continuing evil stories were proving a great

hindrance in the work. Mr. Su came back from a tour in the country saying that it was useless for him to try and preach or sell books. The people seemed afraid of him and could not be induced to listen. He brought back the report that in a certain village, a stranger was sauntering along the main street, and a villager, becoming suspicious, asked him if he was one of 'those kidnappers.' The stranger, inclined to have a little fun, said 'Yes.' Whereupon the villagers were called. They battered him until he was senseless, and then scalded him with hot water. The man died, of course. Placards were being posted up all over the country saying the worst that could be said of us, and calling upon innkeepers not to dare to give any foreigner a night's lodging. This injunction had its effect. On many occasions in the course of my country tours, I was unable to gain admission to inns or even buy a meal.

"This state of things could not be tolerated. The placards were torn down wherever found, but in some instances not without opposition. These, with other grievances, we laid before the British minister at Peking. He at once took the matter up and demanded of the high Chinese authorities that they put a stop to this reviling of missionaries lest a massacre might result. Soon proclamations were posted up throughout Changte prefecture denouncing the inventors and disseminators of these evil reports and assuring the people that the missionaries were there by treaty right and that anyone molesting them must suffer the penalty of the law. At once, as if by magic, the air cleared and a change set in, in our favour."

Here is a vivid picture of the hard side of village work in those days: "Paul tells us about fighting with beasts at Ephesus, but I assure you it is more like fighting with devils in some of these Chinese villages. I have preached the gospel in the worst dens in Toronto's slums. There I found the basest characters ready to respect genuine earnestness, but so beastly are the people in some of these places that let a man be as earnest as Gabriel and he will not escape insult. Other villages again seem to be made willing from the first visit. And we go again and again to be cheered by growing interest.

"This I can say that on no occasion where we stood with our backs to a wall and used the Word of God did we fail ultimately in gaining a victory. But it is anything but pleasant for a foreigner to get into the midst of a Chinese crowd without a friendly wall for backing. No one will as a rule molest him within range of his eyes. It is always the man behind his back that will shove or kick. The missionary turns around to remonstrate against such rudeness and everyone looks innocent, but just then his unprotected back comes in for more abuse. Several times I have got out of such crowds under a shower of clods and bricks. But with my back to a wall I have been able to stand as much crushing as my tormentors and have always held my ground."

We cannot pass from Chuwang without a word of tribute to our "beloved physician," Dr. William McClure — strong, reliable, sympathetic, yet quiet and humble; a gold medalist of McGill, and one who was looked upon in Montreal as "the coming man" in his profession. But he counted it all as nothing that he might have some share in "the great adventure" the Church was making in China.

What must it have meant, then, for him when many, many months passed without a single "good case" coming to the hospital, owing to the suspicious fears of the people. But we, who were with him, kept praying for our Doctor upon whom the sadness of disappointment was creeping. Then the answer came. Several critical cases passed safely through Dr. McClure's hands which began to win the people's confidence. Two or three years later, the hospital records stated that *thirty-two thousand patients* had been treated that year by Dr. McClure, in what one might term "a poor mud hovel" of a hospital.

More than forty years have passed since then, and, as I pen these words, this greatly loved and honoured servant of the Master has just bidden me farewell, as, at over eighty years of age, he once more sets out on his long, lonely journey to China.

VIII.

CHANGTE AT LAST!

How often do we attempt work for God to the limit of our incompetency rather than to the limit of God's omnipotency.

HUDSON TAYLOR

WE COME to the greatest and most important forward step Goforth had yet taken. For two years, at each succeeding Presbytery, he had earnestly sought for permission to secure property in Changte city and open up work there, but the majority was against this step, feeling as they did, that to open a third station, with the present force, would weaken the two stations that had already been established.

But Goforth kept on praying and believing for Changte. At last, the answer came. At the Presbytery meeting in the spring of 1894, permission was granted for the opening of Changte, but *conditionally*. The main condition was that the site for the Mission station must be outside the city wall, and in close touch with the north suburb. The second condition required Goforth and McGillivray to promise they would not ask either of the other stations for evangelists or help in any way that might weaken those stations.

However, Goforth had got all he wanted—permission to go ahead. The following morning at daybreak found him on the road to Changte. His whole soul was bounding with joy and hope for he could see the fulfilling of the promise given six years before on that early morning when entering the Changtefu region from the north. All the way that day, he prayed that God would give him the very best site, the site of His choice, for the Mission station. How fully, how wonderfully, God answered his prayer! Within twenty-four hours of his reaching the city, he had received thirty-two offers of property, among them, the very site that he and McGillivray had often looked upon as the ideal site for a mission station! But long trying negotiations had to be gone through before the site actually became Mission property. This work, Donald McGillivray undertook, thus setting Goforth free for a brief furlough.

That summer, the whole Chuwang region was visited by great floods. The water in the Mission compound stood at six to eight feet deep. The Goforths had packed, when leaving for furlough, household goods, such as clothes, linen, curtains, books, etc., in trunks and bureau-drawers. All such were ruined by the dirty flood water. When the water subsided, weeks of great heat caused black mould to form on everything. Furniture that was loosened could be mended, but all else was irreparably destroyed. Thus, for the second time, the Goforths experienced the loss of most of their temporal possessions.

Goforth could say with Paul, of these and later losses, "I do count them but refuse that I might gain Christ and be found in Him." But to his wife who had gathered together since the fire in Chefoo, only sufficient to make a simple but cosy home, the news of the floods came to them in Canada, as a sore trial.

Later, when life could be seen through the perspective of time, she came to see the truth of these lines:

> *"The blow most dreaded often falls*
> *To break from off our limbs a chain."*

For these and later losses were but setting them free for the nomadic life later on.

Little need be said of that first furlough. Though in Canada but a few months, Goforth addressed many meetings, sometimes eight to ten a week. But his heart was in Honan; so early in the autumn he returned, leaving his wife and three children, little Helen being but a few weeks old. On reaching Changte, he found McGillivray had gone successfully through the difficult task allotted him, and for which, with his fine knowledge of Chinese, he was so eminently fitted. The ideal site for the mission plant was actually in the hands of the Mission.

Much, however, had to be done. A preaching chapel close to the busy front street had to be built and some simple one-story Chinese rooms erected. On the arrival of spring, word was sent for Mrs. Goforth to come. From the first, Goforth and McGillivray arranged between them that the former take charge of the main station, while the latter gave himself to touring outside with Mr. Wang, now his evangelist as well as teacher.

The following letter dated from Changte, from her husband was received by Mrs. Goforth just as she was leaving for China:

"We had another busy day yesterday with soldiers and enquirers. The roads are horrid, the barrows go slowly. I consequently had time to talk to people by the way. I have had several good talks,—it is joyful work to serve the Master.

"I have never felt so rested in any place in China. It seems as if this is the place God has allotted for us to fix our dwelling-place. To have the open fields on two sides and the mountains to the west is surely all we could hope for. Ten converts from Tsaiyuan have come in today to welcome me back, one of whom has brought the deed of a house which he wants to give the Mission for a meeting-place in his native town. This has indeed been a happy day. I had six of the neighbours in last night to worship. The Lord is using Sir'rh (the young gate-keeper) to bring them in.

"In the morning we study Luke's Gospel, and in the evening the Psalms, with the Chinese. On the Sabbath my subject, forenoon and afternoon, in speaking with them, was 'The Sacrifice of Christ.' Oh! how wondrous! Again and again, I could scarce keep the tears back.

"I have had a good forenoon's study, having had my breakfast by six o'clock; but this afternoon I was receiving visitors until the present—seven-thirty. A believer from Taokung has come and will spend the night with us. I am glad to have so many coming to see us. There are three men in the city now who may be considered enquirers. I am delighted with the attitude of the people towards us. The Master is working in the hearts of men. Oh, for His grace, sufficient not to permit the hindering of His work!"

The autumn of 1895 was a red-letter period in the

lives of Jonathan Goforth and his wife. For almost seven years, Changte had ever been before them as their goal for a permanent station and home. For this they had steadfastly believed and prayed. It was therefore with great joy they started off from Chuwang early one October morning. To the three children, the long day's journey in the springless cart over bumpy uneven roads was just a picnic, but not so to the mother, who was having her first experience of travelling in what Dr. R. P. Mackay, their "beloved secretary," called "the excruciating cart."

How can one describe those early days at the new station! The foreign women and children, about whom all kinds of rumors had been circulated—mostly bad, —drew literally thousands to the Mission compound. Goforth was kept at high pressure from dawn till dark. Building operations were still in progress and as is necessary in China, he had to measure wood, count bricks, weigh lime, and keep a constant watch on the workmen. His Bible, even under these circumstances, was always with him, for opportunities that might come to sow the seed. Besides all this, he had to preach to the crowds which daily filled the chapel, and in the midst of this pressure, frequently would come a note from his wife from the women's court behind, "Do come and help me! Crowds of women—so tired from preaching I can hardly speak!"

So back Goforth would go and together they would sing a simple Gospel hymn written by Pastor Hsi, two lines to a verse and each line repeated four times, and sung to the catchy tune of, "We won't go home till morning!"—the whole a simple epitome of the Gospel

This delighted and quieted the crowds for the message that followed. And so the days went by for nearly three weeks, when both began to realize the strain could not be kept on indefinitely.

Goforth felt it was of the greatest importance that every effort should be made to take full advantage of these first early days of curiosity which would soon pass. Truly it could have been said of both of them at that time: "I will turn my face to the wind and lift my handful of seed on high."

Early one morning, before the crowds began to gather, Goforth came to his wife with his Bible open at Philippians 4:19 and said, "Rose, we simply cannot stand this much longer. I feel almost at the end of my physical powers, and you are nearly as exhausted as I am. Now listen, it says, 'My God shall supply all your need according to His riches in glory by Christ Jesus.' It says, 'all your need.' Surely, we need an evangelist to help us. Do you believe God can supply our need and fulfil this promise to us? I do. Then let us unite in prayer that God will send a man who can relieve me in the chapel. I can then help you without too much strain and be able also to look after the building." They knelt down and as he prayed, his wife thought, "But how — how can we expect to get a preacher? We have promised not to ask help from the other stations and we have no converts. *It is as if we were praying for rain from a clear sky!*"

But the Lord that worketh wonders heard Goforth's cry. The day following his prayer for help, Wang Fulin, a converted opium slave from near Chuwang,*

---

*For his full story see, **Miracle Lives of China**, page 33.

appeared at the Mission on his way to Changte city, seeking employment. He presented a truly pitiable spectacle. Emaciated, his face still having the ashy hue of the "opium fiend," his form bent from weakness, a racking cough every few moments shaking his frame, and clothed or rather partly clothed, in beggarrags. The man's story was a sad one. Since he became a Christian he could no longer carry on his "trade" of public story-telling. The family had come to a point of absolute destitution, even to the eating of leaves off the trees. Wang Fulin had at last decided the day before (when Goforth was praying), to leave home for Changte city. Goforth did not stop to hear more, but ordering a good meal to be served the man, went back to consult with his wife. "Was this the answer to their prayers?" they asked themselves. Yet, could anyone outwardly be more unlikely? They determined, however, to try him for a few days. He could at least testify to what the grace of God could do in saving an opium slave.

Within an hour or two of his entering the Mission gate, Wang Fulin was *cleansed* and clothed in one of Goforth's Chinese outfits and seated in the men's chapel preaching to a large audience! From the very first day of his ministry, there was no doubt of his being the messenger sent in answer to prayer. He had in a wonderful degree the unction and power of the Holy Spirit. His natural gifts as a speaker had been developed during the many years of street story-telling. Now all was consecrated to the one object,—the winning of souls to Christ. He seemed ever conscious that his time was short and always spoke as a dying man to dying men. From the very first, men were won to Christ. Of the two first-fruits of his ministry, one was a doctor of note and the second a wealthy landowner. For three years during those early days of stress and strain, he was spared to help in laying the foundations of the Changte Church. Then God took him. He was ever remembered, later, as the "Spirit-filled preacher."

The following note of thanksgiving from Goforth was dated December 16, 1895, less than three months after the family arrived at Changte.

"I am constrained to say 'Glory to God in the highest' for He is graciously manifesting His divine power these days. During the last five weeks we have had such a number of men coming day by day that we have kept up constant preaching on an average of eight hours a day. Wang Fulin, the converted gambler and opium smoker helps me. We take turns in preaching, never leaving the guest-room without someone to preach from morning to night. The men keep coming in in increasing numbers. I noticed once today when preaching that the guest-room was filled, while others were listening outside the door and windows. Almost every time we speak, men seem to be brought under conviction. Men will sit a whole half-day at a time listening. Some seem to get so much interested that they seem to forget that they have miles to go home after sundown. Interested ones come again and again. Each evening, when almost tired out, we have to turn men away and tell them to come the next day. This evening I had to turn away three enquirers, along with others, when it was too dark to see.

". . . Today has been the best of all the days.

Never in Canada or here have I before realized such power of the Holy Spirit. We say but little about the idols but hold up Christ crucified. He will draw them away from these vanities. God's time to favour the people of this city and surrounding villages has come. Oh that we may walk humbly before Him, for we have never seen His power on this wise before."

February 23, 1896. "The days of blessing continue. These days the people bethrong us. It is not only idle curiosity which brings some of them. Not a day passes but some come to enquire definitely about the doctrine. It is so easy to tell such of the way of life. So many women come these days that I have to help Mrs. Goforth to talk to them. I speak for awhile to the women that she may rest. Then I go out to the chapel to talk to the men. This is kept up from morning to night. It is heavy work, but it is grand to use all our strength in the Master's service.

"Mr. McGillivray, what with teaching a class of enquirers and speaking several times each day in the chapel, is worked to the uttermost. This is a great opportunity for reaching the women. Sometimes dozens of them are here at a time. It is perfectly proper for me to speak to them, with my wife at my side.

"It has been our privilege to see the manifest signs of Holy Ghost power among them. None but the Holy Spirit could open these hearts to receive the truth, as we see some receiving it every time we speak. I never saw anything approaching to it in

previous years. It cheers us beyond measure and
makes us confident that God is going to save many
people in this place."

Thus the work at Changte seemed from the first
to have the seal of God upon it. Converts were multiplied. Donald McGillivray, each time he returned from
a tour, reported much encouragement.

So many inquiries came to Goforth down through
the years asking for a statement regarding his position
on Divine healing that we give the following story of
his early position and how he came to somewhat modify
on this subject. About the time the Goforths left for
China, Dr. A. B. Simpson's *Divine Healing* and Dr.
A. J. Gordon's *Ministry of Healing* were being widely
read. Goforth brought both these books to China and
was inclined to take the *extreme*, or should we not say
highest view in favour of Divine healing. Sad experiences through which he and his wife had passed, had
strengthened him in this position by the time the following experienced occurred.

A few months after settling at Changte, Goforth
was suddenly taken ill, his symptoms all pointing to
probable pneumonia; high fever, pains in head and
chest, and difficulty in breathing. The nearest doctor
was at Chuwang, but though Mrs. Goforth plead to be
allowed to send for help, her husband absolutely for-
bade her doing so, saying he had taken the Lord as
his healer. Anxious days followed for the wife as
Goforth, white and still, consistently refused even the
putting on of a poultice. The crisis passed and he
began to recover, but before he had fully regained his
strength, he was taken down with violent chills and

fever. Regularly, every second day, the attacks came on him—first chills, then fever, followed by violent sweating and ending with a period of utter exhaustion. After the third attack, Mrs. Goforth became so alarmed, her prayer now became the cry of desperation that help might come before it was too late.

In the midst of praying thus, Donald McGillivray returned from his touring and Dr. Menzies arrived from Chuwang. After seeing Goforth, the doctor said, "If he will not take quinine, and he says he will not, I fear two or three more such attacks as he has been having, will prove fatal, but if he will take quinine I see no reason why he will not be himself again in a week."

Mrs. Goforth went to her husband and reported what the doctor had said. She knelt beside him and pleaded with tears that he take the quinine. He was very weak, scarcely able to speak. At last he said, "For your sake, I will take it. But we must face this whole question again, I am too weak now."

One or two slight attacks followed, but as the doctor had said, in a week Goforth was practically as well as ever. Later, the whole question of Divine healing was searchingly gone into, for Goforth realized that a "chain is no stronger than its weakest link." In discussing this question with others, he would never dogmatize as to what stand others should take, but was content to say, "As for me, I must leave my Lord to reveal His will in each case as it comes. Sometimes we seem clearly led to use means and to regard a doctor as God's minister. Again, we have seen God honour simple faith, and a miracle of healing was wrought." As far as the writer can recall, these cases of healing were, in the Goforths' experience, either when medical aid could not be obtained or when human means had failed.

In a letter dated April 12, 1896, Goforth writes:

"Since coming to Changte five months ago, we have been cheered almost daily by the manifest tokens of the Holy Spirit's power. He has been making the people willing to hear beyond all our expectations. During this time upwards of 25,000 men and women have come to see us and all have had the Gospel preached to them. Preaching is kept up on an average of eight hours a day. Sometimes fifty or more women in our yard at one time. The signs of blessing among women were even more cheering than among the men. I am sure the friends of Missions would rejoice greatly to see what we have seen. Almost every time we held up Christ as Redeemer and Saviour, the Holy Spirit moved one or more. It has been our privilege to see at one time from ten to twenty of these heathen women deeply moved and earnestly enquiring the way of salvation for a couple of hours at a time. Some of the interested ones have returned to hear more, and others will return. We have no doubt but that many who have been moved by the Spirit of God during these months, will be centres of light in their own districts."

The following letter tells of facing a real menace to the work, that of a Romanist invasion.

"We are much perplexed about a new danger which threatens to absorb our infant church in North Honan. It is a Romanist invasion. In one town where we had a very encouraging work of about three years' standing, the Romanists have captured almost the whole number of enquirers.

"The inducements they offer are well nigh irresistible from a Chinese point of view. They promise to protect them from all persecution, to board any one free of charge who will go to them and study the doctrine, to provide free schools for the education of their children, and promise financial aid as well as promising to employ as many as possible.

"We knew that they were trying to induce some of our converts to the southeast of this city to join them. We took steps to warn the converts of the designs of Rome and cautioned them about being misled. Imagine our disappointment when we found that eight men, the representatives of our work in that region, had gone over to the Romanists. It means the sweeping away in a week the work of years. We could offer no such inducements and we have a horror of making 'rice Christians.'

"We cannot fight Rome by competing with them in buying up the people, but we will continue to preach the Word and let the light shine in. Let the people of the Lord unite in prayer for us. One of the brethren remarked the other day that this was the most discouraging thing we had met with since commencing work in Honan."

Goforth writes some months later that practically all those mentioned in the above letter as having gone over to Rome, had returned in spite of the inducements.

About this time Donald McGillivray was called to Shanghai to engage in translation work. His departure was a great loss to Jonathan Goforth.

IX.

ALL THINGS TO ALL MEN

God's best gifts are not in things but in opportunities.
Anon

EARLY IN 1896, Presbytery decided the time had come for the erection of a semi-foreign bungalow for the Goforths. Since moving to Changte, they had been living in a Chinese house, quite unsuitable for their needs. While their new home was being built the Goforths feared that it might prove a barrier between themselves and the Chinese and perhaps hinder the progress of the work which was going on so hopefully; so they prayed that God would overrule, and not only prevent the new building from being a hindrance, but make it a means of increased blessing to the people. As with so many of their prayers, they came to see that the answer lay in their own hands. A price had to be paid —"open house to all." This price they resolved to pay.

The new home was completed by the fall of 1897. Its architecture was simple, being Chinese in style on the outside while the interior was like an ordinary bungalow in the homeland. As it was the first building of its kind to be built in that region, the house was naturally an object of great curiosity to the Chinese. The board floors, the glass windows and the shutters, the foreign furniture, the organ, the sewing-machine, (the "iron-tailor" as it was called), even the kitchen stove which let its smoke and gas go out through a chimney instead

115

of into one's eyes and through one's house,—all these were things of wonder to the Chinese. And as for the cellar! Who had ever heard of people having a big hole underneath their house! That must be where the "foreign devils" kept the bodies of the kidnapped children. And so, when it became noised through the district that the foreigners were willing for people to see through their "strange house," multitudes availed themselves of the opportunity.

Goforth led the men through the house in bands of ten or twenty or more at a time, while his wife took charge of the women. But first there was the Mission compound to be explored. Dr. Menzies had made a pump. It became the talk of the whole countryside. Such a wonderful thing that could bring water up from the bottom of a well without a bucket! They had heard about Paul's tricycle. A self-propelled cart they called it. Paul would give them an exhibition by wheeling several times around the yard. They had also heard of the baby-carriage. Florence would wheel the baby in it up and down a few times for their edification.

Then Goforth would stand up on the veranda of the house and say, "Men, I have something to tell you. I want you to stand here and listen. If you go roaming about the yard and will not pay attention, I shall not let you see through the house." The house, being the main attraction, they were always ready to listen while Goforth gave a short Gospel address.

Afterwards they were shown through the house. Nothing escaped their curious eyes. Beds were turned back, drawers opened, the sewing-machine examined, the organ played, before they appeared satisfied. We regret to say that a very careful watch had to be kept while leading bands of visitors through. The Chinese had, at that time, great capacious sleeves and they were very dexterous at poking knives, forks, spoons, saucers, pictures and knick-knacks up them. We took what precaution we could, but things would disappear. We found it impossible to keep a pair of foreign-made scissors about the place. Some of the sewing-machine fixtures were taken. One visitor even got away with the carving knife.

Goforth made a special point of allowing them to see the cellar and assisted them in lifting lids off every box and jar and even helped them to turn over the coal, so as to convince them we had nothing to hide from them. This did more than anything else to kill the ugly rumours about the jars of children's flesh that were supposed to be secreted in the cellar.

The high-water mark in visitors received was reached one day in the fall of 1899, when 1,835 men passed through the house. On the same day, Mrs. Goforth received about 500 women. This particular day had been looked forward to with great uneasiness by missionaries and native Christians alike. On that day the city god, Chenghwang, was to be brought out for his semi-annual visit to a temple near the Mission compound, and a great fair was to be held in connection with this important event. On the same day, thousands of government students were to assemble in the city for the annual examinations.

The day, when it came, was one never to be forgotten by those at the Changte station. Goforth had no time to eat dinner that day. His wife handed him a cup of hot milk now and then which kept him going till nightfall. Sometimes there were as many as five hundred men down at the front gate clamouring to get in. Something would have to be done to ease the pressure. Goforth would go out to them and say, "Men, I can take about one hundred and fifty of you at a time. I will take that many through and let them out the back gate, after which I will take another lot through." "All right," they would say. Yet immediately the gate was opened, the whole five hundred would try to get in at the one time. Fortunately the gate was fairly narrow, and when Goforth felt that he had let through as many as he could handle, he would brace his hands against the door frame on either side, blocking the way, while some of the Christians cleared the door and closed it.

There was one incident on this day which Mrs. Goforth always recalls with a smile. Usually she played the organ for her husband's visitors, but on this particular day she was too much engaged with her crowds of women, so Goforth had to be his own organist. Knowing that he could not distinguish one note from another, and hearing the organ being played, she peeped into the living-room. Imagine her feelings at seeing her husband seated at the organ with all the twenty-four stops drawn out, his hands pressed down on as many notes as possible, the bellows going at full blast and a crowd of delighted Chinese standing around. One remark heard above the *din* was, "He plays better than his wife."

As can well be imagined, this constant receiving of visitors was exhausting work.

"I have often been receiving and talking to band after band of men in my study from morning right on till evening," wrote Goforth at that time. "About sundown, I sometimes feel so tired that I wish the last had come for today, but I may glance out to the front and there the gatekeeper is bringing in a fresh lot. Am I to say to these men, "I cannot see you today. I am tired. Come some other time." No! How do I know but that the Lord has sent these men specially to me and tired and all as I may be, I bring them in and treat them kindly and tell them of our wonderful Redeemer."

Some missionaries felt that the Goforth's policy of keeping "open house" was a great mistake, that it meant cheapening themselves and the Mission before the people. The future, however, was to reveal abundantly the value of this policy. Deep-seated prejudices were overcome, friendly contacts were made with the highest and of all classes, and many hearts were opened to the Gospel.

"Some may think," writes Goforth, "that receiving visitors is not real Mission work, but I think it is. I put myself out to make friends with the people and I reap the results when I go to their villages to preach. Often the people of a village will gather around me and say, 'We were at your place and you showed us through your house, treating us like friends.' Then they will almost always bring me a chair to sit on, a table to lay my Bible on, and some tea."

From the front windows of the Goforth's house, one could see through gates of two courts, clear to the "Great Gate" opening on to a busy thoroughfare. All through these early years at Changte, again and again, a man could be seen running at full speed from the front, calling for Pastor Goforth to "come quickly—a mob is gathering!" On such occasions his wonderful gift and power to handle crowds was tested to the full. There were times when the mission and missionaries were in the gravest danger.

A testing, at times heart-breaking, period for the Goforths began the summer of 1898 when their little daughter Gracie showed signs of a strange disease. Though examined by more than one doctor, the trouble was not diagnosed till several months had passed when the child was found to be in a hopeless condition from enlarged spleen brought on by pernicious malaria.

For almost a year, Gracie lingered. During those last months she spent as much time in her father's arms as his work would permit. Sometimes she lay in her little carriage drawn up beside her father's desk and at such times all she seemed to crave for was to gaze on the father's face or slip her little hand in his when free. The tender love of the parent for his suffering child and her great love for him was extremely touching to those who witnessed it.

The doctor had warned the parents that the end would probably come in convulsions. The thought of this impending was agony, for both Gertrude and Donald had passed so. But the good Lord knew all and kept to them His promise—"He stayeth His rough wind in the day of the east wind." Isa. 27:8.

One evening, the father had gone to rest early as it was his turn to take the vigil at midnight. Miss Pyke had just come in. Gracie seemed no worse, only a little restless. Suddenly, she partly rose and said in a strong commanding tone, "I want my papa." Not wishing to disturb the tired-out father, the mother hesitated, when again Gracie said, "Call my papa. I want my papa!" Miss Pyke whispered, "You had better call him. He can walk with her a little, and that will ease her." (The child was so heavy from dropsy the mother could not lift her.)

A few moments later the father had taken his beloved little one in his arms, laying her head gently upon his shoulder as he started to pace the floor. The mother slipped into the adjoining bedroom and sinking on her knees, cried to the Lord to spare Gracie suffering. If she were to go, to take her without pain or struggle. Then the words came as a flash, "Before they call I will answer, and while they are yet speaking, I will hear."

At that moment, Miss Pyke entered saying, "Gracie is with Jesus." While the mother was on her knees, Gracie, who had been resting quietly in her father's arms, suddenly lifted her head and looking straight into her father's eyes gave him a wonderful, loving smile, closed her eyes, and without a struggle, was gone.

The following evening, October 3, the precious remains of little Gracie were laid away in a tree-sheltered corner of the mission compound. On returning home, Paul was found to be ill with measles and dysentery. A week of anxiety followed, then as he began to recover, nature had her way with the utterly worn-out father. For weeks Goforth lay seriously ill with a bad attack of jaundice. He was still very ill and a sight to behold with eyes like brass or amber and a complexion not unlike that of an Indian, when the mother herself, exhausted with long nursing and over-strain, went down to, and almost passed, the borderland. Outside missionaries and Christians were praying for the *two* lives hanging in the balance—then joy and thanksgiving arose as the cry of a little child was heard!

Time was passing, Christmas week was at hand, and still Goforth continued weak and shaky and unfit for work. At last, impatient at his slow progress, he determined, in characteristic fashion, to follow his own ideas as to how to regain strength. One morning, having borrowed a hunting outfit and gun from his neighbour, he started off duck-hunting accompanied by one of the newly arrived missionaries, Mr. B., and Paul. For several days this was kept up. The second day, however, nearly ended in tragedy. Mr. B., evidently unaccustomed to carrying a gun, was behind Goforth with barrel pointing forward. Something happened to fire the gun. Goforth heard the sound of a bullet whizzing past his ear and turning quickly, found Mr. B. white with horror at what had happened and Goforth's narrow escape.

The duck-hunting experiment proved a great success, for by Christmas day, the Goforths' larder was richer by several birds and Goforth himself once more feeling fit for full time service.

The back of the mission compound led out into the open country. Goforth's study was not more than fifty yards from this gate. One day, as a high official accompanied by a number of "underlings" was being received in the study, a loud persistent banging on the gate was heard. By the time Goforth, followed by the official and his men, had arrived on the scene, the one on the outside was making such a noise and pounding on the gate in such a way the Chinese became alarmed. Mr. Griffith had arrived and took a stand with a club close to Goforth, making ready to strike if the one outside meant mischief. Well indeed that he did so, for the instant Goforth had unlocked the gate, the man outside aimed a blow with a heavy meat chopper at his head— but Griffith was too quick and struck the weapon aside! The man was found to be a raging maniac. The official was for having him taken to the city and executed at once, but Goforth plead so for the poor fellow's life that he was put in charge of his family. It would probably have been better if the official had had his way, for the following day, the insane man killed his own brother. Later, he was shot. There were no asylums in China.

Something of Jonathan Goforth's "passion for preaching," his utter fearlessness, and his gift for training men, may be seen in the following extracts.

"Right here at our doors is the city of Changte with a population of about 100,000. We must needs look after them. Taking Christians with me, we will go from street to street preaching and singing the Gospel in true Salvation Army style, although without the aid of flag and drum. It ruffles the temper of some of the 'upper ten' Chinese residents on those streets, but we can't help that. We must awake them from the sleep of death. It is hard for some of these Christians to testify for Christ on the street. Some of them have had no education and when they stand up to speak they are afraid and tremble, yet a little practice gives confidence and power. In this way we have trained about a dozen men, besides the helpers who may be called upon in an emergency. We dread 'dummy' Christians and strive to have all enabled to give a reason for the faith that is in them." . . .

. . . "I have heard a man suddenly exclaim when the sun had travelled far westward, 'Oh, I've got listening to this wonderful story and forgotten all about my dinner!' Imagine the people in our country forgetting their dinner if the pastor preaches a little overtime. It is an old story with us. Not so with the heathen. I have known them to stand listening for hours and night after night, when we ceased preaching to go home, I have heard one hundred to two hundred men cry out—'Stay and tell us more!' I have had rough men urge me to repeat some address they had heard me give in some other part of the city. The addresses thus asked for are as a rule those which reveal the love of Jesus in dealing with sinners. It is no weariness to the flesh to tell out the Gospel to people so willing to hear. Time flies and our strength is renewed like the eagle's."

Perhaps no phase of his missionary service brought out the strength and power of Goforth's character more than his work among the students. We give the following abbreviated description of that work as it comes from his own pen.

"Sometimes as many as five thousand students from the five counties came up to Changte city for examinations. They were most difficult to handle. In fact, the first year, I simply did not know how to handle them, but I did the best I could.

"The students would frequently come into the

chapel and gaze about them with lofty airs. On my inviting them to be seated, they would pay no heed, continuing to look around and cast knowing glances at each other. As this was causing disorder, I would say more firmly, 'Gentlemen, be seated.' My only response would be a snicker of laughter. Then, with considerable emphasis, I would again insist, "Gentlemen, we preach the gospel in this place and cannot permit disorder. Sit down!' At this, they would bolt for the door, convulsed with laughter, upsetting all inside who were inclined to listen.

"I determined to be ready for them on their return the following year. I sent to Shanghai for a large globe and several maps and astronomical charts. The maps and charts were hung about the study, and the globe occupied a prominent place. When the students arrived, I left the preaching in the chapel in charge of Mr. Wang and invited the students back to my study. On entering, the first thing which caught their eye was the globe. Someone would exclaim, 'What is that big round thing?' I would explain it was a representation of our earth. Then several would say, 'You don't mean to tell us that the earth is round! Isn't it square and flat?' On explaining a little further and going into the movements of the earth, with a look of blank astonishment, several might exclaim, 'You surely don't mean that the earth turns over at night! Why! wouldn't we all tumble off?' Then would come the explanation of the law of gravitation—and so on, until it began to dawn upon the self-sufficient students that the foreigner had something worth listening to.

"A few enlightening geographical facts worked wonders in lowering their pride. Then, they would turn to the astronomical charts asking the meaning of the balls and circles. They all became intensely interested in every fact of astronomy given them. It was very interesting to watch the change in their attitude and the expression of their faces as we told of the sun, its size, its distance, and so on. By this time, all the pride had oozed out of the students. One of them exclaimed one day—'Why, we Chinese are like people sitting at the bottom of a well gazing at the heavens and imagining we see the whole expanse!'

"The student is now teachable and will listen readily when I tell him about God the Father and His Son, Jesus Christ. Many hundreds of students were received in this way. So great was the success of this plan which I had adopted that I came to feel it was inspired of God."

All through that winter of 1899-1900 the political situation was becoming daily more threatening. The very air seemed electric, yet foreigners all over China made no move for safety. The general feeling among missionaries and merchants alike was that the threatening storm would pass as many others had done. It was a case of "Wolf! Wolf!"

During the months before the crash came, the progress of the Gospel throughout the Changte region was never so hopeful. Goforth and his wife had made a map of their own field. Each centre where a Christian community had sprung up, was indicated by a red dot. By May of 1900, there were over fifty of these red dots.

How the children delighted in watching them increase, Florence exclaiming one day, "Oh, won't it be lovely, Father, when the map is all red!"

As late as May of that fateful year, the Goforths arranged for a visit to the distant out-station of Hopei, situated among the foothills west of Changte. Some of their colleagues kindly took charge of the four older children, baby Wallace accompanying his parents.

At Hopei, they had one large room facing on an open court. For a week intensive preaching was carried on by Goforth and his helpers in the courtyard, while Mrs. Goforth and her two Bible women told out the Gospel story to the women in the room. The paper-covered windows of this room which faced on the street were soon filled with holes, behind which always a bank of curious eyes peered in. Smallpox was raging, as could be seen by the number of children covered with pox among the crowds inside thronging to see the foreign woman and her child. The gospel seed-sowing of that week was as " bread cast upon the waters," but the day came when an abundant spiritual harvest was reaped in that region.

On returning home, the Goforths found their colleagues much concerned at a sudden stoppage of all mail. Mail received by the post-office and sent on, gradually came back from the north and was returned to the Mission. They were thus cut off from any communication with the outside world. The drought continued. Even the trees were becoming seared and yellow. Night and day the air was rent by the cries of the people for rain. Rumours of all sorts were abroad. One of these was that bands of fifty or more men were planning to march on the Mission station with the purpose of destroying the property and massacring the foreigners.

In the midst of all this the Goforths' eldest daughter, Florence, a beautiful golden-haired girl, between seven and eight years of age, was taken ill. In a few days meningitis developed. Dr. Leslie, at Chuwang, was the nearest doctor. Though the roads were dangerously beset by bandits, a messenger was dispatched for him. The doctor left at once, but arrived only a short while before the child passed away, the evening of June 19.

"A peace there is in sacrifice secluded,
A life subdued from will and passion free:
'Tis not the peace that over Eden brooded,
But that which triumphed in Gethsemane."

X.

THE ESCAPE

Who delivered us out of so great a death, and will deliver: on whom we have set our hope that he will also still deliver.

THE APOSTLE PAUL

BEFORE GIVING a brief account of our deliverance on that awful journey in 1900, I wish first humbly to submit the following, for well I know there will be those who will read these pages whose dear ones were *not* delivered but whose lives were given up for Christ in glorious martyrdom for His Name's sake.

When in Canada, following the experiences now to be recorded, we were faced with the question, put in various ways—"How can you say as you do, that it was by God's power and grace that you were all brought through? If this were so why did He not deliver the hundreds of missionaries and native Christians who were even then being done to death throughout China?" Truly a vital question, which could not be lightly set aside! Humbly and prayerfully we pondered this "WHY" in the light of Scripture. In the twelfth chapter of Acts we read of Herod's succeeding in putting James to death by the sword, and directly after comes the story of how Herod was hindered in carrying out his intention to kill Peter who was delivered by a miracle. Then who could read that marvellous eleventh chapter of Hebrews with its record of glorious martyrdoms and miraculous deliverances without being thrilled! In face of these and many other passages, while still unable to answer the "WHY" we saw our Almighty God used His own prerogative to glorify His name whether in the glorious martyrdom of some or in the miraculous deliverance of others.

The days while Florence's life hung in the balance were days of intense suspense. Every effort to learn of what was taking place to the north failed utterly. Then, just after Florence died, came a message, delayed many days en route, from the American Consul in Chefoo, saying: "Flee south. Northern route cut off by Boxers." This was quickly followed by another still more urgent message.

The missionaries and Christian leaders gave themselves to prayerful consultation. We missionaries all favoured remaining, but the Christians became more and more urgent that we flee without delay, contending they could escape more readily were we not there. The missionaries finally yielded and hasty preparations were made for the long and hazardous journey,—fourteen days by cart to Fancheng, South Honan, and ten or more days from there by houseboat on to Hankow.

There were indications from the first that God's purpose was to save us, though some of these could not be discerned till later. The journey was to be made by large farmer-carts resembling gipsy-wagons. To break the terrible heat from the sun, wadded quilts were gathered from every available source and carefully spread out of sight between coarse straw mats, and placed over the carts as awnings. Well it was that this was done as we shall see later. The day before leaving, an official courier from the north rode through the city of Changte at breakneck speed. He had a burnt feather in his cap which the Chinese said indicated his message was of life and death importance. We did not know till Hankow was reached that this courier carried a sealed packet from the Empress Dowager to the Governor of Honan at Kaifengfu, the capital, commanding the massacre of all foreigners. Without knowing this, the missionaries who had planned to take the direct route south which led through the city of Kaifengfu, were led, at almost the last moment, to change to a much longer one running westward and far from the "death-trap" which would have awaited them had they gone into Kaifengfu.

The missionary party from Chuwang arrived at Changte June 27. Less than an hour later, a Christian brought the news of all mission property being destroyed there and their homes being looted. Before daybreak, the following morning, the caravan started. There were ten heavily laden carts. Besides ourselves and our four children, the party consisted of three men, five women, and one little lad, Douglas McKenzie, also, three servants.

I have already said this is but a *brief* story, for were I to attempt to give in detail each day as it passed, I might well write another such book as *A Thousand Miles of Miracle*. Of those first ten days I can only say that each day as it came seemed harder than the last. The intense heat, the sickness of one of the chil dren, the bumping over rough roads in those springless wagons, and, ofttimes, at the close of day, no place to sleep but the bare ground with a quilt beneath us, made one think *then* nothing could be harder, but *afterwards* those first days seemed as nothing. More than once the cry was heard, "Kill, kill," but we were brought through unharmed.

On the evening of July 7 we reached the small walled town of Hsintien. For some days the people had been becoming more and more menacing. An engineer party which had joined us south of the Yellow River, somewhat apart from us, decided they would not stop at Hsintien but press right on to the large important city of Nanyangfu, twenty-five li distant. This greatly increased our danger as the engineers were armed and had with them a mounted armed escort. There was no doubt but that the leaders of this party were thoroughly scared. One said, "If I get out of this, not a million dollars would tempt me back to this land!" As a compromise, they left us one mounted soldier from their escort.

The engineer party was scarcely out of sight when crowds began to gather outside the inn door which was barricaded with carts, etc., but every moment a break was threatened by the stones hurled against it. Money was demanded, and things looked very serious. A letter was sent off about midnight to the engineers, telling of our danger and asking them to return. By daybreak we could see the crowd outside becoming ever more dense. Our whole party had by this time begun to hope against hope for the engineers' return, but this hope was given up when a letter came saying the official

at Nanyang was very threatening, ordering them to
leave at once. They were sorry, but were starting on
immediately! On hearing this, the carters became panic
stricken. The poor fellows huddled together in a corner
of the yard refusing to move.

Much time was being lost. Finally our men drew
up a statement promising full indemnity to each man
for any possible loss of carts, animals, injuries, etc.
Then they began slowly and unwillingly to harness up.
While this was being done, a call came for us all to
meet in an empty room for prayer. My husband took
from his pocket *Clarke's Scripture Promises* and began
to read from where the book opened. The passages
were as follows:

"The eternal God is thy refuge, and underneath
are the everlasting arms: and he shall thrust out the
enemy from before thee; and shall say, Destroy
them."

"The God of Jacob is our refuge."

"Thou art my help and my deliverer; make no
tarrying, O my God."

"I will strengthen thee; yea, I will help thee; yea,
I will uphold thee with the right hand of my righteousness. . . The Lord thy God will hold thy right
hand, saying unto thee, Fear not; I will help thee."

"If God be for us, who can be against us?"

"We may boldly say, The Lord is my helper, and
I will not fear what man shall do unto me."

Never indeed was there a more timely message
given to mortal man than these words given to us at
that time. During the reading and through the time

of prayer that followed, God's presence became wonderfully real. I could not see into the hearts of others, but I can say for myself that every trace of agonized panic with which I had been threatened, was banished forever, and in its place came a sweet peace which God's Word truly describes as "passing all understanding."

Quietly and calmly all got on the carts, which one by one passed through the gate into the street. To our surprise all was quiet—the dense crowd made no move to hinder us. But my husband began to suspect something serious when no one attempted to respond to baby Wallace's advances as his father held him up before the crowd. Many times on the preceding days the Chinese love for little children had apparently saved the situation as angry looks turned to smiles and laughter as the wee boy laughed and crowed at the crowds.

Just as we passed through the town gate, my husband turned pale. Pointing to a crowd of several hundred men with arms full of stones, daggers at their belts, and other weapons in evidence, he had just uttered the words, "There is trouble ahead," when the attack began. The whole cavalcade by this time had passed down to a dip in the road. First came a fusillade of stones, which our assailants expected would crash through the brittle straw mats, but this the quilts prevented. Then came the firing of guns and the rush forward. Some of the animals had their backs broken, the carts became tangled, bringing all to a standstill.

Jumping down from our cart, my husband rushed

forward shouting, "Take everything, but don't kill!"
At once he became the target for the fiercest onslaught.
(Can anyone read the following without in his heart
believing in an Almighty God's over-ruling hand?)

One blow from a two-handed sword struck him on
the neck with great force, showing the blow was meant
to kill, but *the wide blunt edge* struck his neck leaving
only a wide bruise two-thirds around the neck. The
thick pith helmet he was wearing was slashed almost
to pieces, one blow severing the inner leather band
just over the temple, went a fraction of an inch short
of being fatal for the skin was not touched. His left
arm which was kept raised to protect his head, was
slashed to the bone in several places. A terrible blow
from behind struck the back of his head, denting in
the skull so deeply, that, later, doctors said it was a
miracle the skull was not cleft in two. This blow felled
him to the ground. It was then he seemed to hear
clearly a voice saying—"Fear not! They are praying
for you!" Struggling to his feet, he was struck down
again by a club. As he was losing consciousness he
saw a horse coming down upon him at full gallop. On
regaining consciousness, he found this horse had thrown
his rider and fallen on smooth ground, close beside
him, and kicking furiously, the animal had formed a
barrier between his attackers till he was able to rise.
Standing dazed, a man rushed up as if to strike, but
whispered, "Get away from the carts!" By this time
the thousands who had gathered to watch the attack began to crowd forward for what they could get of our
things, but the attackers felt the loot belonged to them

and ceased their attack to fight for their rights. The confusion which followed gave us a chance to get away from the carts.

It is not possible to give here the details of each one's escape. Later, each had his or her testimony to give to a mighty and merciful deliverance. The days which followed showed, in some respects, just as great evidence of God's purpose to save us.

As to myself and the children: The cart was surrounded by fierce men, seemingly crazy to get our things. One struck at the baby's head, but I parried the blow with a pillow. From behind and before, boxes, bedding any and everything was carried away. Helen and the baby were with me, and Paul came running straight through the melee without getting hurt. Just then a man from behind struck at me with his dagger, but by throwing myself back I barely prevented its reaching me.

My husband, staggering and dripping with blood, came to the side of the cart saying, "Get down quickly. We must get away!" As we started off, one man relieved me of my shoes, another snatched my hat away, but we were allowed to go, but only for a short distance, when a number of men began following and pelting us with stones. Putting the baby in my husband's arms I turned and plead for the children. Surprised perhaps that I could speak their language, they stopped and listened a moment. Then the leader called out, "We've killed her husband—let her go." With this they left us.

Not far distant a village could be seen, and this we

endeavoured to reach for Mr. Goforth's strength was failing. Men and women were out in force as we neared the village. At first, the men sought to drive us away but as my husband sank to the ground apparently bleeding to death, the women all began to weep. This moved the men to pity and as I knelt beside my husband with the children weeping bitterly, they gathered around seeking to help. One man whispered, "I have something to stop the bleeding," and running into a hut nearby, quickly returned with the palm of his hand piled up with a fine gray powder with which he filled the great open wound at the back of the head, instantly stopping the flow of blood. Then several men joined in helping my husband into the village, to a small mud hut about eight feet square with one tiny window. Here they laid him on a straw mat spread on the ground. A round mat was given me. They locked us in saying it would be safer so. Through the tiny window hot water was handed for bathing our bruises which were becoming extremely painful, especially those at the back of my head and neck. From time to time, bowls of millet gruel and dried bread were passed in to us. We could hear the men planning how at nightfall they would start off with us by cart to Hankow and so save us.

But, oh, could one ever forget the suspense of that day! Mr. Goforth lay quite still but very pale,—at times so death-like, I feared the worst. Never for one moment during the eight hours in that hut did I cease to cry to God for his life, and for our comrades and our precious Ruth of whom we had heard absolutely nothing. With what unspeakable joy and thankfulness therefore about four o'clock that afternoon did we welcome Mr. McKenzie, and learn from him that no one had been killed, but Dr. Leslie had been seriously crippled. Our little Ruth had been saved by the faithful nurse, Mrs. Cheng, spreading herself upon her and taking upon herself cruel blows meant for the child.

The whole party had spent a day of great suffering by the roadside. All had united in praying the Lord to move some of the carters to join them with their carts, for the party could not proceed without them, Dr. Leslie being in the condition he was. To some of us, the greatest miracle of our *Thousand Miles of Miracle* was that five of the carters did come with their carts, all that were now needed, as baggage and bedding was gone.

When Mr. McKenzie announced all were now waiting on the road for us to join them, Mr. Goforth immediately rose. As I started forward to support him, he put me gently from him, saying quietly, "Only *pray*. The Lord will give me strength as long as He has work for me to do." Steadily and without assistance, he walked some distance to where the party waited.

As we were leaving the village the people crowded around as old friends. One poor old man insisted on my taking a pair of his old shoes, so worn as to scarcely hold together, saying they might keep my feet from the rough ground. Women came with old soiled children's garments, urging that the nights were cool and the children might need them.

"Why were they so kind?" one man was asked. He

replied, "We are Mohammedans. Our God is your God and we could not face Him if we had joined in destroying you." A remarkable fact is that rarely is a Mohammedan village found in China as they congregate in cities for protection. Truly, "God moves in a mysterious way."

Joining the rest of the party we found our cart which held three before the attack, now had nine aboard —our two selves, four children, Mrs. Cheng, a man servant, and the carter!

As the great city of Nanyangfu loomed in sight the walls appeared black with the crowds awaiting and outside the gate for a mile, crowds lined the roadway. How—how indeed, did we pass through that mass unharmed? When we reached them, our carts swayed and at times almost overturned with the pressure upon them from all sides. Clods of earth and bits of brick were pelted and that fearsome cry, "Kill, kill!" came from multitudes. Yet we passed on till the inn was reached. The open yard of this inn was very large, which became packed with a mob of probably over a thousand.

As we left the carts, we were literally driven into one room which soon became crowded to suffocation, for the heat was intense. The whole party was at least outwardly calm and quiet, except Mr. Goforth, who could not forbear doing some plain speaking. Whether this had any effect on what followed, is doubtful, but after an hour or more, the mob outside demanding that we be brought out, the room gradually emptied, and all the men of our party, (except Dr.

Leslie), with Mrs. McKenzie, Douglas, our four children and myself, were lined up shoulder to shoulder on the narrow veranda.

Till darkness dispersed them, we remained facing that great seething mob. There were jeers and insults and cries of, "Kill!" But no weapon which many had in hand prospered. Again—why? What but the restraining hand of God!

Soon after dark, the messenger who had been sent to the official with a letter demanding protection, returned greatly agitated. As he was waiting, he said, in a corner of the court for the official's answer, he overheard two soldiers discussing the official's plans for the massacre of all our party. The gist of the plan was that none should be killed inside the city lest he (the official) be blamed later; but a party of soldiers were to be at a certain place by the road the missionaries were to take and none were to escape. Then the official could say bandits had done the deed. So sure was this man we were all to be killed that night, he at once set to work trying to persuade the other Chinese with us to return to North Honan with him. Failing in this, he set out alone that night and on reaching Changte, reported all as having been killed!

The missionaries faced a serious question. Would they again demand protection or would it be better to start on? All agreed it was better to face death in the open than in that stifling inn. To save his face and camouflage his real plan, the official sent a few soldiers *to guide us to the right road!*

We started off in the dead of a very dark night.

Just as we had all passed through the city gate, Mr. Goforth noticed a light being flashed every few seconds from above the gate. These he felt convinced were signals to the waylaying party that we were coming. Just then, the carts came to a standstill, and a carter rushed up saying Paul and Mr. Griffith were not on their cart. For two hours search was made for them, even back to the inn—but no trace of them could be found. Then, as dawn was at hand, it was decided we must go on, leaving behind one cart and a trusted servant.

At this juncture, one of the most remarkable evidences of God's plan to save us, took place. While we were waiting, the soldiers had got on the carts *and had fallen asleep.* The carters too, were drowsy, and when we came to a fork in the road, the animals were left to take their own way, which was *not* the road of the way-laying party, but leading away from it. When the soldiers awoke, they were furious, but after a time of threatening, left us and returned to the city. It was ten o'clock before we finally again reached the right road and were then far from Nanyangfu!

The whole region was in a greatly disturbed state. Our carts were surrounded and stopped probably a dozen times that morning by wild mobs. They would pull us about, searching for what might be found, but finding nothing, we were allowed to proceed. One villainous looking man with a spear, led one band. At first he seemed prepared for any violence, but as he looked at our wounded men and at the little children, his heart softened with pity. Taking advantage of this, I held up the torn dirty garments and told how the

Mohammedans had given them. This seemed to quite overcome him. Turning to the crowd, he said, "We must not hurt these people,"—and then to us, "It is very dangerous for travellers; I will go with you for a way."

It was indeed a mercy he did, for the next mob was very wild. One man snatched the battered pith helmet from Mr. Goforth's head and when an effort was made to reclaim it, the snatcher tore it to bits before our eyes with a wicked taunting laugh. At this same place, men tried to drag our faithful nurse off our cart, but the man who had come along with us stopped them, saying, "The children will need her. Let her alone!" When we were safely started again, our kind "villain" friend left us and ran ahead. Soon we came to a great crowd of several hundred, but it seemed strange to find them entirely lacking in hostility. We found it was because our kindhearted friend had told them of what we had suffered, and so prepared the way for us.

Ahead of us was a large walled city. How gladly would we have avoided it had this been possible, but the animals needed rest and fodder and our whole party was in a state of exhaustion. One can only faintly imagine the condition of Dr. Leslie and Mr. Goforth whose wounds, though now thirty hours old, had not received antiseptic treatment.

Our entrance into this city was a repetition of the evening we entered Nanyangfu. Most of us had probably got beyond thinking clearly, but it is doubtful if any thought we would ever get from that city alive.

The inn yard was very large and as our cars stopped, the great crowd pressed upon us. *Then again* God undertook for us! Through the crowd, two well-dressed young men of official class pressed forward shouting, "Ku-Mu-shih" (Pastor Goforth). These turned out to be sons of an official at Changte, a friend of Mr. Goforth's, who had with their father been received in our home at Changte.

A few moments sufficed to explain the situation. Then the young men turned to the crowd telling them who we were and the good we were doing. What a change came over the people! Then, in the tone Chinese are used to obey, they ordered everything to be done for our comfort. Oh, what this all meant to us! How our hearts rose in gratitude to our Mighty Saviour for giving us such respite!

A message was awaiting us from the engineer party with a package of antiseptic dressings. Dr. Jean Dow was therefore able to attend to the many wounds which so terribly needed cleansing and dressing. (To the writer, one of the miracles of the journey was that, left so long without cleansing, the wounds from those septic swords did not in any case result in blood-poisoning.)

When our new-found friends learned of Mr. Griffith and Paul, they were much alarmed, but said, "You must press on without delay for the country is in an uproar. We will do our utmost to save them. If they can be found alive, we will see that they reach you." They then wrote a letter to the official at the city where we must needs stop for that night. He was a friend of

their father's. They told of the condition of our party
and begged him in their father's name to befriend us.
And finally, these young men arranged for a semi-
official man well known throughout that whole region
to go with us the rest of that day.

While worn and suffering, it was a happy and
thankful party that left the city which but two hours
before, they had entered in such desperate and hopeless
straits. Of those eight hours before reaching the city
where the letter was to be delivered, little need be said,
except that the experiences of the morning mobs were
repeated with the difference that we had with us the
one-man escort who, in each case, saved the situation
for us. At four o'clock that afternoon, a man came
running to our carts with a message from the two young
officials saying Mr. Griffith and Paul had been found
and would reach us that night.

On reaching our destination, Mr. Goforth, without
resting a moment or taking time for food, started off
for the Yamen, with the letter for the official. His
bound head and arm and tattered blood-stained upper
Chinese garment, the left sleeve of which hung in rib-
bons from the sword cuts, made him a marked man.
By the time he reached the locked Yamen gate, the mob
had become dense and menacing. To his intense relief the gate was opened to him at once and closed on
the crowd. The official received him with the utmost
kindness on reading the letter, and promised to have
an armed, mounted escort ready for us by daybreak to
accompany us as far as Fancheng where we hoped to
get boats. Mr. Goforth returned to the inn under es-

cort. We learned later that this official's wife came from a Christian family and was herself a Christian.

A word of myself and the children: On arriving at the inn, I was so exhausted as to be scarcely able to reach the brick bed in the inner room. Throwing myself down with the baby beside me, sleep came at once. Later, I was told that when Paul and Mr. Griffith arrived about midnight, they tried to waken me, but shaking and shouting had no effect—I just slept on. Then about half-past two, I suddenly came to myself, realizing the situation. Can I ever forget the scene which met my eyes as I reached the door of the large outer room! By the dim light of the one taper lamp could be seen the forms of the rest of the party stretched out on the earthen floor, sleeping the sleep (as I had done) of utter exhaustion. But in a very short time, all were stirring and by daybreak were on the carts beginning what was the safest but *hardest* day's travel of that entire journey.

We started by daybreak, and, with but a short rest at noon, travelled rapidly over those rough roads for almost twenty hours, reaching Fancheng about midnight where we found the engineer's party awaiting us. After twenty-four hours in an indescribably unsanitary inn, the entire party boarded several small house-boats for the remaining ten days to Hankow.

The journey thus would have been enjoyable and restful but for the fact that no longer having any bedding or pillows, the bare boards became apparently harder each day and the boat people's poor food which we had to share—well, we all got upset and when nearing Hankow the children began amusing themselves with a new game—imagining what they would like best to eat. One said, "Ice-cream!"—but most seemed quite content if they could just have some bread and butter. Then suddenly there appeared a steam tug coming up-stream to meet us! Oh, what joy there was among the children when they found there was actually bread and butter in plenty for them and *milk* too!

Our story has grown long, perhaps too long. But many facts and stories have had to be omitted. Those who have read thus far, however, will want a word further. Reaching Hankow where we had hoped to get outfitted we were not allowed to go ashore, but were taken at once on to a steamer bound for Shanghai. I was able to borrow some garments for the children and even for my husband from those on board, but could find none to meet my own need. On reaching Shanghai we were all taken—the mission centres were overflowing—to a *fashionable English boarding-house!* As we entered the large vestibule, a company of young people were having afternoon tea. They were all in immaculate summer tennis costume. Had a menagerie suddenly passed through the hall, these young people could not have shown more hilarious surprise. Can we wonder?

Of our Heavenly Father's marvellous provision for us all, especially the children, for we were ordered to Canada by the first steamer, and of His sustaining grace when reaction and break came, these are already recorded in *How I Know God Answers Prayer.**

*Harper and Brothers, New York.

Just a word of explanation regarding Mr. Griffith and Paul. When reaching the city wall at Nanyang, Mr. Griffith noticed a break in the wall just beside the gate through which the carts had to pass. His cart was last, and thinking to escape with Paul more easily if off the cart, took the child with him and went through this gap, but must have started off by mistake on a road leading away from that taken by our party. In this way they became lost. But as we all looked back over that whole day, this act of Mr. Griffith, though seemingly a calamity at the time, was, in reality, the saving of the whole party.

The following extracts from an address by Dr. Goforth, written probably in 1901, are here given by special request.—

"Who Caused the Boxer Movement in China?

We believe the first great cause of that uprising was the land-grabbing greed of the great nations. Their seizures, or proposed seizures of Chinese territory was the great irritant. . . .

Germany, filled with the idea of becoming a great colonial power, had sought for years to get a slice of Chinese territory . . . seized Chiaochow Bay and laid claim to the whole of Shantung, a province of one hundred and eight counties, as her sphere of influence. . . .

As soon as Germany had seized Chiaochow, the Russians were very much put out, for, they had thought of securing that same Bay as a winter port for their fleet. Away north at Vladivostock the ice becomes too thick and they wanted an ice-free port. . . . But Russia, in order to compensate herself, seized Port Arthur and claimed all Manchuria as her sphere of influence.

At this, Great Britain was greatly stirred. She feared that by allowing the Muscovite to hold the gateway to the Chinese capital, she must take second place in the councils of Peking. Therefore, to checkmate Russia, Britain seized Weihaiwei across the Gulf from Port Arthur, on the promontory of Shantung. But Britain never led anyone to suppose that she would be satisfied by the little rocky port of Weihaiwei. . . . No, Britain for years in public print had been telling the world that the Yangtse valley was her sphere of influence and that she would defend it against all comers. . . .

France, too, coveted some of the Celestial Land. She had already waged an unjust war with China and had annexed Annam. But her greed was not yet satisfied for she claimed the four southern provinces, Kwangtung, Kwanghsi, Kueichow and Yunnan as her sphere of influence and with a high hand commenced to push her Tonquin railway up into China. . . .

Italy likewise, so roughly handled by the Abyssinians, sought to recoup herself by curtailing the possessions of the "Sick Man of the East." Her fleet hovered around the province of Chekiang for months, trying to gain a foothold and hoping to relieve China of the burden of garnering in the wealth of such a fine province. . . .

Even little Japan, with all her heathen doctrines of right and wrong was not restrained from imitating the land-grabbing greed of the great Christian nations.

She had already captured Formosa and proposed to absorb the province of Fukien, a fine tea-growing district of the mainland. . . .

Many of the Chinese mandarins had Chinese secretaries who could read English as well as anyone. What appeared in public print about these seizures and proposed seizures of Chinese territory was known all over China. What were the poor Chinese to imagine? They no doubt thought the big Christian nations after all had no conscience—without right or reason they proposed to take our country from us.

Now apply the same treatment to ourselves. Imagine several of the big nations attempting the crying injustice of carving up our Dominion to gratify their greed. Do you suppose we would meekly allow them? . . . The Chinese, in their ignorance, feared that all foreigners, whether missionary, merchant, or engineer, were in league to bring about the partition of China. It seemed to them, as a people, from the Empress Dowager down, that the only way to escape the evil was to destroy and expel the foreigners. Therefore they arose in their crude and cruel fashion and made the attempt. Had they succeeded it would have been a calamity for China. The movement was not approved of by the best Chinese statesmen. Had all China accepted the Boxer method for the preservation of their country, not one of us would have escaped from the interior and Chinese doom would have been hastened."

Dr. Goforth then goes on to speak of some of the minor causes of the upheaval. Among these he mentions "the legalized iniquities of Shanghai"; "the high-handedness of many foreigners in their treatment of the Chinese"; "the demand of the Roman Catholics for official recognition in courts"; and the "opium curse (always laid by the Chinese at Britain's door)."

III.
1901 - 1925

If thou forbear to deliver them that are drawn unto death, and those that are ready to be slain; If thou sayest, Behold we knew it not; doth not he that pondereth the heart consider it? and he that keepeth thy soul, doth not he know it? and shall not he render to every man according to his works.

PROVERBS 24:11, 12

XI.

IN GOD'S CRUCIBLE

But Thou art making me, I thank Thee, Sire.
What Thou hast done and doest Thou knowest well.
And I will help Thee: gently in Thy fire
  I will lie burning on Thy Potter's wheel—
  I will lie patient, though my brain should reel.
Thy grace should be enough the grief to quell:
And growing strength perfect, through weakness
    dire.

GEORGE MACDONALD

DURING THE months in Canada, following the Boxer experiences, Mr. Goforth was called upon far and wide to tell the story of the escape but his main messages were along quite other lines. He soon came to see the church's interest in foreign missions had sadly waned. He saw, too, the great increase of worldliness in the church, some of the highest church leaders being swept in to this tide, and, with great sorrow and concern, he sensed the danger of the "Higher Criticism" then coming to the fore. As Dr. Buchanan expressed it, "Like his Master, Goforth had a great compassion for the needy and helpless and a two-edged flashing sword for the self-satisfied Christian Pharisee." Yes, and for any and everything which he was convinced lowered the standard of the Cross.

Many times he was heard to say, "Even before I

153

gave myself to the Lord Jesus Christ, I had given up cards, dancing, the reading of questionable literature and other such things because I felt they were but a waste of precious time which might be spent in more worthwhile ways. After my conversion, I saw these and many other things were so many leakages of spiritual power." Graft, sweating of the poor, (fed by women's thirst for bargains), were horrors of cruelty to him that must be and were denounced. Many received his messages with gladness, but others, the reverse.

In spite of his naturally optimistic spirit, there were times when he felt crushed at the apparent growing apathy of the home church regarding the untouched, unreached millions of "the regions beyond." His heart was in China, so when letters arrived telling of arrangements being made for some of the missionaries to re-enter North Honan for the reorganizing of the work there, Goforth, leaving his wife and family in Canada, at once turned his face China-ward to join in the rebuilding of the mission.

By May of 1902, Mrs. Goforth received word from her husband to come as soon as possible. On July 1, she left Toronto with five children, the oldest, eleven, the youngest, Constance, eight months. It had been arranged by Goforth and his wife that he would meet her on arrival in Shanghai. On reaching the Bund, a telegram was handed Mrs. Goforth saying, "Goforth Typhoid Changte." For a moment all went dark, but the Lord just used this time of extreme testing as an opportunity to show what He could do.

After a week of anxious waiting in Shanghai, try

ing in vain to get some word through by telegraph to Changte, Mrs. Goforth with her children, proceeded up the coast to Tientsin, Paul and Helen being left at Chefoo to attend the China Inland Mission schools there.

During the weeks Goforth lay ill at Changte, the post-office in Peking, by some mistake, returned all letters addressed to Mrs. Goforth back to the Changte station. The result was—no word other than the brief telegram at Shanghai reached her of her husband's condition, though for a whole month she waited in Tientsin daily looking, but in vain, for some word from Changte.

Then one day, Goforth appeared, having travelled alone the two weeks' journey from Changte. He was a mere ghost of himself, emaciated and still weak from his long siege of typhoid, but he was as buoyantly happy and optimistic as ever.

We have come to what can only be written as a personal story. Were it not that the facts now to be recorded most vitally affected Jonathan Goforth's whole after life, I would set it aside as other "personal" stories have been, for I wish to keep before me ever the fact that this is a record of Jonathan's life, not mine. To live over again in the writing, the events of those weeks, will not be easy, but it should be done.—

A few days after my husband arrived, we were all once again on a houseboat with everything ready for the three weeks' return journey upstream. I could see Jonathan was just waiting for the opportunity to lay something important before me. Indeed he was simply bubbling over with eagerness. Then it came out. In brief it was as follows:

The personnel of our old Changte station was entirely changed. Two married couples and two single women from Chuwang (a station not to be reopened), had been added to the staff. The whole Changte region had been divided into three distinct fields, the part allotted to Mr. Goforth being the great region northeast to northwest of the city, with its many towns and almost countless villages. With great enthusiasm my husband laid bare his plans for the evangelization of this field.

"My plan," he said, "is to have one of my helpers rent a suitable place in a large centre for us to live in, and that we, as a family, stay a month in the centre, during which time we will carry on intensive evangelism. I will go with my men to villages or on the street in the daytime, while you receive and preach to the women in the courtyard. The evenings will be given to a joint meeting with you at the organ and with plenty of gospel hymns. Then at the end of a month, we will leave an evangelist behind to teach the new believers while we go on to another place to open it in the same way. When a number of places are opened, we will return once or twice a year."

Yes, it was a very wonderfully thought-out plan and should be carried out *if there were no children in the question!*

As I listened, my heart went like lead! The vision of those women with their smallpox children at Hopei, crowding about me and the baby, the constant danger to the children from all kinds of infectious diseases that this life would mean, (for the Chinese cared nothing of bringing infection to others), and the thought

of our four little graves—all combined to make me
set my face as adamant against the plan. My one and
only reason, however, in opposing and refusing to go
with my children, as my husband suggested, was because it seemed a risking of the children's lives.

Oh, how my husband pleaded! Day by day in the
quiet stillness of that long river journey, he assured
me that the Lord would keep my children from harm.
He was *sure* the Lord would keep them. He was *sure*
God was calling me to take this step of faith. Then
as we drew near the journey's end, he went further.
He said:

"Rose, I am so sure this plan is of God, that I
fear for the children if you refuse to obey His call.
*The safest place for you and the children is the path
of duty.* You think you can keep your children safe
in your comfortable home at Changte, but God may
have to show you you cannot. But He can and will
keep the children if you trust Him and step out in
faith!"

Time proved he was right, but, as yet, I had not
the faith nor the vision nor the courage to regard it in
that light.

I must digress for a moment to tell of an incident
that occurred on the one-day cart journey from the river
to Changte. We had two carts, mine was ahead, when
a sudden bend in the road brought us into a great crowd
watching an open-air theatrical. The carters tried to
get past by whipping up the animals—mine succeeded,
but Jonathan's cart was surrounded. The whole mob
became menacing. When I looked back I saw several
men trying to drag my husband off the cart.

Oh, how I prayed, for I knew if they could succeed in getting him under their feet, he would certainly be killed! I begged my carter to stop, but he was white with terror and was lashing the animals into a gallop. Just ahead was a flimsy bridge made of mud and corn-stalks, which usually was crossed with the utmost care at a snail's pace. To my horror, the carter went on this bridge at full speed, but to my joy and relief, when able from the violent shaking to look back, I found Jonathan's cart just behind! Later, in talking over this incident, my husband said, "Except for the experiences on that memorable journey in 1900, I doubt if I was ever in more imminent danger."

We reached our Changte home on a Saturday evening. Sunday morning I left the children with the faithful nurse, Mrs. Cheng, who had saved little Ruth from the Boxers' blows. They all seemed perfectly well. Two hours later I returned to be met by Mrs. Cheng saying, "Wallace is ill." The doctor was called who pronounced it "one of the worst cases of Asiatic dysentery he had come across."

For two weeks we literally fought for the child's life during which time my husband whispered to me gently, "O Rose, give in, before it is too late!" But I only thought him hard and cruel, and refused. Then, when Wallace began to recover, my husband packed up and left on a tour *alone*.

The day after he left, my precious baby Constance, almost one year old, was taken ill suddenly, as Wallace had been, only much worse. From the first, the doctors gave practically no hope. The father was sent for. Constance was dying when he arrived. We had laid her on a cot in the middle of my husband's study. Our faithful friend, Miss Pyke, knelt on one side. My husband knelt next to Constance and I beside him. The little one was quietly passing, all was still, when suddenly I seemed to apprehend in a strange and utterly new way the *love* of God—as a *Father*. I seemed to see all at once, as in a flash, that *my Heavenly Father could be trusted to keep my children!* This all came so overwhelmingly upon me, I could only bow my head and say, "O God, it is too late for Constance, but I will trust you. I will go where you want me to go. But keep my children!"

Oh, the joy that came and peace—so when my husband turned to me saying, "Constance is gone"—I was ready and comforted, knowing that her life had not been in vain. Our little Constance's remains were laid beside her two sister's graves on her birthday October 13, 1902.

The evening our little one passed away I sent for a Mrs. Wang, whom I had come to love and honour for her fine Christian character and her outstanding gifts. When she came I said, "Mrs. Wang, I cannot tell you all now but I have decided to join forces with my husband and am going with him in opening up work outside. Will you come with me?"

The tears sprang to her eyes as she replied, "Oh, I cannot. I have a child and to take her into all kinds of conditions outside would be too risky."

Thinking it best not to urge her I said, "Go home and pray about it and tomorrow after the funeral come and tell me what you decide."

The next evening as she entered, though her eyes

were overflowing, she said with a joyous smile, "I'm coming with you." For years while carrying on the work of which we shall now write, we two worked, prayed, and wept together for our Chinese sisters in the region north of Changte. From this time on, the following lines by Whittier had new significance:

And as the path of duty is made plain
May grace be given that I may walk therein.
Not like the hireling for his selfish gain,
Making a merit of his coward dread,
With backward glances and reluctant tread,
But cheerful in the light around me thrown
Walking as if to pleasant pastures led
Doing God's will as if it were my own,
Yet trusting not in mine, but in His strength alone.

XII.

FOLLOWING THE GLEAM

*I will go before thee, and make the crooked places
straight: I will break in pieces the gates of brass, and
cut in sunder the bars of iron.*

GOD'S PROMISE THROUGH ISAIAH

BEFORE GOING on with the Goforths into their new
life, it will be well to gather up a few threads regarding the Changte station, for many changes were taking
place. Rapidly it was becoming a fully manned and
fully equipped mission station. The personnel had
come to include besides ourselves, three married couples
and three single women workers. All these missionaries
were true to the fundamentals of our Christian faith
and all had the evangelistic vision. With one exception
all had travelled and suffered together on the memorable journey in 1900.

Some things which must be recorded from this on
can be better understood if a question, which has
reached me, be answered just here. The question is,
"Was Jonathan Goforth easy to get on with as a missionary!" While it is not easy to answer such a question, it is important and searching and must therefore
be faced.

In regard to his ordinary, daily contact with others,
the answer should be a decided, "Yes." He radiated
kindness, gentleness, and love. He was not "touchy"

or quick-tempered in the ordinary sense. But, on the other hand, as a missionary when facing important issues in Presbytery that affected *his own work,* he was *not* easy to get along with. Jonathan Goforth was a *pioneer* through and through. He had ever the *forward* vision and with his strong convictions concerning Divine guidance *of himself,* he naturally came often into conflict with other members of the Honan Presbytery, for what body of, say twenty strong personalities, could easily bend to one of their number, when some had perhaps equally strong convictions opposed to his? It must be said, however, in justice to Jonathan Goforth that he demanded for himself only what he was gladly willing to accede to all other members of Presbytery, namely; freedom to carry on his or her work as each one felt led. Not a few in Honan Presbytery came to see, as time went on, that too many hard and fast rules had been made. Some, (especially new arrivals), were "sticklers" that these rules must be obeyed though times and conditions had changed. The majority vote of Presbytery always must carry. It is easy therefore to see that ofttimes Goforth found himself hampered and held back from following fully what he deemed was for him the Holy Spirit's leading.

The plan Goforth was now proposing to follow, for the opening up of his own field was a most radical one. Therefore, it was necessary to get the consent of his co-workers before it could be carried out. The new plan met with distinct opposition from the doctors and mothers, because of the danger to the children, and from others, because renting of places outside was contrary as it seemed to them to the principle of self-support. Goforth, however, contended the places he proposed to rent were not as chapels, but as places from which he could carry on evangelism.

Keen contention followed, but Goforth was so sure the plan was a God-given one, he was determined to carry it out and suggested as a compromise that he might be allowed a three-year trial of the plan, during which time he would finance the cost himself. This was finally agreed to. As will be seen, this was all in God's plan, for it led to the first steps in trusting Him for financial needs in connection with the work.

One of Jonathan Goforth's outstanding characteristics was his keen sense of justice and fairness. To some associated with him it seemed, at times, this trait was carried too far and led him into unwise generosity in dealing with Chinese. But even to risk over-reaching or taking advantage of another was to Goforth abhorrent. In the light of this trait, the following story can be better understood.

When the day of reckoning came for China following the Boxer outrages, word was sent from the various foreign Ministers in Peking to their Nationals asking for a statement of losses sustained. Our Mission statement was to be in Canadian currency. A considerable period passed before the indemnity was actually paid and in the intervening time the currency exchange had greatly altered to the advantage of the foreigner. Thus Goforth (we will not speak of others) found he received in Chinese currency much more than his claims amounted to. To keep it all seemed to him quite clear would be to defraud the government. To return the over plus to Peking would probably mean putting it into the pockets of whoever received it, to be spent in unworthy ways. He therefore decided to use it in some way for the benefit of the Chinese.

Two plans came before him. The first was to buy a small telescope which, with his knowledge of astronomy, (his one hobby), would be invaluable in his work among students. The second plan, however, came more and more to eclipse the first and was finally decided upon. It was to purchase a piece of ground close to the mission compound of Changte and erect on it a number of small two or three-roomed Chinese cottages where employees of the mission, such as school-teachers, evangelists, or hospital assistants, could live with their families. For years Mr. Goforth had felt deep sympathy for these men, who, for many months of the year were not able to see their families. A small rental sufficient only to keep up repairs would be required. Each cottage would have its own garden and the whole done in Chinese style, would be enclosed by a high wall and main gate.

The scheme was carried out in every detail and the place named "Peace Village." The property was then handed over to the mission. Perhaps I need scarcely add, before it was completed, more than double the indemnity surplus had been expended, but Goforth enjoyed a clear conscience.

FAMILY EVANGELISM

The touring months were from February to June and September to December. The Goforths now planned to give most of this time to the opening up of their field as we have indicated. Many things must needs be adjusted to the new life, and some things loved and prized by the family had to be given up, such as flowers, bird, dog, and cat—the Changte home being of necessity closed while they were absent.

The general plan was to have a small native compound rented at a town, if possible, with two courts; for while Mr. Goforth was prepared to trust for the children when taking them into the new and dangerous surroundings, he determined to take every possible precaution to safeguard them. We have often been asked by missionaries and indeed some in the homeland to tell how we managed to live as a family under those outside conditions. A few brief details must suffice for this as our manner of life and plan for work was practically the same at every centre opened.

As we could not take furniture about with us, we had to be content with what was found at a place, which usually consisted of one table, two chairs, a bench for the children and the ever present "kang," i.e. brick platform bed, reaching across the full width of the room and convenient not only for the "family" bed but a most convenient place for many other things. On reaching a place a regular routine had to be gone through. While our cook was seeing to the building of a brick stove, which usually took an hour, someone was dispatched for a few bundles of straw; then curtains were quickly hung, one across the kang end of the room, the other sheltering part of the opposite end for Mr. Goforth's "study." Here an extra table, if available, was placed. Fresh newspapers came in handy for the window sills, one making a handy place for Mr. Goforth's books, the other acting as dressing-table with looking-glass and toilet articles. By this time the straw had come and been laid on the kang. Careful watch had to be kept during the process of spreading it as lumpiness would mean wakeful hours for parents at least. A few coarse straw Chinese mats over the rough bricks or uneven earthen floor and tacking up blue cotton curtains completed our "settling."

While the above was in progress (which was a delightful picnic for the children), Mr. Goforth was busily engaged with his evangelists getting the preaching place in shape. A number of fine gospel, illustrated texts were pasted around the walls; a large lamp suspended directly above the preaching platform, and, behind it or to one side, the hymn scroll was hung. This scroll had from twelve to fifteen simple Gospel hymns such as *Down at the Cross, Jesus Loves Me, Whosoever Will*, etc., written in large Chinese characters on white cloth. To one side in the part roped off for women, the baby organ was placed. Then with a few chairs and as many benches as could be procured the place was ready.

We have spoken of curtaining off a portion of the general room for Mr. Goforth's "study." This could only be done when the room was large enough. At many places he had to be content with just standing by the window with his back to the rest of the room. Though naturally there were few moments during the day when absolute quiet reigned, yet never once was his wife able to recall his having shown impatience or express annoyance at the noise. Mr. Goforth's habits of study and prayer were as regular under these outside conditions as when at home in Changte. He always rose at five in summer and six in winter. Ten minutes was given to the "daily dozen," and within half an hour of rising, he had started his intensive Bible study with pencil and notebook. Breakfast was always sharp at seven. From eight to nine a Bible-study class was held with his evangelists. Then commenced the regular work of the day, when with his band of Chinese helpers, street preaching began. Sometimes they all went farther afield as invitations came from surrounding villages. When distant places were visited they would be away all day and at such times Goforth ate by the roadside the same as the evangelists. One of his rules in life was as far as possible to become "all things to all men." Often he returned very tired but always rejoicing at the opportunity he had had to lift up Christ as an Almighty loving Saviour, and, to see, as he did practically every time he addressed a heathen audience, the Holy Spirit using the Word as a sword.

Whether speaking to one or one thousand, Goforth was never known to attempt to deal with souls without his open Bible. As in Toronto during his student days, so down through the years, his Bible was his ever-present companion. In starting work at a new centre, he made it a rule always to take a fresh passage of Scripture each time he addressed a heathen audience. The Chinese have great honour for what is written, especially ancient records. One of the secrets of Mr. Goforth's unusual power in dealing with heathen audiences was, no doubt, his habit of taking full advantage of this.

We have spoken of Goforth's *day* schedule, but the evening meeting was the great meeting, always. This was held for the most part in a large unused shop which opened entirely to the street. As I recall these meetings, my heart thrills at the remembrance of the dense crowds that gathered and the delight of the men and women at the organ and the singing. One evangelist was appointed to explain a hymn, taking each evening a new hymn and explaining it verse by verse, the verse being sung perhaps half a dozen times before going on to the next; then when the last verse was ended, going back to sing the hymn right through. By this time the audience, at least some of them, had begun to grasp the message of the hymn and even tried to join in singing! Oh, friends, who wrote in those days pitying us, would that you could have experienced, as we did day by day, and also evening by evening, the keenest joy a human being I believe can experience, for as days passed we saw men and women transformed by the message of God's love in Christ. Short gospel addresses, and more hymns, kept the crowds steady. The evangelists were often kept till after midnight dealing with enquirers. (As this is my husband's story, I cannot dwell on my side of this life except to say my Bible woman, Mrs. Wang, and I received the crowds of women in the courtyard in the daytime, where straw mats were spread for them to sit on and taking our part among the women in the evenings. Some have spoken of children as "little hinderers"; we found our children to be "little helpers!")

It is quite impossible to give in detail the story of all or even many places opened in the way we have described. As time passed, at every centre opened, Christians multiplied. A statement frequently made by Mr. Goforth, which, to some, seemed incredible, but nevertheless is true, was that "every new place *without one exception* where we lived as a family for at most one month and carried on this aggressive evangelism, we left behind what later became a growing church." This statement was not made in the spirit of pride or boastfulness, but humbly, as a witness to what the glorious Gospel of the Grace of God would do *if given a chance.*

This country life, while often not easy to the flesh, was one of constant opportunities to see *what God could do.* There were times when every human prop seemed taken from us, and God alone remained as refuge. To illustrate this, one story out of many, is as follows:

It was our third or fourth visit to Pengcheng, an important centre, sixty li northwest of Changte. A large straw-mat tent had been erected as Christians from the surrounding region were to gather for the special meetings. Heavy rain had soaked the tent causing it to leak like a sieve, leaving pools of water on the ground below. Then, just as we arrived, the weather turned bitterly cold and windy. The tent was like an icehouse in spite of two stoves going.

Almost at once Mr. Goforth caught a severe cold which rapidly grew worse with apparently high fever, (I had not my clinical thermometer with me), and severe pains in head and chest and difficulty in breathing. In spite of my protests he insisted on taking his meetings, but about the third day he came in at noon looking so very ill I became alarmed. He would take nothing to eat, and lay down saying he would be ready for the afternoon meeting.

I was in despair. Changte was too far away for help from friends there and the roads were in an almost impassable condition. I could only cry to the Friend Who never fails. Then thinking Mr. Goforth was asleep, I slipped out and sent a messenger around to call the Christians to the tent. When they had gathered, I told them of my anxiety and of Mr. Goforth's symptoms. As I ended by saying, "Oh, pray for him!" I broke down and wept. Oh, what prayers then arose—earnest, heart-flow of prayer such as I had never heard! As I listened my heart was comforted and I thought, "Surely God will hear such prayers!"

This continued for some time, then fearing Mr. Goforth might arrive, I gave out a hymn. A few moments later he walked into the tent in his old brisk way, looking quite well. As soon as I could get to him at the close of the meeting I said, "Jonathan, you seem quite better." He replied, "Praise God, I am." He then told how a short time after he had heard me go out the fever seemed to leave him, his head and chest ceased to pain, he could breathe easily and he felt quite well. The symptoms did not return.

> *"Say not my soul 'From whence can God relieve*
> *my care?'*
> *Remember that Omnipotence hath servants every-*
> *where."*

On one occasion, we started from Wuan for Pengcheng. The route we were to take, over a rocky mountainous region, was supposed to be the most direct, taking one long day. We were, however, much delayed in starting. By almost nightfall we found ourselves at the town of Hotsun, scarcely halfway to Pengcheng. The road ahead was infested with highwaymen. We had stopped at an inn and would have arranged to put up there for the night but the innkeeper insisted on our moving on that night. Our position was a most difficult one. The crowd had gathered about us in the court, and we had not even the privacy of a room. Mr. Goforth sent the evangelist out to find a place. Bowls of boiled dough strings with scrambled eggs had been brought (to be eaten with chop sticks!). The crowd had become so packed about us we could scarcely move our arms.

Just then the evangelist returned saying everyone refused to take us in. Mr. Goforth whispered to him, "Try again and we will keep praying, for we must not go on tonight." We dared not close our eyes lest the superstitious people, crowding about us, would think we were mesmerizing them. So while struggling with those long slippery dough strings and eyes open, we kept our hearts uplifted to the God who hears and answers prayer that he would give us a resting place. Our bowls were scarcely empty when the evangelist returned, his face fairly shining. He said, "Pastor, it is just wonderful! A wealthy man in the town who owns a fine large compound just across the road, and newly done over for the visit of an official, says you can have the whole place as long as you wish to use it and free of rent!" Yes, it was indeed wonderful! Yet, but one more instance of how our Master could and would undertake in time of need.

This courteous act on the part of a leading man gave us "face" before the people, which resulted in crowds flocking to see us and to hear our message. So many requests came for us to stay, Mr. Goforth decided to remain three days. During those three days literally thousands heard the Gospel and when we went on, a foundation had been laid which in time became a growing, self-supporting church.

Dr. Goforth's description of our stay at Pengcheng is as follows:

". . . this town is so crowded and houses so dear, that we have to put up with a good deal in the way of bad smells. At the south end of the house there is a pig pen with half a dozen pigs; at the north end of the house there is another pen with as many more pigs; while right in front of the house were five large kangs full of stuff, which Chinese like the smell of, but which does not suit foreigners! Add to this the smell of sulphur gas from many burning pottery works . . . . .

"We stayed amid these surroundings for eight days with the children. They were happy, busy days. Mr. L. and I accepted men and women for baptism on Sabbath and recorded besides seventeen on the Catechumen roll. . . . At the afternoon service nearly forty sat down to partake of the Lord's Supper. There were about ninety Christians present at the services. The Spirit of God was with us and blessed us all. . . . . . God is owning work done in this region. We have this year recorded fifty-two catechumens in this district. . . . . ."

The following is not given by any means as a *sample*

of travel in those days, for it was the most tragically hard experience of all the years of hard, hard journeys that followed. Had it not been for the discovery of an old letter, written more than thirty years ago to the home folks, the story would probably have been forgotten.

"The threatened uprising of an anti-foreign sect similar to the Boxers in the Changte region, prevented our going to Tzuchou as we had planned to do. We heard that in this district of Wuan, some fifty miles to the northwest of Changte, there were none of the anti-foreign sects which were giving such trouble around our main station, so we turned our faces toward this place.

The helpers succeeded in renting a very suitable native compound, and by September the 25th we were ready to start. Miss McIntosh gladly accepted our invitation to accompany us as the trouble with the would-be Boxers had put a stop for the time being to all outside work among the women, and this gave her an opportunity of helping in the opening-up of an entirely new field.

We had received permission from the engineers of the railway then being built to travel by construction car as far as Hantan, an hour's run up the line. We stayed at the inn there over night. Early the following morning we started for Wuan, some twenty miles to the west. We had three carts. Miss McIntosh, with her Bible-woman and Ruth in the first, myself and baby Mary and the Chinese nurse in the second, the third containing Mr. Goforth, Helen, Wallace and an evangelist. The first twenty li (seven miles) was passed over without any special trouble, though I thought the roads were the worst I had ever seen (the old corduroy road at home was nothing to it). Then, about eleven o'clock, we came to a hilly, rocky region, when our troubles began in earnest.

We had not bumped (literally) over a li of boulders, before over went the first cart! Fortunately, no one was seriously hurt, though Mrs. Chang received a nasty bruise in her side, and Mrs. Wang's little girl was much shaken and frightened. But this upset made us all on the alert and very soon the carters informed us we must get out and walk. At first we were inclined to think this quite a pleasant change, but when we had walked until quite tired out over those steep, rocky roads, we got into the carts again to get a little lift by the way, but were, in a few moments, told to get out again and walk— the way then indeed seemed hard! Words fail in attempting to describe the hardness of the hours that followed, yet the children seemed to enjoy it all!

More than once, Miss McIntosh and I lay down on the roadside and tried to rest, while the poor carters, Mr. Goforth helping, struggled to get the carts over the almost impassable places. Again and again the carts had to be lifted, one by one, over rocks . . . . .

It was after darkness had set in that the women's cart upset the second time. Mr. Goforth's cart upset twice, once completely turning over. Fortunately, all were walking at the time.

Finally, Miss McIntosh and Ruth had the novel sensation of going over! It was just after this that my cart went over, but I screamed so frantically at the carter, he stopped just in time and I got out with the baby.

Shortly before we reached Wuan, we came suddenly

upon an immense crowd, watching an open-air theatrical performance. By this time we had come to comparatively level roads and, keeping well back in our carts, we succeeded in getting through the crowd without them noticing that we were foreigners. When at last we stopped in front of our hired house in Wuan, and later found ourselves safe and sound in the preaching room with our baggage around us, it was with hearts filled with gratitude to the God of all mercies that He had brought us in safety through those terrible experiences.

Although we had not partaken of food since our eight o'clock breakfast, we could eat nothing, all were so utterly exhausted, except the children, who were sleepy but happy and enjoying all as a picnic, and we just spread our coverlets any way on the brick beds without even straw to soften them. The next morning, when attempting to rise, one of the ladies fainted,—the other felt the effects of that journey for many months.

Quite early that first morning, the City Official, Mr. Yen, arrived with his retinue. He at once sternly rebuked Mr. Goforth (though he was really not to blame) for having brought women and children over such roads in *carts*. He ended up by saying, "From now on my official sedan chairs are at your disposal. If you do not make full use of them, both coming and going, I will consider it a personal offense."

Mr. Yen, and also his wife, later became warm and intimate friends. Mr. Yen once said to Mr. Goforth, "I cannot understand how this Bible you gave me can have such power. Before I began to read it, I frequently gave unjust judgment in court for gain. Now I must judge justly or I cannot sleep!"

Pages could be written of that memorable first visit to the city of Wuan, but space can be given for only one incident. One day Mr. Yen, when calling on Mr. Goforth, brought with him a friend, a Chinese gentleman of the finest type. After the first courtesies were over, this man turned to Mr. Goforth, apparently struggling with deep emotion, and said he had a story which he had long wished to tell some foreigner. He then went on to relate how he had witnessed, in 1900, that terrible scene in the Governor's court at Taiyuanfu, Shansi, when the missionaries were massacred. His voice trembled as he told how deeply impressed he had been with the calmness of all when facing death. He told how one young girl stepping forward, in a clear, ringing voice plead in Chinese with the Governor for the lives of all. For a few tense moments the great crowd was hushed and there seemed to come a moment's ray of hope. Then the cyclone of fury broke and soon the heaps of soulless bodies told that man had done his worst.

"These which are arrayed in white robes, who are they? . . . These are they which came out of great tribulation. . . . The Lamb which is in the midst of the throne shall be their shepherd and shall guide them unto fountains of waters of life. And God shall wipe away every tear from their eyes" (Rev. 7:13-17, R. V.).

XIII.

GLEAMS OF REVIVAL

Verily, verily I say unto you, He that believeth on me, the works that I do shall he do also; and greater works than these shall he do. . . .

OUR LORD JESUS CHRIST

THERE IS something very strengthening to one's faith when looking back through the perspective of time, to be able to trace clearly the guiding of a Divine hand. The writer realizes, very keenly, she has now come to "sacred ground" in the story of Jonathan Goforth's life.

He was nearing his forty-fifth milestone when a strange restlessness seemed to take possession of him. He dwelt much with his wife on the verse at the head of this chapter, and earnestly he longed to see in his ministry the "greater works" promised. Mr. Goforth had, up to this time, been undoubtedly a successful missionary, judged by ordinary standards, but he himself was never satisfied with what he felt to be "just touching the fringe" of the appalling multitudes needing Christ. His whole soul burned intensely, that our Lord's promise, "and greater works shall ye do," might be fulfilled in him. It might truly be said of Jonathan Goforth that he "delighted to do God's will." His love for the Word amounted to a passion and to learn God's will through the Word was for him to obey *at any cost!*

We were, as a family, living at one of the out-centers, when some unknown friend in England began sending us pamphlets on the Welsh revival. Scenes of that marvelous movement were vividly described. Eagerly Mr. Goforth looked for these pamphlets, which, for a considerable time, came weekly. While reading them aloud to his wife, he was repeatedly so thrilled and moved that he could scarcely proceed for emotion. A new thought, a new conception, seemed to come to him of God the Holy Spirit and His part in the conviction and conversion of men.

At this time, far off in India, Dr. Margaret McKellar, one with whom we had had most congenial fellowship in the student days of 1887, but had not seen nor corresponded with in the intervening years, was led of God to send Mr. Goforth a little booklet entitled *A Great Awakening*. Never can I forget the day and circumstances when this blessed leaflet reached us. We were living in a large "barn" of a room at Tsichou, forty li north of Changte. The children were playing on the great platform bed at one end of the room (it was probably raining or they would have been outside), when Jonathan came to me with the leaflet opened, saying,—

"This is a remarkable booklet. It contains selections from Finney's 'Lectures on Revival.' Just listen to this." And then he read a portion of the front page of the second part as follows (we give the passage in full because of its being the factor used of God to lead him into the very life for which he had been so yearning and dimly groping):

"A revival is a purely philosophical result of the right use of constituted means. It is not a miracle, nor dependent upon a miracle. There has long been an idea prevalent that promoting religion has something very peculiar in it, not to be judged by the ordinary rules of cause and effect. No doctrine is more dangerous than this to the prosperity of the Church. *Suppose a man were to go and preach this doctrine among farmers, about their sowing grain. Let him tell them that God is a sovereign and will give them a crop only when it pleases Him, and that for them to plow, and plant, and labor as if they expected to raise a crop, is very wrong, and taking the work out of the hands of God. And suppose the farmers should believe such doctrine. Why, they would starve the world to death.* Just such results would follow the Churches' being persuaded that promoting religion is somehow so mysterious a subject of Divine sovereignty, that there is no natural connection between the means and the end. *I fully believe, that could facts be known, it would be found that when the appointed means have been rightly used, spiritual blessings have been obtained with greater uniformity than temporal ones.*"

Again and again he read the passage over, dwelling on the parts I have italicized. So evident was his emotion, the children became hushed and gathered about us, sensing something unusual. At last, my husband said, "It simply means this: The spiritual laws governing a spiritual harvest are as real and tangible as the laws governing the natural harvest." Then, solemnly, almost as if making a vow,—"If Finney is right, and I believe he is, I am going to find out what these spiritual laws are and obey them, no matter what the cost may be." Dr. Campbell Morgan says, "Obedience is the one qualification for further vision." AND THE FURTHER VISION

CAME TO JONATHAN GOFORTH AS HE LEARNED AND
OBEYED GOD'S SPIRITUAL LAWS.

At once, he sent home to Canada for A. J. Gordon's
Ministry of the Spirit, S. D. Gordon's *Quiet Talks on
Power, The Autobiography of Charles G. Finney,* and
Finney's Lectures on Revival. In the meantime, he
procured a wide two-inch margin Chinese Bible and,
with his English Bible, set himself to an intensive study
of the Holy Spirit. With fine pen he made full notes
on the wide margin of his Chinese Bible as he went on in
this study. Soon he began to use these notes as outlines
for addresses, especially to Christians. He had given
but eight or ten of these, all on the Holy Spirit, when
signs of deep conviction of sin came to be seen on the
faces of the Christians such as he had never witnessed
before. Then came times of breaking down and confession of sin with definitely increasing results in conver-
sions.

A short time after the booklet had reached us, we
returned to our home at Changte and, as the days passed,
Mr. Goforth became more and more absorbed in his
intensive study of the Holy Spirit. Not that his regular
work was ever neglected, but every possible moment,
when free to do so, he gave himself to this work,
rising before six, sometimes five, in order to get unbroken time at his Bible. I became anxious and one day
when entering his study I found him on his knees with
Bible and pencil before him. I said, "Jonathan, are
you not going too far in this? I fear you will break
down!" Rising, and putting his hands on my shoulders,
he faced me with a look I could never forget. I can
only describe it as "glorious" and yet sad, as he said,

"Oh, Rose, even you do not understand! I feel like one who has tapped a mine of wealth! It is so wonderful! Oh, if I could only get others to see it!" From that time on, I could only step aside, as it were, and watch to see "whereunto this thing would grow."

The latter part of the following February, Mr. Goforth left for the great religious fair at Hsunhsien. It was estimated that more than a million pilgrims climbed the hill outside that city during the ten days of the fair for worship of the great image, Lao Nainai (Old Grandmother). This fair was by far the greatest opportunity of the year for reaching numbers with the Gospel and all missionaries and native evangelists possible gathered there for intensive evangelism.

On this particular year, 1906, a great snowstorm had so blocked the roads, few pilgrims had arrived. Goforth therefore decided to use this slack time with the Chinese workers in prayer and preparation, giving them something of what he himself had been receiving.

One evening, while speaking to a heathen audience which filled the street chapel, he witnessed "a stirring in the people's hearts" such as he had never seen before. While speaking on "He bore our sins in His own body on the tree," conviction seemed written on every face. When asking for decisions, practically everyone stood up. Then turning about, seeking for one of the evangelists to take his place, he found the whole band of ten standing in a row with awed looks. One whispered, "Brother, He for whom we have prayed so long, was here in very deed tonight." During the days that followed, at every centre where the Gospel was being proclaimed, men came forward seeking salvation.

Soon after his return to Changte, Mr. Goforth came into severe clash with one of his colleagues. Both men had strong wills and each felt he was right. Finally, they were persuaded by other missionaries to meet alone, and on their knees, the matter seemed amicably settled. But there remained in Goforth's heart a secret sense of resentment amounting, in reality to unforgiveness. On the eve of starting on a long communion tour of his stations, he became convicted of his hypocrisy, and after a time of quiet confession and humbling of himself before the Lord, all unchristian feeling towards his brother vanished, and love reigned. Then, as he went forward on that long tour, God used him mightily.

For more than a year longer until the spring of 1907, Mr. Goforth continued his work as we have endeavoured to picture it, and with conspicuous success, but with no vision or thought beyond the Changte city and his own field to the north.

Then began the opening of doors into new and undreamt of and still wider service. A short time before Presbytery was to meet, two letters reached Mr. Goforth, (we were then in the country), both from senior missionaries and both urging him to consider favorably a call to Japan for a year's work among Chinese students there. It was a work he had proved himself eminently fitted for and a work he loved. So sure were we that we were to go to Tokyo, our annual order for stores was not sent off with the mission order.

When Presbytery met and the question came up as to who should go to Tokyo, one of the young missionaries immediately arose and moved that Mr. L. be appointed for this work. Another young missionary jumped to his feet and seconded the motion. Within a few moments the whole thing was passed and Mr. Goforth not even mentioned! To say the least, we were both dumbfounded! Then, in less than ten minutes, the same routine had been gone through and Mr. Goforth chosen to accompany our foreign mission secretary, Dr. R. P. MacKay (then visiting the Far East) on his trip to Korea. Another member of the Presbytery who had been asked by Dr. MacKay privately to go with him on this journey, had been left out! It all seemed, at the time, at least to some of us, little less than a jumble, but looked back upon in view of what took place later, it was not difficult to see God's hand was guiding definitely at that meeting.

When purchasing their boat tickets in Tientsin for Korea, Dr. MacKay and Mr. Goforth were on the point of getting return tickets, but at the last moment decided on single fares. Had they not done so, this story might never have been written.

After three weeks' visiting the main centres in Korea, they returned to China, taking the northern overland route around through Manchuria, with hearts stirred to the depths at what they had been witnessing. Three mission stations were visited en route. At each place Mr. Goforth was the speaker at the impromptu meetings arranged for them. Simply he told of what they had been seeing in Korea of the Holy Spirit's working. At each place came earnest requests that he return to hold a ten days' mission. When for the third time the same invitation came, Mr. Goforth began to wonder whether "the thing was of God," and promised if the way opened, he would return.

When later, Goforth laid the whole matter before the Honan Presbytery, and asked for permission to accept the call to Manchuria, some were strenuously opposed to his going, but after long discussion, it was finally decided to allow him freedom from his field for *one month, including travel.* Six months, however, passed before he was finally free to leave. Not until seated on the train did he fully realize the magnitude of the task before him. Giving talks to his evangelists as he had been doing, was far different from what would now be expected of him when facing Manchurian audiences. He reckoned that at least forty different addresses must be given. Feeling overwhelmed, he began to pray for the Lord's help in getting outlines into shape. Then the inner Voice spoke in an unmistakably clear way, "Give them just what I have given you." He obeyed, and through all the wonderful forty or more meetings in Manchuria his addresses were from the closely written notes on the margin of his Chinese Bible jotted down during the time of his intensive study of the Holy Spirit. Later, Goforth wrote:

"When I started on the long journey to Manchuria in February, 1908, I went with the conviction in my heart that I had a message from God to deliver to His people. But I had no method. *I did not know how to conduct a revival. I could deliver an address and let the people pray, but that was all."* . . .

"When the invitation had been extended to me, the preceding year, to conduct a series of special meetings in Manchuria, I had stipulated as to the conditions of my acceptance, first, that the two branches of the Presbyterian Church in Manchuria, namely, the Scotch and the Irish, should unite for the services; and, secondly, that the way should be prepared by prayer. Imagine my disappointment, therefore, when on reaching Manchuria I found upon enquiry that not one extra prayer-meeting had been held. But the last straw which was laid on the back of my already wavering faith was when I learned, after the evening service on the opening day, that the two Presbyterian bodies had not united."

He then tells of going to his room at the close of the first meeting and on his knees, in utter despair, crying to the Lord for help. The promise came, "Call upon me and I will answer thee, and will show thee great things, and difficult, which thou knowest not." Jer. 33:3, R.V. Early the following morning, before the call for breakfast had come, an elder in the church was ushered into his room and knelt (where he had knelt the night before), sobbing out his heart in confession of sin. He said, "During your addresses yesterday, I was searched as by fire. Last night I could not sleep a wink. . . ."

The following graphic picture of Jonathan Goforth at the time of his revival ministry in Manchuria, comes from Rev. James Webster, who for many years worked under the Scotch Presbyterian Mission there, and who accompanied Mr. Goforth from place to place during the time of the Revival.

"His message was the simple, old-fashioned one. We heard, to begin with, of the revival movement through which the Korean Church has passed, the rapid progress of Christianity in the Hermit Kingdom, the amazing increase of converts, the strength and independence of the churches, the number of schools and colleges, all established within the past few years, and all self-supporting.

"He was as well versed in the statistics of our church as in that of Korea. There followed a merciless comparison between the progress there and here during the last decade,—a very humiliating contrast. He had not come to praise up the Manchurian mission, but asked us to inquire seriously the cause for the extraordinary difference. It could not be explained by the long continued unrest and the turmoil of the wars in Manchuria, for Korea had had its own share. Nor was it because of the cruel political situation in Korea, in the hope that the profession of Christianity might induce western nations to assist them. Notwithstanding their sufferings the Korean Christians were anti-revolutionary, showing a loyalty and a forbearance under oppression which had been an example to their countrymen. The greatness of the work in Korea was 'not by might, nor by power but by my Spirit, saith the Lord.'

"The watchword of the Revival of 1859 was, 'Ye must be born again'; of 1870, 'Believe on the Lord Jesus Christ,' but of Mr. Goforth's message, it was *'Not by might, nor by power, but by my Spirit.'* This doctrine, presented in many aspects, iterated and reiterated, amply illustrated, emphasized and pressed home, has been his one theme in Manchuria. He has not dealt in abstract theories about the work of the Holy Spirit. 'We speak that we do know and testify that we have seen.' There is a note of certainty about it all. He is perfectly sure of it in his own mind, and he says it out with all his might. He believes that idolatry and superstition are not the fruits of the Spirit and he says so. He believes equally that men and women who have renounced these practices and have been baptized in the faith of Christ, but are still living under the influence of hatred, jealousy, uncleanness, falsehood and dishonesty, pride, hypocrisy, worldliness and avarice, are living in that which is in active opposition to the Spirit of God. While living under the influence of these, and cherishing them in the heart, men and women bearing the name of Christ can obtain no such blessing as has come to the Korean Church. . . .

"The Cross burns like a living fire in the heart of every address. What oppresses the thought of the penitent is not any thought of future punishment, but their minds are full of the thoughts of their unfaithfulness, of ingratitude to the Lord who has redeemed them, of the heinous sin of trampling on His love.

'Sorrow and grief replace my bliss,
  I have no wish that any joy should be,
I have no room for any thought but this,
  That I have sinned, have sinned and grieved Thee.'

"This it is which has pricked them to the heart, moved them to the very depths of their moral being, and caused multitudes, being no longer able to contain themselves, to break out into a lamentable cry, 'God be merciful to me a sinner.'"

Jonathan Goforth went up to Manchuria an unknown missionary, except to his own narrow circle. He returned a few weeks later with the limelight of the Christian world upon him. But for the grace of God, the suddenness of it would have been his undoing. But God's servant, so evidently anointed for special service, quietly, calmly, and humbly met the calls for revival missions which began to literally pour in from all parts of China. The Honan Presbytery faced an unusual and difficult problem, for Goforth's field must be considered. At their meeting in the spring of 1908 at Weihuifu, the Mission's central station, it was finally decided that Goforth should be freed for the revival work—at least for a time.

Mr. Goforth's evangelists and some of the leading Christians from his field had been anxiously waiting at Changte, to hear the decision of Presbytery. On hearing that Mr. Goforth was to leave them, they at once came to me in a body, begging that I take charge of my husband's field in his absence. Knowing I could not decide this myself and that it was most unlikely Presbytery would agree to it, I endeavoured to put them off. But when the men sank down on their knees, begging with tears streaming down their cheeks, for me not to leave them, but to take my husband's place, I agreed that a deputation should go immediately and lay the matter before the Presbytery which was still in session. Presbytery, however, decided "there was no Presbyterian precedent for such a course."

Preparations at once began for the break-up of our home, for it had been decided by Presbytery that I should return to Canada with the children. The following conversation though it lifts the veil on the family life is given you. Only thus can certain phases of Jonathan Goforth's character be glimpsed.—

A few days before the break came we were walking in front of our home at Changte, and naturally feeling keenly the prospect of a long separation. I determined to see how far my husband would go in putting the work first in his life, so I said, "Jonathan, I'm going to ask you a straight question. Suppose I were stricken with an incurable disease in the homeland and had but a few months to live. If we cabled you to come, would you come?"

He hesitated before answering. "You are asking me to face an issue which we hope may never come."

"But," I persisted, *"would you come?"* He saw I was in earnest and must be answered.

After hesitating some moments—perhaps praying—he said, "You have supposed a case and asked a hard test question. Before answering it, I want to suppose a case and ask *you* a question. Suppose our country were at war with another nation and I, a British officer in command of an important unit. Much depended upon me as commander as to whether it was to be victory or defeat. Would I, in that event, be permitted to forsake my post in response to a call from my family in the homeland, even if it were what you suggest?"

"No, Jonathan," I replied, rather sadly. "I must confess you could not, for a soldier's first duty is to king and country."

Much that followed was too sacred for these pages, but finally Mr. Goforth ended by turning to his Bible. He read: "As his share is that goeth down to the battle, so shall his share be that tarrieth by the stuff: they shall share alike." (I Sam. 30:24). "And remember," he went on, *"your promise was always to let me put the Lord and His work first."*

Then, in his characteristic way, he turned from "grave to gay" by saying with his glowing look *that always won out,* "Now remember, when at home, be sure and give the children plenty of apples to eat!" . . . .

A week later, the mother with five children, the youngest, Frederic, two years of age, started on the long homeward journey while Goforth gave himself wholly to the revival missions.

One of the first revival missions was held at Chefoo —on the Shantung Peninsula. In the following Goforth tells of some tragic experiences—

"A large mat shed specially erected holding ꞏ1,000 was many times filled. From the first there was deep conviction of sin. God was very present. Frequently there would be many praying at once and with deep emotion. Dr. Hunter Corbett, the oldest missionary in China, said he had never heard such praying. At the close of these ten-days' meetings, I started by mule litter for Tengchoufu, less than a day's journey inland. But a few miles from the city of Chefoo, when attempting to cross the river, the hind mule stepped into some quicksand and was drowned. The front mule and driver were rescued with great difficulty. My bedding, books, clothes, etc., were all soaked, but, as I had alighted from the litter just before the accident happened, I escaped. I returned to Dr. Corbett's home on Temple Hill, and some days passed in getting things dried out. Then, with two other missionaries, I took passage by a small coast steamer run by Chinese.

"We left Chefoo at 8 A.M. Monday morning. It

was a six hours' run along the sea-coast to Tengchoufu. But, four hours out, a north blow sprang up and we plunged through the waves for several hours, finally fleeing for shelter to the islands north of Tengchou. The wind was stronger and colder on Tuesday and by Wednesday, it was blowing a gale with driving snow. It was terrific by Wednesday noon. Our anchor was slipping, timber junks were anchored in front of us nearer the shore and they might at any time snap their cables and drift upon us. Behind was a wide reach of shallow water. The captain felt he must change his anchorage and seek a place behind a higher part of the island but felt it to be a great risk in the teeth of such a gale. I prayed as they raised both anchors and got shifted to a safer spot. Never have I been on board ship when the danger seemed so great.

"The ship was not supposed to feed its passengers. On Monday we had had breakfast before starting but no more the rest of that day. On Tuesday at noon, we begged the crew's cook to give us some millet gruel he was preparing, but it was not till evening he gave us each a bowl of rice. Wednesday about 2 P.M. we each received about half a bowl of cold rice which the cook had scraped out of the kettle after the crew had eaten. We went to bed supperless but after we had been asleep some time the cook wakened us up and gave us each a bowl of hot millet gruel. Thursday the wind had lessened, but it was very cold. I walked up and down the little deck weak with hunger, trying to keep warm. About twelve I thought nothing looked so tempting as the dinner the cook was taking to the crew. It was 1 P.M. before we received a bowl of rice. It was cold, but delicious! Then Mr. W. who had managed to get ashore, brought us some Chinese cakes. He said he had met a man selling hot, steamed, sweet potatoes and had eaten two pounds without stopping!

"We started for our shelter about 5 A.M. Friday and landed before daylight. Three of the missionaries were down to meet us. Much anxiety had been felt for us as this had been the fiercest blow this autumn. We had expected to reach here in six hours and it had taken us ninety-six!"

XIV.

WHEN REVIVAL BLESSING CAME TO CHANGTE

Create in me a clean heart. . . . Renew a right spirit within me. . . Restore unto me the joy of Thy salvation. . . . Then will I teach transgressors Thy ways and sinners shall be converted unto thee.

DAVID, KING OF ISRAEL

STORIES OF Mr. Goforth's revival missions have already been recorded by himself in *By My Spirit*. The writer, therefore, has decided to give in these memoirs simply two pictures of the revival movement as it reached and affected Goforth's own station of Changte.

The first of these pictures or stories is from Goforth's loved and honoured colleague of many years, Dr. Murdock McKenzie, a great man with a great head and a great heart, a level-headed Scot who held tenaciously to strict Presbyterian ways. Therefore, we prize the more, the graphic picture he portrays of those days of blessing. The following are but extracts from a much longer and fuller story:

"Would that you could have been with us the last few weeks, that your hearts might have been stirred to their depths, and that you might have seen with your own eyes the wonderful works of God. Surely God has been in this place and we were conscious of it. I cannot attempt to tell you all I have seen, but will give simply some impressions.

"There is but one word can express our experiences

during these days, and that is "Wonderful!" What has happened? Nothing more than God has promised from the beginning,—when the Holy Spirit is poured out He will convict the world of sin. The church in Changte has been baptized by the Holy Spirit and cleansed, and the cry of all here is, 'Why did we so long despise His working, and trust in other ways to build up His kingdom.'

"During part of October, Mr. Goforth was in Shansi Province and there God's Spirit was present in power. We therefore trusted that when he came to us, we would not be denied the blessing. But, oh, how far beyond our expectation was the result!

"As Mr. Goforth's object in these meetings was not a revival among the heathen but among the Christians, it was necessary for us to call in to the central station all who could come from the seven counties of this district. . . . As to Mr. Goforth's addresses, they were earnest Gospel talks, straight home to the heart, well illustrated with incidents from Korea, Manchuria, Shansi, and other places.

"On Monday morning, his text was from Rev. 3:15, 'I know thy works that thou art neither cold nor hot.' After the addresses an opportunity was given for prayer, when several broke down in tears unable to proceed. One of these was Mr. Fan, assistant teacher in the girls' school. He made public confession of his sins and asked God's forgiveness. In the afternoon the text was from John 11:30, 'Take ye away the stone,' and a powerful appeal was made to all to allow nothing to hinder them from receiving the blessing.

"An opportunity was then given for prayer, and

thereupon ensued such a scene as never before had I seen, nor again do I expect to see. A man started to pray, but had not said more than half a dozen words when another, then another joined in, and in a moment the whole company was crying aloud to God for mercy. Oh, the intensity of feeling, all the pent up emotions of a lifetime seemed to be poured forth at that time. All the sin of the past was staring them in the face, and they were crying in anguish to God for mercy.

"Nothing in my mind can more fitly describe the scene than to compare it to the suddenness and violence of a thunder-storm. It starts with the patter of a few heavy drops, then comes the downpour lasting half an hour or so. But while it lasts how terrible it is. So it was here with this storm of prayer. It started with the one or two. Then came the burst from many hearts —all the pent up emotions long held in check. There was no restraining it, and no attempting to do so. . . .

"Some were praying for help to confess their sins, and to allow nothing to be unconfessed. Some could only sob, "O God, forgive me; O God, forgive me!" Some were imploring the Holy Spirit not to leave them. As the days passed there was added confidence in tone, due to the increasing knowledge of the power of prayer. As men and women came under the power of the Spirit, confessed their sins, and received new sense of pardon, peace and power, their desire to see others receive a similar blessing was especially manifested in their recourse to prayer, and their entire reliance on the Holy Spirit to confer that blessing.

"Sometimes one who had wandered far away from God, and now came back to Him publicly confessing his sin, would ask for the prayers of the people. At once as if with one heart and voice all would respond. Again, the cry of a son or daughter for a father or a mother's salvation, the appeal of an anxious one for prayers for relatives, the yearning of a helper for the people of the district over which he had been placed as shepherd, each brought its response in a volume of prayer by the congregation. . . .

"When prayer was asked for the Emperor and Dowager Empress, who were ill, an immediate and hearty response was made. There was no confusion, no seeming incongruity in all praying aloud at the same time, it seemed a most natural way to approach God. Never did we realize the power of prayer as we did at that time. The whole atmosphere was one of prayer.

"Especially do we think with wonder and gratitude to God of those afternoon and evening prayer-meetings amongst ourselves. We would first spend a little time in talking over the situation, the subject and persons for whom special prayer should be offered, and the answers already received, and then we would spend the rest of the time in prayer.

"Looking back on that time now and recalling the great number of definite petitions presented, and definite answers already received, almost immediately, one cannot but praise God for all His goodness and all His wonderful works to the children of men. We would go direct to the general meeting from our knees, and, oh, the gladness and the glory of it! We saw one after another of those we had been praying for going forward to tell how God had met with them, and brought conviction of sin to their hearts.

"Teachers in the schools, assistants in the hospitals, preaching helpers, male and female, servants in our houses, Bible women, gatekeepers, visiting Chinese Christians from other missions, the boys and girls in the schools, all were definitely remembered in our prayer circle, and not one of them failed to receive the blessing. As one after another of those went forward our hearts were full. We could but bow our heads and listen to His voice saying to us, Be still and know that I am God. Stand still and see the glory of God. . . .

. . . "Sad were the cries of some concerning relatives who had passed away to the other world without them even having said a word to them about the Saviour. Many spoke about opportunities of speaking about Jesus which they had neglected. Others had been neglecting to read the Bible, and to pray daily and so had become cold and dead spiritually.

"That which weighed most heavily on the consciences of all was that we had so long been grieving the Holy Spirit by not giving Him His rightful place in our hearts and in our work. While believing in Him we had not trusted in Him, to work in and through us. Now we believe, we have learned our lesson that it is 'not by might, nor by power, but by my Spirit saith the Lord of host.' May we never forget that lesson."

We prize equally with Dr. McKenzie's story the following account of the Changte Revival by Dr. Percy C. Leslie. Dr. Leslie had lived and worked at Changte for years and was greatly honoured for his devotion to the work and his sane, reliable judgment.

"For a long time we have been looking forward to special revival meetings. We need reviving. There is no doubt about that. And there is no room to doubt God's readiness to revive us again. Korea, Manchuria, Shansi, and other centres have been wonderfully moved and Mr. Goforth has been the central figure in much of this widespread movement. Now he is back in his own Honan. The week in Weihuifu, the middle one of our three main Honan stations, witnessed a real work of grace among the Christians there. Now for Changte! What is in store for the thousand and more throughout the seven counties of this prefecture who call themselves by Christ's name? . . .

"Sixth day, Friday: This has been the great day of the feast thus far, but not the last. Two more days. Let them bring the best He has in store for us! At the morning meeting there was no time for an address. . . .

"Eighth day, Sunday: Great throngs today; well on to seven hundred in the morning. Men crowded to the front to make confession and no time was obtained until afternoon for Mr. Goforth to make an address. It is becoming more difficult to bring the meetings to a close. Indeed, it is one long meeting, lasting all day, with intermissions for food. Each meeting lasts about three hours and an eager crowd awaits the call for the next. Messages and written letters have been sent to different sections of the field, urging them to hurry and come and share the blessing; this all by the Chinese themselves, and an urgent request has been presented by them to extend the meetings for several days, to give an opportunity for those who have been 'compelled to come in' to get wakened up. . . . At the evening meeting many of the visiting Chinese and foreigners took part, among

them Miss Margaret King of Montreal, claiming that
she had had the best day of her life.

"Tenth and last day, Tuesday: Confessions and
prayers filled up most of the time; men who had been
waiting for two days or more got an opportunity at last
to unburden themselves. Others who had been holding
out against the still small voice of conscience, were at
last moved to utterance. A gracious harmony united
the hearts of all, and all were one. A short farewell
message from Mr. Goforth was given at night, an earnest
exhortation to go on from this beginning to something
better in the Christian experience of each life. The
Word of God and prayer life are essential for persist-
ency and consistency.

"One of the indications of the sincerity and intensity of the prayers, was the brevity of most of the petitions; having prayed for the request suggested, they
stopped.

"We remember that the Chinese are not so readily
distracted by noise around them as we are, and prayer
under such conditions is not so difficult as we might
suppose. But how explain the missionaries praying;
some in Chinese, some in English, men and women,
strictly Presbyterian, ordinarily restrained, with Scotch
reserve sticking out at all points, raising their voices
with the multitude; and all because their hearts were
being lifted up as were the Chinese brothers and sisters. . . . . .

". . . It was pitiful to see the distress of some of
these men, strong characters, pillars of the church, weeping in the presence of men because they had been in
the presence of God and His light had revealed them

to themselves; the rank and file also, men with paltry sins to acknowledge, others with blood on their hands, all with tender consciences, conscious of sin against God and only hoping for His forgiveness. Confessions that torture could not wring from men, sins and faults that a few days ago they would not accept reproof for, now they willingly and openly confess. The missionaries were not exempt, and not a few took their places with the other "penitents" in acknowledging shortcomings. Surely 'the Lord shall sit as a refiner and purifier.'

"At 5:30 one morning I discovered a little group in the tent pouring out their souls before God. Men in confession told how their skepticism of the Spirit's power had been shattered and they themselves humbled before Him in the seclusion of their own hearts. One of our strongest men, a preacher, who had boasted that he would never shed a tear during these meetings, was discovered in his room, by a friend, sobbing in great agony of soul. Relief came only after long prayer.

"It was something unusual to have our entire staff of fourteen adults all in from the field. We were reinforced by seven others, six of them from other missions and representing three provinces besides Honan, and I don't think I ever saw such a beautifully unconscious exhibition of Christian unity. There was only one idea, and all were united in seeking its realization. Mr. Goforth's buoyant confidence was perhaps not shared by all from the first, but before the meetings were over, the faith that removes mountains was exultantly present. Such prayers,—in directness, in simplicity, in assurance! It was an inspiration to be in such an atmosphere.

"The missionaries attended the meetings regularly and not a few took part with their Chinese brethren in making acknowledgment of faults and shortcomings, not for any thought of example to the Chinese, but simply because God was moving their hearts and they were led to see themselves under God's searchlight. It was a time when we were all brought very close together, not only missionary to missionary, Chinese to Chinese, but Chinese to missionary and vice versa, and all because all were getting near to Christ and He was saying again,—'That they all may be one. . . I in them and Thou in Me, that they may be made perfect in one.' "

XV.

FURLOUGH 1909-1910

He has no enemies, you say?
My friend, your boast is poor:
He who hath mingled in the fray
Of duty, that the brave endure,
Must have made foes. If he has none
Small is the work that he has done.
He has hit no traitor on the hip;
He has cast no cup from tempted lip;
He has never turned the wrong to right,
He has been a coward in the fight.

ANON

ACCOUNTS OF the revival movement in China appearing in *The Presbyterian Record* and other papers created, for a time, an interest and mild stir in the homeland. Some read the stories with skepticism, wonder and such questioning as—"What does all this crying mean?"—"Confession of sin! I don't believe in it"—"The whole movement savors of fanaticism, Pentecostalism, and other 'isms!'" Some of the clergy, the ministers, declared such demonstrations were "quite foreign to Presbyterian procedure," yet in the *Life of W. C. Burns*, that most saintly and distinguished of Presbyterian missionaries, there is a chapter describing scenes in his ministry, when in Scotland, which could well be a description of Jonathan Goforth's meetings in China. Nevertheless, there were some in the homeland whose hearts opened in sympathy to the revelations of what their

Chinese brethren and sisters were going through when the Holy Spirit came as a "refiner and purifier of silver."

We give but one concrete case of this. The wife of a certain elder in the homeland was known for her lack of interest in, and even opposition to her husband's Christian life and service. The elder died. Occasionally the woman attended church. One Sabbath morning, arriving early, to while away the time she began to read in an issue of *The Presbyterian Record*, which had been placed on the seat, an account of one of the revival missions being conducted by Mr. Goforth in China. The story gripped her very soul. Taking the *Record* home, she reread the story, then getting down on her knees, she confessed her sins to God and yielded herself to the Lord Jesus Christ. Feeling the need of getting right with man as well as God, she went to her minister and his wife. To them she told a sad, sad story. One part only may be given here and that because of its lesson. She had for years carried on systematic thieving, not only in stores, but in homes visited.

When the story was ended, she quietly said: "What must I do now? I am willing to pay any price God wants." The minister then showed how things she had taken must be returned and full restitution made. To this she agreed, and in the days that followed she humbled herself to the dust by going to all who could be reached, confessing to her sin and making restitution. In cases where some had died or were lost sight of, she valued what she had taken and put the amount into the church. The minister's wife, two months later, told her husband that at the Women's Missionary meeting this sister, when asked to lead in prayer, rose and offered the most touchingly beautiful and humble prayer she had ever listened to.

Early in 1909, at the close of some wonderful meetings in Tungchow, near Peking, Goforth left immediately for Canada via London, where he was scheduled to give a series of addresses on "Prayer" under the auspices of the China Inland Mission. While in London, he was taken to see an invalid lady, who, he was told, had been used in a remarkable way as an intercessor for others. During their conversation, she told Mr. Goforth that when she heard of his proposed meetings in Manchuria, she had felt a great burden laid upon her to pray for him. She then asked him to look at her notebook, in which was recorded three dates when a sense of special power in prayer had come upon her for him. A feeling akin to awe came upon Goforth as he recalled those dates as being the very days when he had realized greatest power and had witnessed the mightiest movements in Manchuria.

At the close of his week's meetings in London, Mr. Goforth left for Canada, reaching his home in Toronto but a few days before the General Assembly was to meet in Hamilton. He came back to Canada full of hope that he might see in the beloved homeland similar evidences of the Holy Spirit's working as he had been witnessing in China. Much time was given to prayer during the days preceding the General Assembly. When at last he rose before that great audience of ministers and church leaders, Goforth spoke for twenty minutes with such power and intensity, a marked stillness reigned throughout his address. His plea was for them as leaders, teachers, and professors, to humble themselves before the Lord and seek the Holy Spirit's outpouring as did the Korean missionaries. This he held out as the Church's only hope if retrogression and disaster were to be avoided.

The message was welcomed by some with hope and gladness; by others, it was received with distinct opposition. The former saw in Goforth a Spirit-filled man of vision who feared not the face of man. To the latter, however, he was a fanatic to be shunned. Not till a year later was Goforth to learn how deep-seated was this opposition to him. During the ten months that followed the Assembly a few, but very few, churches opened their doors to Jonathan Goforth for revival missions. To those who did, tokens of blessing came, but only the droppings. Had Goforth lost the Divine empowering? Did the Lord see his servant needed humbling? Or were God's children unwilling to pay the price of full surrender? Who can say? While many were the bright glints of hope and cheer during the 1909-10 furlough, it must be said it was, on the whole, a period to Goforth of great disappointment.

The World's Missionary Conference was to meet in Edinburgh, June, 1910, and as Mr. Goforth was appointed a delegate, it was decided the Goforths as a family should return to China by way of England. Before giving briefly some facts regarding those four wonderful months in Britain, an incident at the World's Missionary Conference must be recorded.

It was Sunday night. The Conference had closed. We were going down the steps and had almost reached the street when an old Knox College schoolmate of Mr.

Goforth's passed us and stopped to say farewell. It was the parting of the ways, he returning to Canada, we to China. Drawing him to one side, out of the crowd, Goforth said, "Tell me frankly, what has been behind the attitude of many of our church leaders towards me these months I have been on furlough? You know me, that I'm not touchy, or one given to imagining slights, but the reserved coolness on the part of many of my fellow ministers has been too obvious to be mistaken. Tell me, frankly, what was the reason?"

The other hesitated, then said, "Goforth, you have only yourself to blame. It was that address before the Assembly, a year ago, that did it!"

While Mr. Goforth was known by name in Britain through reports of the revivals in China and Manchuria, so many distorted stories had been circulated concerning him, it is doubtful if any openings would have come for him to speak in Britain, had it not been for Mr. Walter Sloan of the China Inland Mission, a man widely known and highly honored. It was he who by practically guaranteeing Mr. Goforth, succeeded in getting a number of important doors open to him. Among these were a week's revival mission at two important conventions in Ireland, one in Edinburgh, one in Glasgow and one in Wales. The most important, however, were the ten days at Spurgeon's Tabernacle in London and the week at Keswick. At this latter convention, Goforth shared with Dr. S. D. Gordon the main morning hour, each having a large tent holding a thousand or more. For the first two or three days of the Keswick meetings, it was clearly discernable that Mr. Goforth was "on trial." Then confidence and interest steadily grew. It is well known that the Keswick leaders have always stood solid against emotionalism or undue excitement of any kind. It was therefore a surprise for many to learn of Goforth's being welcomed on a Keswick platform.

The following incident occurred towards the close of the week. We were the guests of the chairman, Mr. Albert Head. One noon at luncheon the Rev. F. B. Meyer was a guest and sat at my right hand. He at once turned to our hostess and said, "Please excuse me from eating as I have something I want to ask Mrs. Goforth." Then, pushing aside his plate, he turned to me, saying (I give as near as I can recall them his exact words): "I have just been to your husband's meeting and have heard him for the first time. I have a question to ask you, but I don't know just how to put it. Has your husband ever had an experience that has brought him into very close touch with God? I do not mean a supernatural vision of God, but something unusual in that way, for he is a remarkable man with a remarkable vision."

"Yes, Dr. Meyer," I replied, "I think he has." He bent his head to catch every word and listened intently as I told briefly the story of my husband's deliverance at the hands of his would-be murderers in 1900, and of the marvelous way he was sustained for duty in the days following. I told him that I had never known his faith in God to fail and of his ever-conscious sense of God's presence. As the company rose from the table, Dr. Meyer exclaimed with a deep sigh, "I thought so!"

I often wondered what the other twenty or more guests must have thought of us that day, but it was worth while,—though I did miss my luncheon!

The Keswick Executive met on the last Saturday evening and at the close of the meeting, a deputation was sent to Mr. Goforth with the surprising proposal that he remain a year in Britain, holding meetings as a Keswick missioner, his salary and all expenses to be met by them. The deputation stated that all the committee had come to see *his message was the message of Keswick.* Goforth would have accepted this offer at once, but before he could do so, the consent of the Board in Toronto must be obtained. A cable was sent, but the answer was in substance, "Return to China. Your field is there." Without a demur Goforth obeyed.

An incident occurred during the mission in Glasgow which should be recorded, as it reveals something of Goforth's attitude towards "ranters," for on several occasions while in Britain a meeting was almost broken up by one or more such mistaken ones:

Pastor Findlay had told Dr. Goforth he was specially concerned about the Saturday afternoon meeting, as he expected a number of the Glasgow ministers to be present. He said, "They have only heard reports of you and now are coming to judge you first-hand." When Saturday afternoon came, the place was crowded, and, as Pastor Findlay had hoped, many ministers from various denominations were in evidence. The first part of the meeting went on as usual, then Mr. Goforth rose to speak. His address was listened to with a stillness that could almost be felt. As his custom was, he gave an invitation at the close of his address for any who wished to pray and left the meeting open. Several very fine, earnest, humble prayers followed, when suddenly a woman jumped to her feet, and, with face raised, and arms outstretched, she repeated rapidly in a loud, shrill voice, the one word, "Blood!" Immediately she was joined by another woman, crying out the same word in the same way. At once dozens in the audience rose and started for the door. Goforth announced a hymn, but it was some moments before the singing could get started and by that time most, if not all, the ministers had gone! Poor Pastor Findlay!

The following interesting item was found among Mr. Goforth's papers:

"When I was in England, in 1910, I heard the origin of the name 'Goforth'. Hundreds of years back there was an upright man who had to make a choice between violating his conscience and leaving his home and loved ones. He chose the latter course and was dubbed 'Goforth'. All our ancestors fought under Cromwell. They were the stern, austere type who did not approve of breaking the Sabbath Day by even cooking a meal on Sunday. During my visit to Yorkshire, in 1910, I found this same spirit characterized the family."

XVI.

AFTER FURLOUGH—TESTINGS

All God's giants have been weak men who did great things for God because they reckoned on God being with them.

HUDSON TAYLOR

TOWARDS THE end of August, we reached the beautiful seaside health resort of North China, Peiteiho, where we stopped over for a week to consult with some of our North Honan colleagues who were still there. We learned for the first time that the Home Board, in conjunction with the North Honan Presbytery, had decided Mr. Goforth must give more time to the work in Honan and less to revival work, and, that we were, for the time being, to live at Weihuifu, the central station of the Mission, and there help out for a year or two. Unwilling to take any hasty step contrary to the ruling of Presbytery, Mr. Goforth decided to fall in with this ruling.

Gladly would we omit the following, but it meant so much to both Mr. Goforth and his wife, it undoubtedly should come in as a part of his life-story. We have already told of the Goforth's losses by fire, by flood, and the Boxers. The fourth loss was, to the writer, the hardest to bear. We can only say it all came about because "someone had blundered." Those who know anything of conditions in a foreign mission station know well how great changes may take place in

210

a year or eighteen months, while a missionary is on furlough.

When leaving our home more than two years before, all furniture and household goods of every kind, large and small, had been stored in a back room, loosely, and apparently safely locked up. On our return, we found the room had been required for some new missionaries, and for lack of a proper storage place, some of our things were taken care of in the various mission houses, but a young, inexperienced missionary, *who had not learned the value of locks in China*, stored many of the loose things, as dishes, kitchen utensils, beds, small furniture, etc., in a leaking, thatched cowshed! When, in the privacy of their own room, the "weaker vessel" broke down and wept bitter, rebellious tears, Goforth sought to comfort her by saying, "My dear, after all, they're only *things* and the Word says, 'Take joyfully the spoiling of your goods!' Cheer up, we'll get along somehow." Our loss, however, turned to be others' gain, for the next Presbytery, when the matter was brought up, decided that a storage room should be built at each main mission station for the safe keeping of missionaries' goods while they were absent on furlough.

For more than a year, the Goforths' headquarters were at Weihuifu. Many country tours were made by them, but without the children, for a fine Christian girl, Miss Agnes Clarke, daughter of China Inland missionary parents and graduate of the Chefoo school, had been secured as governess. During this period, about half of Mr. Goforth's time was given to the outside Revival missions, for the Lord continued to use him as a re-

vivalist. There is one incident of this time which should
be given here, though the sequel comes later.

We were at a country center when a letter came from
one of Goforth's old evangelists at Changte, asking him
to invite his son, Hopinfu, to join us, saying the lad
had given up his position as teacher at the Changte
school and was "going to the bad." The invitation was
sent and the young man came. He loved Mr. Goforth
as a father, but seemed utterly downcast and even desperate. He, however, attended all the meetings and on
the third day broke down weeping. He seemed shaken
to the depths and yielded himself to the Lord Jesus
Christ and found peace. Mr. Goforth urged him to remain with us through another series of meetings. He
did so and before the meetings were over decided to
give himself to the preaching of the gospel. For two
years or more, Hopinfu remained with us. He was
young, gifted and full of enthusiasm and the life of
our band. The sad story of how he left us comes later.

Glad, indeed, were the Goforths when the June,
1914, Presbytery decided they should return to Changte
and take over their old field. When once more in the
old home and facing again the problems of how best
to cover his field, Goforth found himself faced with two
serious handicaps. During his absence from the field,
Presbytery had made a rule allowing, at the most, only
two mission-paid evangelists to one missionary. When
Mr. Goforth left his field, almost five years before he
had a band of fifteen trained evangelists, but on his
return, with one exception, all these were now working
with other missionaries. He could, with reason, have
asked for the return of some of these, but with his

characteristic generosity he decided to start again, believing that in some way the Lord would raise others up.

The second problem was how could he so work the field without sufficient workers that Presbytery would be satisfied that the field was not being neglected, though part of his time was given to revival work elsewhere. I can never forget how, one day, when this question was pressing hard upon him, he drew himself up and, with arm outstreched and flashing eyes, he repeated the following lines, which ever since his student days had been an inspiration to him:

> *"Slacken not pace yet at inlet or island,*
> *Straight for the haven steer,*
> *Straight for the highland!"*

Early one morning, when we were in the country, Mr. Goforth had been pacing the courtyard with such rapid strides and set face, I knew he was agitated about something. When he came in I asked, "What is the matter—is anything wrong?" "Yes," he exclaimed, "I feel bound, hampered, hindered! *Oh, that God would give me an opportunity before I pass on to demonstrate to missionaries and to the home church what results would follow if we but gave God a chance by broadcasting this wonderful message of salvation by every possible means in our power.* I am convinced the simple Gospel story has never had a chance in China."

The story of how God gave him this desire of his heart is told in the final part of this record.

A sadness comes over me as I attempt to write of this period in Jonathan Goforth's life. I knew, as none other, the sorrow and heartache he felt as he learned of the inroads of higher criticism, "the modern menace," was making in the homeland, and also because of the increasing evidence of its reaction on the foreign field. He felt powerless to stem the tide and resolved to preach, as never before, salvation through the Cross of Calvary and demonstrate its power in his own life.

During the five years of Goforth's absence from his field, many of the centres which were but small groups of Christians when he left were now growing churches. He could well have spent all his time visiting these churches, but the pioneer spirit within him urged that he open at least a few new centres each year. How gladly would I tell the full story of those two wonderful years, when, time and time again, we saw the power of God manifested in a truly miraculous way! Some of these stories are told by Mr. Goforth himself.* All I can give space for here is the story of one place, and possibly to just touch upon a few others.

The latter part of August, following our return to Changte, we started for the small village of Suntao, thirty li north of Changte, which was important as a market centre to a wide farming region. On leaving, Dr. Leslie remarked, "I fancy you are making a mistake! This is the farmers' busiest season. You may not get many visitors." "Well, perhaps so," Mr. Goforth replied, "but if no one comes we can get down to Bible-study as well there as here."

The only helpers Mr. Goforth had with him were old Mr. Tung, a good, saintly man, but weak physically; the other, Hopinfu, young and inexperienced (of whom mention has already been made). On arriving at Suntao, we had to pass through a shop to reach our courtyard.

*Miracle Lives of China, Harper Brothers, New York

Three men were in the shop, and all looked and laughed at us in a jeering, most insulting way. One of these men turned out to be our landlord, the second, his youngest son, and the third man, named Feng, the shop accountant. Of these men we will have more to say.

The room we were to live in was of the "barn" class. On one occasion, it was found to contain a coffin. I would not enter then until Mr. Goforth lifted the lid and assured me it was empty! It made, however, an excellent receptacle for papers and a desk large enough for both when closed.

But to return to the first visit. An empty shop just opposite was rented for a preaching hall. Crowds began to come from the outset, both men and women. After three days' constant preaching, Mr. Goforth was so hoarse he could scarcely speak. His need of immediate relief was imperative.

A messenger was sent to Changte, asking for help. In response, several evangelists arrived, but they were only loaned. Goforth tells how, one day, "the burden for evangelists became so heavy, it was like a weight forcing me to my knees. I told the Lord that He was the Lord of the harvest and that he must send more harvesters. There was a time of intense looking to God, almost amounting to agony, and then the burden lifted and I knew that God had answered." He came to me with all strain and anxiety gone, saying, "I am as sure the Lord is going to give me evangelists as if I saw them before me now," and time proved he was not mistaken.

The three men who had been insulting, when we women first passed through the shop, were among the first to come out on the Lord's side. The shop-keeper's eldest son, who had been away for some time, was furious on returning to learn the back courts had been rented to "Foreign Devils." He owned and managed a gambling den adjoining his father's store, but as the gamblers all spent their evenings at the preaching hall, the place had to be closed. The fellow vowed he would not listen to the preaching, but some of the preachers, as well as Goforth, had loud, carrying voices and their every word could be heard in the shop. There was one hymn, each verse of which ended with, "He died for me." It was a great favorite and was sung almost every night. Try as he would, the young man could not get away from the words, "He died for me." Ashamed that others should see him listening, he would go out in the dark and hide outside the preaching hall and listen. One night, he was walking home across the fields alone. Looking up to the starlit heavens, he cried, "God in heaven, I believe what they say of you is true—that there is no other God." Going on a distance, he stopped and cried, "If Jesus is your Son, and if he can save me, give me a vision that I may know for sure." That night he dreamed a wonderful Being stood beside him and said, "Jesus is the Son of God and Jesus alone can save you."

The next day, when the preaching began, to the surprise of everyone, young Chen seated himself on one of the front benches. Day by day he came, morning, afternoon and evening, drinking in the words of Life. Before many days had passed he came out boldly for Christ. In due time he became one of Mr. Goforth's most earnest evangelists and continued so till his death a few years later.

Among the men born into a new life on that first visit to Suntao were robbers, gamblers, opium sots, and others bound as by chains by vicious habits. We have given considerable space to the above story because it is a fair sample of many other centres. Of that first visit to Suntao, Mr. Goforth wrote later:

"A year ago I prayed the Lord for evangelists and received an assurance He would answer my prayer. Now, what is the result? The Lord has sent me two Chinese B.A.'s, both excellent speakers. He moved a consecrated elder to give up his business at great loss to himself, for the preaching of the gospel, and this man has been appointed by the mission as my evangelist. A scholar, who was an opium user and a gambler, was converted at Sun Tao last year. His progress has been most remarkable and it looks as if he is going to make one of the front rank preachers. Also, two brothers, who were among the first converts last year, helped me in the preaching, and their father, also a convert of last year, provides their food."

Great was our joy to find, when visiting places opened years before, great changes had come in the attitude of the people, high and low, toward us. A notable instance of this was at Pengcheng. It was not an uncommon thing during the early visits to that city to be spat upon when on the street. But on our last visit, we were received outside the town by a deputation of the city's leading men, who escorted us to a fine temple which had been prepared for us by having the idols in the main building put back into a place of dark shadows, while the front, sunny part had been swept and garnished for our occupation. Government school students, of low and high schools, were brought by their teachers to hear the Gospel. There were times, when seeing such abundant fruit of our labors, we could but exclaim, "What hath God wrought!"

Young Hopinfu came to be of great help to us. He designed and directed the making of a traveling gospel tent which cost much less and was more suitable to our needs than a foreign tent. He was proving himself more and more invaluable to us in many ways.

A summer school was held at Weihuifu for the training of would-be workers. It was at a time of the year when Mr. Goforth was engaged in the revival meetings, so the young man was sent to this class or school. The following autumn, when Mr. Goforth started out on the touring life, he decided to take the First Epistle of Peter for morning Bible-study with his evangelists.

We had all noticed a strange change in Hopinfu. He seemed restless, unsettled and morose. After the third morning's Bible-class, the young man came to Mr. Goforth and said, "Pastor, the first Epistle of Peter was the study Mr. . . . took with us this summer. I have listened to you for three mornings and if you are right, he is wrong, and if he is right, you are wrong. I cannot judge between you. The foundations have gone from under me. I am leaving. I join the army." In spite of all that Mr. Goforth and the other workers could do, he left us that day, saying to the last, "I have no sure foundations on which to stand!" Oh, the sadness of it!

It will be remembered that one of the conditions of Goforth being allowed by the Presbytery to work his new plan in opening up his field north of Changte was that he must finance any extra expense himself. As time passed and new centres were opened, each place meant added expense in rent and upkeep. When Goforth started out with wife and children, as we have recorded, it was in reality the first step of faith for *money* since his Knox College days. As far as the writer can recall, Mr. Goforth had never, up till this time, received any money from any source for the work except through the regular mission channels. About the time the third cen-tre was opened, the need for financial help began to be keenly felt, for even Goforth could see his salary could not be stretched beyond a certain limit, especially with six children at school. Then the Lord undertook for His servant.

Just at this juncture, a letter reached us from a Miss C. Dinwoodie in Australia, a perfect stranger—indeed, we could never discover how she had heard of us. This lady sent a cheque for fifty pounds, saying she wished to become partners with us in the Lord's work. She stated very plainly that her donation was not for the general running of the Mission, but was to be used by Mr. Goforth in his own work and she asked that in his accounts the word "Investor" be used in place of her name. This dear, God-raised-up partner, for years stood behind us while we were in need of financial aid, though we never wrote to her telling of any special need, always her gifts came as needed.

On one occasion, a time of testing came to the writer. We had been in the country some weeks, and, on the journey home, Mr. Goforth remarked that if money did not come we must draw on our salary, our special fund being exhausted. To this, his "little faith" of a wife strenuously demurred.

Finally, the husband had the last word, which was, "Oh, let us trust Him. Who knows but that a cheque is awaiting us at Changte?" On reaching home a pile of mail was heaped up on the dining-table. Opening the first letter to hand, I read: "Dear Mrs. Goforth, I am a stranger to you. I've never seen you or your husband. I am a Methodist, not a Presbyterian, but I have an old mother, not very well, who has got the idea into her head that you need money. So to quiet her I am sending you the enclosed cheque for fifty dollars. I hope you will find some use for it."

Oh, how humbled I felt! For several moments I could not summon up the courage to hand the letter to my husband, for I expected to hear him say, "I told you so." The good man, on reading it, just smiled, but there was a triumphant look in his eyes which needed no words. Some months later a second letter came from this same lady in answer to my acknowledgment, which read (as near as I can recall): "My mother was dying when your letter came, but she was able to take in all you wrote. The joy of knowing she had been God's channel to help you in China carried her joyfully through those last three days before she passed away." Mr. Goforth's faith never seemed to waver, even when, as a family, times of severe testing came. He would never borrow, nor ever go in debt, and God always honored His servant's trust in Him.

Before going on to a distinctly new period in Goforth's life, we must first give the story of how God gave him one who became his fellow-laborer in the Gospel for more than twenty years—till the end of Dr. Goforth's career as a foreign missionary.

Soon after our return to Changte, a young missionary who had been put in charge of the Changte City preaching hall for non-Christians, came to Mr. Goforth for advice, saying the attendance at the chapel had dwindled till scarcely anyone came. Mr. Goforth then suggested the following plan: that the city official, a friend of his, be asked to give them the best possible site for the erection of a tent and that a month's aggressive evangelistic campaign be carried on, partly for Christians and partly for non-Christians. Mr. Goforth promised to give a month for the leading of this mission.

The plan was carried out, the official giving a great open court, in front of the Chenghwang Miao—Temple of the city god — which was tented in, holding a thousand people. My twenty-four stop organ was carried to the tent, also the church benches and other things. Banners, hymns, scrolls, and pictures made the place attractive. A choir of ten schoolboys led the singing. Our children returned for holidays just as the meetings began and Wallace helped greatly as an attraction with his violin. Those who were through that mission can never forget the joy and enthusiasm of those days. But we are concerned especially with the last night, which was the "great day of the feast."

Su Chuanting, or Mr. Su, as we call him, was passing the tent in a 'rickshaw, on his way for a night's spree. When he heard strange sounds coming from the tent, he said to the 'rickshaw man, "What's that?" The reply came, "It's the foreign devils, holding some kind of a circus." Mr. Su had been drinking and was in the jolly stage. Paying off his fare, he walked unsteadily into the tent and looked in wonder and amazement at the foreign woman playing at a box and a foreign child with his violin. He started up to the front and seated himself on the very front seat, where he hoped to get a good view of this strange circus!

Just then, Mr. Goforth rose and read these words from his open Chinese Bible, which of itself greatly impressed Mr. Su: "This is a faithful saying and worthy of all acceptation, that Jesus Christ came into the world to save sinners" (I Tim. 1:15). Mr. Goforth began by telling what "sinner" meant. Mr. Su later told how angry he became that this foreign devil would dare tell all the people about him, and, literally, show up all his sins and faults. Then, gradually, as he became sober, the truth went home and when the invitation was given for any who believed what had been said, to indicate it by raising the hand, he looked around, expecting, as he afterwards said, that every hand would be up, for it seemed so wonderful to him. But there were none, and saying to himself, "The cowards," he himself put up his hand. Later others followed. Then as several men passed into the inquiry room, Mr. Su followed.

The following day he came to Mr. Goforth, saying, "Pastor, take me with you everywhere you go. I want to learn the secret of how it could be possible when last night as I stood in the inquiry room, my whole past life seemed to drop from me as a garment. I have no desire for those things which bound me with chains. I want to learn this secret that I may help others."

Mr. Su gave up a good salary of twenty-five dollars a month and started off with Mr. Goforth, for a long time getting barely his food. Mr. Su never went back, and made such astounding progress in the following twelve months, the other evangelists came to Mr. Goforth, asking that he might lead a Bible class with them. This was all the more surprising as jealousy is an innate characteristic of the Chinese. We shall hope to hear more of Mr. Su in Manchuria.

XVII.

SAVED FROM HIMSELF

Come ye apart and rest a while.
OUR LORD JESUS

A DEPUTATION from the United States to the American Presbyterian Missions of China passed through the Changte station. The deputation was escorted by Dr. Walter Lowrie, a friend of Mr. Goforth's, and one of the most honored and beloved missionaries of China.

For hours Goforth was plied with questions by these gentlemen regarding his field, his plan of work, results, statistics, and so on. When they rose to leave, one turned to him, saying, "Mr. Goforth, I congratulate you, for you have come nearer in your field to the objective we have set for the evangelization of China than any field we have yet seen or heard of." Their objective was that no Christian need travel more than ten miles to reach a place of Christian worship.

During the autumn of 1915, Mr. Goforth's Alma Mater—Knox College, bestowed upon him the honorary degree of Doctor of Divinity.

It is possible some who have gone with us thus far may have read between the lines that Goforth was attempting the impossible—to carry on the intensive evangelism and general care of the churches in his own field, and also give months each year to the equally strenuous revival missions for others, was more than any physical frame could stand.

Throughout the year 1915 it was increasingly evident to all, as he became persistently attacked by abscesses and carbuncles, that if Mr. Goforth did not slacken his pace, something would happen; but, in spite of the pleadings of his wife, the advice of his colleagues, and the warning of Dr. Leslie that he was "burning the candle at both ends," he would just smile and keep going on as hard as ever.

Again we lift the veil from a home scene. **Mr.** Goforth had promised to hold revival meetings in several China Inland Mission centres south of the Yangtse River. The journey promised to be a hard one, both in distances and manner of travel. The trip was to take several months. But difficulties and prospects of hardness and danger never weighed for a moment with Mr. Goforth. They did, however, weigh now with his wife, being as she was, at this time, very much below par. It was to her a vexatious question whether to remain at home or go with her husband. She dreaded the journey, yet how could she allow her husband, who never thought of himself, to go off in the condition he was, *alone*. One hour it was "go," the next, "stay," until the very afternoon before Mr. Goforth was to leave, the last decision had been to *stay*.

Then our little Mary took matters into *her* hands. Cutting out several pieces of paper the same size, she wrote "stay" on some and "go" on others. Then, mixing them in a hat, she brought them to me saying, "Mother, you just must go with father! Now draw." To please her, I drew, and the paper said, "go." Delighted with the result, the child put a number of slips between a book and again commanded me to draw! Thinking it only a bit of play, I drew and the result was again "go." As she prepared for another try, I inwardly determined that this last would settle the question, though I had persistently said I was *not* going. Again she brought the paper arranged for me to draw and again the slip said "go." Less than half an hour later our home was as busy as a hive of bees. The children were put in Mrs. Griffith's care till they left for school in Chefoo, and the following morning saw us starting on that long, strange, strenuous, and fateful journey.

The first objective for meetings was at Yuan Chow. Many times Mr. Goforth was heard to speak of this mission as one of his most precious memories. Mr. Porteous, the missionary in charge, had a very sweet tenor voice. Again and again when all were on their knees, he would lead softly in that beautiful chorus:

> "Lord, Crucified, give me a heart like Thine;
> Teach me to love the dying souls around,
> Oh, keep my heart in closest touch with Thee;
> And give me love—pure Calvary love,
> To bring the lost to Thee."

At the close of those ten days' meetings we started in chairs over the mountains with the sound of the music and chorus ringing in our ears. That whole region was indescribably beautiful. Every turn in the road brought fresh vistas of mountain ranges and valleys lit up with rich colors. A combination of trees frequently seen was the almost black, heavy, camphor tree, with the tall, pale-green, feathery bamboo, and other trees of deep green, all closely grouped together. The rice fields in the valleys, then at the brilliant gold-green shade, stood

Lord Crucified.

LORD, Cruci - fied, Give me a heart like Thine : Teach me to love the
dying souls a - round. Oh, Keep my heart in closest touch with Thee ;
And give me love-pure calvary love - to bring the lost to THEE.

受苦的主
使我能體主愛
助我愛憐
四面迷亡之羊
求主使我
此刻覺主同在
加我愛心
十架愛心
領迷路羊回來

out in beautiful contrast to the patches of red soil visible up the mountain sides.

We must, however, pass over many interesting incidents and places of that journey till we come to the Kwangsin River region. After a chair journey of six days, we arrived at Iyang, where we found Miss McKenzie (one of the most wonderful of those hidden heroines of the China Inland Mission), and a large number of missionaries and Christians, gathered to welcome us. Ten full days followed, and three meetings a day besides many interviews, kept Mr. Goforth strained to the utmost.

The old alarming symptoms, of which he seemed quite unconscious, began to appear. Two more places were visited with long journeys between. Then a Chinese doctor, trained in a foreign hospital, was called in, who attempted to operate on a carbuncle forming on the back of the neck, but he gave up the operation and ordered Dr. Goforth to be taken as quickly as possible to Dr. Main's hospital at Hangchow, south of Shanghai. We made the three days' journey together in a very small houseboat.

When Dr. Main had examined Mr. Goforth and had heard the story of the preceding months, he said, "Goforth, you say you are returning to Changte for work there. If you do, you will be committing suicide, as surely as if you took an overdose of opium." This brought Mr. Goforth to his senses and from then on he became docile and obedient. The doctor's orders were that he should return to Canada as soon as possible. During the three weeks before arrangements could be made for the home journey, Mr. Goforth became much worse, the angry carbuncle at the back of the neck developing in an alarming way. As we boarded the lighter at Shanghai for our steamer late one night, Mr. Goforth was in terrible pain and distress.

How can one tell of the marvellous kindness shown by all on that boat! It is at such times we learn the value of human sympathy. There were a number of young engineers in training on board, who vied with one another in kindly attentions and sympathy for the sufferer, one of them giving up his couch, which was arranged in a sheltered spot on deck, and here Mr. Goforth lay, literally shining for his Master. How those young fellows delighted to sit beside him for his cheery smile, and, when able, his understanding word which drew them to him. The ship's physician (we were told later) had not hesitated to make it known that he feared Mr. Goforth would never reach port. He was, however, much improved on our arrival at Vancouver.

The following letter from Mr. D. E. Hoste, Director General of the China Inland Mission, who was a fellow passenger, sheds a bright light on how Mr. Goforth reflected his Master on that journey:

"I am thankful to be in a position to bear witness to the profound impression made upon me by Mr. Goforth's personality during a voyage across the Pacific in 1916, when we shared the same cabin. He was in a rundown condition, owing to carbuncles, and was suffering not a little from one at the time. I shall never forget the impression made upon me by his unbroken patience, cheerfulness, and unselfish regard for others which characterized his whole demeanour and behaviour. I never saw the least petulance or impatience throughout the whole trip. I was deeply touched as I saw his worn, emaciated countenance and enfeebled bodily frame, lit up and sustained by the grace of the Lord, whose he was and whom he served. Truly a man to love, admire, and learn from, quite apart from his outstanding gifts and far-reaching public ministry. He was a 'winner' in more senses than one."

On reaching Toronto, the Goforths found a welcome haven in the Missionary Rest Home at Mimico, some distance out of the city. Then, by the end of August, they were face to face with a serious financial crisis, the sudden return to Canada and Mr. Goforth's illness having entailed many extra expenses. The hard fact had to be faced that their salary was not sufficient. Mr. Goforth felt he could not lay our needs before the Board and ask for help. The only other alternative was to step out in faith, secure a suitable home in Toronto, and trust the Lord to undertake for the extra expense. This we did, and the Lord never failed us.

While the financial question was being discussed, Ruth, then about seventeen years of age, became very indignant that we should be brought, as she put it, "to a place of beggars." But we assured her that to trust God for what was lacking was not begging. But she seemed only partly convinced. The day came for our taking possession of the new home in Toronto, and on entering, we found a large mail awaiting us. One letter was from Miss Dinwoodie in Australia, whose co-operation with us in the past we have already mentioned. Her letter enclosed fifty pounds with the express wish that thirty pounds be used for work in China, but twenty pounds was to be used for personal needs. I handed the letter to Ruth with the words, "It seems to me as if our Father were beside us saying, 'Take this one hundred dollars as an earnest of what I am going to do for you.'" Tears stood in Ruth's eyes as she handed the letter back. "Oh, mother," she said, "we don't trust God half enough." That little incident was the beginning of a new vision in the life of our dear daughter and ultimately led to her yielding herself as a missionary to Indo-China, where she has been with her husband for some years.

Soon after reaching Toronto, June, 1916, Mrs. Goforth was led into a very deep spiritual experience through Dr. Charles G. Trumbull, Editor of *The Sunday School Times,* a speaker at the Niagara-on-the-Lake Conference.* The following summer, Mr. Goforth and his wife were invited to the American Keswick held that year in Princeton, New Jersey. It was their first prolonged contact with Christians "across the line." Friendships were made there which remained unbroken through the remainder of Goforth's life. The Keswick contact led to Boston, where the "Boston Circle" was formed; but of these, more later.

It was on this furlough we first became impressed with the way God had been raising up intercessors for us. Frequently one or more came up at the close of a meeting, saying they had prayed for us every day for years; some even from the time we had left for China. One day—not now—we shall know the "why" of many victories and perhaps too the "why" of many

---

*How I Know God Answers Prayer, Harper Brothers, New York

failures because someone had failed to "hold the ropes."

The almost three years in which Mr. Goforth had been passing through the siege of twenty-five carbuncles and abscesses had been not only a time of great physical suffering but also a testing of his energetic nature. It was characteristic of the man that, from the time Dr. Main's words convinced him of his need for rest, he yielded himself up without a struggle to rest. His quiet patience and entire freedom from worry and his never-failing buoyant cheerfulness impressed and inspired all with whom he came in contact.

Through a friend's kindness the family spent some weeks in Muskoka. It was blueberry season. Day by day Mr. Goforth started off immediately after breakfast with Ruth and others picking berries. He entered into this with the same zest he had in his revival missions! Later, he insisted it was those "glorious" blueberry-picking days which made him once more ready for China!

XVIII.

GOSPEL NOMADS

Measure thy life by loss and not by gain,
Not by the wine drunk but by the wine poured forth;
For love's strength standeth in Love's sacrifice—
And he who suffers most has most to give.
THE SERMON IN THE HOSPITAL

RETURNING TO China the autumn of 1917, Mr. Goforth again started out to spend part time on his field and part time at the revival missions, calls for which had been accumulating from many parts of China.

To give up his field, leave the Christians, and his faithful band of evangelists, all of whom loved him as a father and whose love he fully reciprocated, was what Mr. Goforth could not bring himself to face. Presbytery became—shall we say?—*restless* regarding what they felt to be "Goforth's untenable position." At the same time another issue arose which led to the final decision, for it was truly a time of crisis.

We have come to what I feel to be the most difficult point of this record. To be faithful to Jonathan Goforth's memory, the following facts must be given. For years, the teaching which was called "higher criticism" and "modernism" had been increasingly taught in the colleges of the homeland, and, as was inevitable, its reaction became more and more evident on the foreign field. Mr. Goforth was never one to mince words when deeply stirred on what he deemed, "a lowering of the standards of truth." Of that time we know not how to write. There was keen contention. I will give simply Goforth's answer to one word applied to him—"Intolerant!"

"Intolerant!" he exclaimed, "if you saw one under-mining the foundation of a structure you, and others with you, had given the best of their lives to build, would it be intolerant to use every ounce of strength in combating the wrecker?"

Mr. Goforth utterly refused to give his vote that both sides, fundamentalists and modernists, be allowed to preach and teach as they felt led. He cited the case of Hopinfu. There was but one thing for him to do—send in his resignation. The Home Board dealt generously with him. They insisted he should remain a member of the North Honan mission of which he was the founder, but recommended that he be set en-tirely free from his Changte field to carry on the re-vival work to which he felt called. His salary was to be continued, but he was to hold himself responsible for all else—as home and travel. The old home at Changte was required for the one taking over Mr. Go-forth's field.

The question of where to make a home or rather, headquarters, was a difficult one, as the future life was to be nomadic. Several hundred miles south of Changte, where the provinces of Honan and Hupeh meet, a beautiful, irregular plateau, on one of the ranges of mountains which reached as far south as the great Yangtse River, had been discovered some years previously. The place was called Kikungshan and the whole plateau had been secured by foreigners as a health resort. The climate was mild both winter and summer. Since this place was central and suitable for residence at any season of the year, the Goforths decided to make their home there.

The purchase of land and building of a home on the mountain was a most difficult problem, not only financially, but, to Mr. Goforth, the most serious question was how to get time from his all-important work to oversee the building. In meeting this, we glimpse how always the Lord's work came first with him. It was risky, so others thought, and would undoubtedly cost more, but rather than cancel a tour through south China, he determined to put the building of the home in the hands of a Chinese contractor and keep to his schedule of meetings.

During the following two years, a tally was kept each time we changed our resting-place, when, we found, we had "moved on" *on an average of every five days* during that time. It is therefore impossible to touch upon or even mention many of the missions conducted during these two years. This first journey to south China seemed a very long one—from Kikungshan to Hankow, then on by river steamer down the Yangtse to Shanghai; from there by steamer to Hong Kong; from thence up the "West" river to Canton, and on up to Wuchow, an important station of the Alliance mission.

After a week's meetings there which were attended by much blessing, we started on the long river journey to Kweilin, an important mission centre close to the watershed of south central China. Streams flowed from the one side southward and eastward to Canton and on the northern side, down to the far-distant Yangste River. The following are some extracts from a letter written to the home folks at this time:

"The journey here, from the time we arrived at Hong Kong, has been most interesting. On the steamer from Canton to Wuchow, we noticed that gates of iron bars were dividing one part of the boat from another. These were kept locked; even the entrance to the upper deck was secured by an iron grating, which was locked each time anyone went up or down. This precaution was taken because of the great danger from pirates. A few years ago one of the finest missionaries, Dr. Roderick Macdonald, was murdered by pirates on one of these boats.

"We made the journey of six days from Wuchow to this place, Kweilin, by small house-boat. And it was small! From our one possible seat, a board, I was able to run the charcoal stove, cook all that was to be cooked, set the table (a valise on a board), and dip water out of the river, without moving from my seat! You would have been interested could you have seen us two old folks getting our meals those six days. Thanks to Mrs. Jaffray's kindness we had plenty to eat. When through with our meals, we two would set to the dishwashing, which needless to say was a simple affair and somewhat of a relief from the monotony.

"Jonathan does love to have a little fun and he certainly had it one day at my expense. Among the things Mrs. Jaffray had packed in the hamper were a number of what looked to us like small oranges. Jonathan peeled one and took a good bite! I did not see his face at the moment. By the time he turned to me holding out the fruit, his eyes were so twinkling with mischief and fun I might have suspected something, but did not. So when he said, 'Just taste it,' I did—for I am fond of *sweet* oranges —but oh, it was not an orange, but a lime!—for sourness like a concentrated lemon!

"There were some real discomforts, such as the violent rocking of the boat passing over the *three hundred and fifty rapids* en route; we could not get over the seasick feeling this movement gave. Then we forgot to bring candles or lamp, so were forced to either sit in the dark on the board seat or get to the hard board bed at six-thirty every evening. I did not feel this as much as Jonathan. The noisy boatmen, the hardness of the bed, the long hours on the horizontal, all combined to keep him from sleep, so it was not much wonder he remarked, 'Well, I certainly won't recommend this trip as a "rest cure" for anyone!' "

"But the wonderful scenery! It was beautiful beyond description. Mountains rose on either side of us almost all the way; as we looked forward we seemed to be passing through one gorge after another. Through many of these forward glimpses we could count several mountain ranges. Then the rich coloring! It was very much the same as we saw when travelling through Kiangsi Province.

"The Lord has been giving much blessing both here and at Wuchow. At other places in the south, all speaking had to be done through an interpreter, but strange to say, this place is a Mandarin speaking region, and we are understood as well as in Honan. It is a very great privilege to be permitted to help Jonathan in this work. Especially do I feel this when at such a station as this where the missionaries are cut off, to a great extent, from outside help.

"It has been to me really touching to see the hunger expressed for the highest and best that God has to give. I feel keenly my own unworthiness for such a ministry, but praise God, we can commit to Him the failures and mistakes, yes, and sins of the past; and He can use these to lift us on to the plane where we can help others up, thus making 'stepping-stones of our dead selves to higher things.'"

Six months later, our Home Secretary, Dr. R. P. MacKay, received the following letter from one of the missionaries at Kweilin:

"In November last, Dr. Goforth visited Kweilin at the invitation of the Christian and Missionary Alliance. Our Church was also asked to join in a united ten-days' special mission. I feel I must write and tell you of how great benefit the mission was to me personally and to our church. After the lapse of six months I am able to say that the results are lasting and increasing, and no one can tell 'whereunto this thing will grow.' For myself, I have received the greatest blessing of my life, and I shall feel eternally grateful to Dr. Goforth and your church in thus giving me the message of life more abundant in Christ Jesus.

"As regards the church, we have been saved out of the snare of the devil, and the fruits of the mission are becoming more apparent every day. Since

the time of the mission the missionaries in Kweilin
have continued in unceasing prayer that the whole
city and district may receive the fulness of God's
blessing. I send this short note of thanks, but I could
never tell more than a fraction of God's mercies to
us at that time and since. Thank God Dr. Goforth
was able to come to Kweilin.

> "Yours sincerely,
> "(Signed) 'J. R. WILSON'
> "Church Missionary Society."

A full schedule of meetings at mission stations
along the river routes, west of Canton, had been arranged for Mr. Goforth. The same tokens of the Holy
Spirit's presence and power were manifest at every
place visited. His wife was unable to accompany him
on this part of the tour owing to a somewhat serious
breakdown. After some weeks in the Matilda Hospital,
Hong Kong, she returned to Kikungshan where she
found their new home nearing completion. The contractor had done marvelously — only one mistake (a
very serious one) having been made, namely, *the
stairs being turned the wrong way!*

It was well on in the summer before Mr. Goforth
returned from the south. Probably two hundred or
more missionaries were then gathered on the hilltop.
We had hoped Mr. Goforth might have two months of
complete rest in the new home from which could be
seen a beautiful valley, over a thousand feet below,
stretching for many miles between ranges of mountains.
For a brief few days only, he was able to enjoy it all
without a care. Then the urgent request came to lead
a series of meetings on the hilltop for the missionaries.

Though longing for rest, he could not refuse, for his soul was ever eager to tell out to others the message of "the fulness of the Christ-life through the Holy Spirit's indwelling." Days of blessing followed. Some said Kikungshan had come to be "a step heavenward."

Almost immediately after the meetings for missionaries, came an invitation from Marshal Feng Yuhsiang, (then General), for Mr. Goforth and his wife to hold meetings among his soldiers. The General and his army were three days south of the Yangtse River in an extremely hot region. Though the city, outside of which was the camp, was situated by a river, the land rose on three sides keeping any breeze from reaching the lowland. The summer of 1919 was an unusually hot one. When the invitation came, word had just been received of cholera raging on the plains. Mr. Goforth never for a moment hesitated in responding to the General's call, but "his weaker self" did shrink from facing the heat and cholera. Two other ladies promised if I decided to take the risk they would go with me.

The last evening had come when a decision must be made. Opening my Bible in a rambling way, my eye lit on these words: "He that observeth the wind shall not sow and he that regardeth the clouds shall not reap" (Ecclesiastes 11:4). That settled the question. The following morning we were en route to Marshal Feng's army. Thus the door opened to one of the most fruitful ministries of Jonathan Goforth's life, and, oh, how I would have regretted missing what we saw on this trip had coward fear prevailed!

The journey of one day by train and three by

steamer was extremely hot. It was as if we were in a Turkish bath day and night. We tried to sleep at night on the deck of the steamer. On Sunday afternoon, August 24, we reached the house of Mr. Caswell of the Holiness Mission. It was amusing to read the General's letter written in English by his Chinese English teacher, in which he said to Mr. Caswell, "I beg you to prepare the treatment for their coming."

General Feng called within an hour of our arrival. He was over six feet tall, and every inch a General, yet without a trace of the bombast so often seen in the higher-class Chinese His manner was a curious and striking mixture of humility, dignity, and quiet power; he had a striking, good face. He at once impressed one as true and sincere, a man to be trusted.

From the first, God was very manifestly working. Twice every day Dr. Goforth had an attentive and keenly interested audience of about one thousand men, chiefly officers. At three of these meetings the wives were permitted to be present; but all the rest of the women's meetings were separate, when God gave me much help in speaking to them. At our last meeting, practically all the officers' wives present said they wished to follow the Lord Jesus.

At one of the last meetings for the men, General Feng broke down as he tried to pray. What seemed to affect him was the thought of his country. As soon as he could recover from his sobs, he stood up, and, facing his officers, pleaded for his country—pleaded with them to join him in putting aside all mean motives, and think and work and pray for their country. One of his staff officers followed, praying earnestly, then one after the other of the officers, with sobs and tears cried to God on behalf of themselves and their country.

An old missionary who was present, and who described the scene to me, said he did not think there had ever been such a scene before when a general wept before his own officers, with all that followed. But the discipline was not broken by it; for when the General rose to leave, the audience rose as one man.

XIX.

HARVESTING ON FAMINE FIELDS

Wheat, that mildews in the garner,
Scattered fills with gold the plain.

ANON.

THE WORST famine in the annals of China faced the people of North-Central China in the late summer of 1920, our old Changte field being the centre of the worst affected area. It was said from thirty to forty millions of people faced stark starvation. Reports coming from Changte were heart-rending and too horrible to publish. The whole Changte staff gave themselves up to meet the unparalleled crisis.

The writer, forced to remain at the Kikungshan mountain home, gave herself as steward for famine funds. During the winter of 1920-21 over one hundred and twenty thousand dollars passed through her hands to the various famine relief centres.

Just as the famine was ending, one thousand dollars was received. Not knowing just what to do with this sum we decided to put it into the famine relief fund in the Hankow bank and wait for guidance. Some months later we heard that the Changte friends greatly wished that a campaign of evangelism might be undertaken through the field, as people's hearts had been wonderfully opened through the relief work, so heroically carried out by all the Changte staff, but to carry out such a campaign needed funds, and they had none. We wrote, asking what the cost would be. The reply came, "about one thousand dollars." What a joy it was again to open the cheque-book, clear up the relief account by writing out the cheque for one thousand dollars, and send it to the dear brave ones who had carried on all through those terrible months. To crown it all, it was arranged that we should return to Changte for the winter and lead a band of evangelists throughout the whole Changte field.

Coming back again on the old battle-ground, what wonderful opportunities lay before us of reaping a harvest of souls, where carefully organized relief work had, but a few months before, saved multitudes from the cruel relentless grip of famine! A band of eight picked evangelists and two Bible women were to accompany us, for a very full programme was planned. All, or most of the main stations throughout the entire Changte field were to be visited, one or two meetings a day for the Christians and the rest of the time to be given to aggressive evangelism for the heathen. Part of the band were to carry on preaching in villages while the main tent meetings were in progress. Then all would gather for the evening meeting.

All through those five months of physically hard labor—under which the health of the writer ultimately broke down—never once was Mr. Goforth heard to complain. When enduring the bitter cold of drafty tents and unheated rooms, hard brick beds, and often the torment from very small but very lively fleas, over forty of which met their fate at his hands early one morning — he remained calm and unperturbed. He made light of what he described as "minor matters," choosing rather to regard the winter's tour as "a glorious victory" for his Lord. It had been settled that names and addresses of those wishing to become Christians should be taken down, these to be passed on to Mr. Griffith for examination and recording as catechumens. At the close of the tour, three thousand names of those who had come forward publicly confessing Christ, were handed to Mr. Griffith. Later, he was able to visit little more than half the places we had touched, and though he was known as a very strict examiner, he recorded fifteen hundred names. The following are just a few incidents taken from a daily diary written at that time:

"On arrival at one place, at least half a dozen Christians were vieing with one another to help us get settled. There was the ever-necessary curtain to be hung, a tick to be filled with straw, bedding to be undone, and so on. Then about six o'clock some bowls of delicious food were brought in from the Chinese restaurant which we thoroughly enjoyed as we had had only a light lunch. By seven-thirty we were ready for the prayer-meeting, Dr. Goforth with the Christian men, and I with the women. Then all walked down the street to a large courtyard fixed up with plenty of bunting, blue and white awning, a platform, benches, etc. The baby organ was in place and a fine audience of heathen gathered. We had a rousing gospel meeting. It is just grand to be out once more in close touch with the people"—

"We hear that about forty families have taken down their gods in the last place visited. Fine large attractive gospel texts are given to each one destroying their household gods. These are put up where the main god had been. Many died here of starvation last winter. Out of one family, only one little child survived"—

"We praise God that what we have seen and heard convinces us that the Lord has been working through the evangelists. Many of the gentry of the town and the officials also have had Dr. Goforth meet with them privately to tell the message. The Christians also at the last meeting for testimony testified to freshened vision of their responsibility to their own people. Many had during their meetings confessed with great brokenness to living cold, fruitless lives"—

"The Christian postmaster from a town a few miles distant escorted Dr. Goforth to where the leading men of the town were waiting to receive him and to hear from him the gospel. An officer and a number of soldiers later escorted him to the headquarters of the local militia, where he found over twenty prominent men awaiting his arrival. He was received with every honour and for over an hour and a half preached the Gospel and answered questions. What a change from thirty years before when two of our missionaries were driven from the same place and a year later Dr. Goforth had to force an entrance into the public inn!"—

"Travelling westward we came into the real hill-country where cart travel is impossible. We made quite a cavalcade. My chair usually led with Dr. Goforth walking beside. Then the evangelists and behind came our three Bible women each on an animal, and lastly the three pack animals with bedding, etc. Such a welcome awaited us! School-boys in gay patriotic caps with flags flying led the way, and as I alighted from my chair a crowd of eager Christian women thronged each other in trying to have some share in helping me over the rough stone and up the steep steps. A whole family who had been saved by the famine relief last winter, turned out of their home to accommodate us. Our whole visit at this centre will ever remain one of our brightest memories"—

"The large village temple here had been so transformed by numerous gospel texts and posters, flags and bunting, one could scarcely have known it for a heathen temple. The idols were pushed quite back out of sight. My organ and the preacher's table stood on the high temple platform and the audience sat on benches in the court below which was covered in by mats"—

"The lantern meetings had to be held on a great threshing-floor just outside the village, the wall of which was used for the screen. A great crowd assembled and were very orderly. Word must have got out that we women were preaching a message specially helpful to the old people for in my day meetings many old women came to listen. One day I asked the ages of some occupying the front benches and they ranged from sixty-five to eighty-three"—

"It was an inexpressible joy to both of us who had fought for years the opposition and distrust at this centre to now see all such hostility crumbling away. Everywhere while there we were treated with the utmost respect"—

"It is only 'a little straw,' but it shows how the wind of public opinion is veering in our favour that when Mr. Goforth and I were walking along the street, the street-vendors squatting before their trays of sweet-meats, on catching sight of us, would immediately rise and stand at attention while we passed. This was indeed a contrast to past years when the same men would probably have sneered and jeered at us and have called after us the then common 'foreign devil' "—

"A truly wonderful movement is going on among the teacher class of this region. It began several years ago while we were holding tent meetings here. It has now spread till a large number of government school-teachers in this county, with the city of Tzushien as its centre, are now Christians"—

"There were large attentive day audiences, while at night almost unmanageable crowds came to the services on the Life of Christ. These evening meetings and elsewhere were conducted entirely by our evangelistic band. Of the permanent results of this mission only time can tell, but this we do know, that during these days thousands have heard the gospel of salvation through the Lord Jesus Christ faithfully proclaimed"—

"On arriving here, when Dr. Goforth saw the meeting-tent, he at once said, 'Why, you have made it far too large. It will hold six or seven hundred!' 'No, no, Pastor,' replied the Christians, 'wait and see if we won't have to raise the back part to accommodate more,' and they were right. It was a wonderful sight to see for the first time cart-loads of heathen women being brought in from the distant villages by their men-folk to attend the meetings"—

"Travelling southward seventeen miles, the picture which remains of this place is a dark one. Our 'Palace

Hotel' was just a dark, damp, dirty hole. The weather was bitterly cold with a piercing wind. Little wonder then that the writer was laid low with what resembled flu or pleurisy. At the close of the four-days' mission, while still suffering with pain and fever, we had to make the journey northward some twenty miles. This journey will ever remain in the writer's memory as one of the hard experiences of China. A cold north wind blew gales of dust and sand in our faces, but external comforts were not for us on our arrival at the new place for there was no room to put up our little stove in the damp, bitterly cold room allotted to us. Here too, sickness kept the writer from attending the meetings, but day by day, Dr. Goforth reported wonderful meetings for both Christians and heathen"—

"Here the mission resembled one we held in Changte city. The Christians had made great preparation for our coming and had secured a splendid place in the heart of the city in the temple court. The interest was grand, but the writer had by this time reached the end of physical strength and was obliged to return to Changte where the W. M. S. Home proved a 'house of refuge.' The kind, loving workers, so stressed to the utmost with their own work, found time to take the tired one in. We shall ever be thankful for that week's quiet rest and care. Dr. Goforth and the rest of the band continued the tour through the remaining out-stations, returning to Changte at the completion of the tour as scheduled."

The following little incident which is not recorded in the diary comes to mind. As Mr. Goforth was leaving the tent at a certain place, he noticed a young lad about twelve years of age following him. Seeing the lad wished to speak to him, Mr. Goforth laid his hand upon the boy's head, saying, "Well, my boy, what can I do for you?" "Please, Pastor," said the lad, "am I too young to give my name? I want to be a Christian." Taking the boy's hand, he led him back to the tent where one of the evangelists was recording names, where after questioning, he was, to his great delight, received, and his name recorded. That evening, as we were having supper in our "mud hut," who should shyly make his appearance but this lad, followed by another boy. "Pastor," he said, "this is my cousin. He too wants to be a Christian." So he came to be called our little Andrew. Later, as the boys left, my husband's face just glowed with joy. "Truly this is a work that angels might covet!" he said.

XX.

"IN JOURNEYINGS OFT"

Oh, if mine own thought should on Thy words falling,
Mar the great message, and men hear not Thee,
Give me Thy mind to grasp Thy mystery;
So shall my heart throb, and my glad eyes glisten,
Rapt with the wonders Thou dost shew to me.
        —BY A MISSIONARY EN ROUTE TO HIS FIELD

FOLLOWING THE winter of reaping on the famine
fields at Changte, the Goforths returned to their headquarters at Kikungshan, in preparation for the second
visit to South China. On this tour Mr. Goforth saw
blessed signs of the Holy Spirit's convicting and transforming power at each centre visited. The first revival
mission was held at Swatow, on the coast south of
Shanghai. At the close of the meetings, we were to
leave for Hongkong by steamer about five P.M. All
that day the wind had been rising. By the time our
boat was due to leave, our captain became anxious,
and decided to anchor by an island off-shore.

At daybreak we were well out to sea, but never had
we experienced such tossing! The writer lay in perfect
peace of mind, expecting each moment the boat would
be engulfed. Mr. Goforth was out, helping with the
one other woman passenger, who continued in violent
hysterics most of that day. By nightfall, the captain
succeeded in getting a somewhat safe anchorage by an

island near Hong Kong, which city we reached safely the following morning.

Two days later, the worst typhoon for many years struck Soochow, ripping up great trees we had walked under but a few days before, and wrenching off the iron-riveted verandahs of the house we had stayed in. Boats were carried more than a mile inland and many hundreds of lives were lost, among these a number of those to whom we had ministered. The storm we had encountered was not the tail-end of the typhoon, but the working up to it.

The following interesting testimony to the importance of memorizing the Word of God, written about this time, was found among Dr. Goforth's papers:

"It is well to be able to repeat Scripture, but it is of very great importance to remember where it is in the Bible. My ideal has always been (though I cannot say I have always attained unto it), that it would be a shame for me, a missionary, to have to go to a concordance to find a portion of Scripture that a Chinese brother might ask me for. My wife seems to regard me as her walking concordance and my Chinese fellow-workers seem to think that I know everything in the Bible, but I am ever wishing I could spend several hundred years at the Bible.

"Since the New Version of the New Testament came out in Chinese, I will in a few days have gone over it thirty-five times in the Chinese text, comparing it with the Authorized and Revised New Testaments. My method now is to go over each verse five times, but ever trying after the first time to repeat it from memory, and even though I am sure of the meaning,

I still read for comparison both English versions. Going through the New Testament once in this way, I reckon as having read it five times in Chinese, taking no account of the English. As a result of this method, when I preach to the Chinese, the Scripture comes readily to mind and the Holy Spirit is able through me to compare spiritual things with spiritual. It is appalling how God and souls are defrauded because we know so little of His saving Word."

The following are extracts from Mr. Goforth's record of one period with Marshal Feng and his army:

"Less than eleven years ago, General Feng and all his men were heathen. Now, for its size, the army under General Feng is the greatest Christian army on earth. It is about thirteen months since we spent thirteen days in meetings with the army. On the last day we baptized nine hundred and sixty men. That same day, four thousand six hundred and six officers and men partook of Communion.

"A few days later, General Feng was promoted to Divisional Commander and sent to support the appointee to the military governorship of Shensi. A Chinese writing from the first city in the Province that the Christian army passed through, said: 'Other soldiers when they came seized our houses and public buildings and made off with anything they took a fancy to, and our wives and daughters were at their mercy, so that the people called them the soldiers of hell. Now General Feng leads his men through the city and nothing is disturbed and nothing is molested. Even the General lives in a tent, as his men do, and everything they need they buy, and no one is abused. The people are so delighted the people call them the soldiers of heaven.'

"A missionary who saw the Christian army victoriously enter the Capital of Shensi, said: 'During the last few years, I have seen the heart-rending sight of army after army take our city and pillage it at will, but this time as I saw regiment after regiment of General Feng's army marching through the city singing hymns, the tears ran down my face for joy.'

"Another missionary, going into Shensi during the recent crisis, met the Christian army coming out. Arriving one evening at a certain stopping place, he saw a great company of soldiers together and found General Feng preaching to them. It is not the ordinary kind of Christianity which can move soldiers to give time and place to the worship of God when on forced marches! . . .

"Thirty-three and a half years ago, when we tried to enter the gates of Kaifeng (the Capital of Honan), we were kept out by armed guards, but when we entered the gates a few weeks ago the armed guards were Christians, the walls by the gates, and the passage through them on either side, as well as important points in the city, have telling exhortations from the Chinese sages and from the Scriptures. There are cartoons painted on the walls, showing the evil of opium, morphine and cigarette-using, etc., etc., and even the fly pest is not passed over. The streets are clean as they have not been for ages. Kaifeng for centuries has been notorious as a city of stagnant ponds. Now the Christian Governor is about to drain them off into a river to the south. All women of ill repute have been sent from the city. If the Governor remains long enough in the Province he will open a reformatory to reclaim such unfortunates.

"Colonel Lu, one of the best men in the army, is

made Head of Police for the whole Province. He is the man who would like to be set free to go as an evangelist through the armies of China. He is the man who so strongly holds that China's pressing need is not Western civilization, but the living God controlling in the hearts of her people. For such a Christian leader to be in control of all the police will mean much for this province.

"Over a year ago, General Chang, a great Christian and a great fighter (for in the recent battle he, with two hundred and eighty men, for hours held back a thousand of the enemy until reinforcements could be brought up), told me that the Spirit of God pressed him to go through the land as a preacher. This time when we called on him he again asked me to urge his request before the Governor. As I held his hand in saying goodbye, I prayed that God would guide. General Chang is the leader of the Evangelistic band of over fifty in this Christian army. General Feng over a year ago decided to have a place in his army for the training of evangelists.

"On arriving at Kaifeng, there was an invitation from the Governor to take supper with him. Consequently, I planned to call shortly before that time, but he sent over for me to come at three o'clock. After being with him for a time, I saw he was very busy, so I said I would go away and return about suppertime. 'No,' said he, 'you stay right here with me. If anything urgent needs to be attended to, I will see to it and we can chat between times.' It is a rapid rise from brigade commander to Governor of the key Province of this land in thirteen months, and in point of influence to be almost second to none in China. Still he seems to be the same humble follower of the Lord as we have known in the past, and gives all the glory to God. When he was ruler of the province of Shensi he urged us to give a year to that Province, but now he asks that we give that time to Honan. In accord with the Governor's request, we are planning to give all October to special evangelistic effort at Kaifeng. After supper we went out to inspect a couple of theatre buildings, to see if they could be used for the coming meetings, and if they prove unsuitable, the Governor says he will erect an auditorium to seat several thousands. Thirty-three years ago I could not imagine that I would ever go through the streets of that hostile city with its Ruler, he on his bicycle, and I in a 'ricksha, going around looking for a preaching place. I am sure if Dr. J. F. Smith, who was with me then, could have been with me on this occasion, he would have shouted for joy.

"To have General Feng as our Governor in Honan brings an unparalleled opportunity and responsibility to all missions located in the Province. What shall the home church do towards strengthening her mission in North Honan? The Governor is as zealous for the living God as was Nehemiah. Will the Canadian Presbyterian Church stand by him and cheer him on by adequately striving to save her part of the Province? At this time of times the Foreign Mission Board is faced with a staggering deficit of $166,000, and rumors of retrenchment are reaching us. What! Retrench? When such an open door invites us? The deficit is staggering, but that sum would not pay the tobacco bill of Canadian Presbyterians for one month! But why a deficit at all? Is it because our gifts to save fourteen millions are so vast? We pride ourselves that we are the banner church of the Dominion in our liberal gifts to Missions. Are we really satisfied that our annual gifts to save fourteen millions of heathen are all that our Lord and Master should expect of us? It is so vast a sum that it would hardly keep the ladies of the Canadian Presbyterian church in face powder for a year! Are we not insulting Him who paid our debt on Calvary? Do we mean it when we sing, 'Were the whole realm of nature mine that were a present far too small,' etc.? Somehow I cannot believe that Canadian Presbyterians are going to approve of retrenchment on the Foreign Field. On the other hand, I am confident that the Home Church will catch the vision and, for Honan at least, will realize that it is the floodtide of opportunity. Here is one of the world's great Christians, Governor of our Province, planning an evangelistic campaign to reach thirty millions. When in history had the Church such an opportunity? On visiting hundreds of wounded officers and men in the hospital wards, I came across one downhearted one and on inquiry I found out that he was not a Christian."

It was while on the above visit to Kaifeng, Dr. Goforth met with what might have been a very serious accident. One dark night, while returning in the Governor's motor from a meeting in the camp, the chauffeur missed his way and drove straight into a deep ditch. Dr. Goforth was thrown forward so violently, his head broke through the heavy glass windshield. He was completely stunned and for a few moments, helpless, but he quickly recovered—though for some time it was evident he had received a severe shock. The following morning at daybreak, he was off to the camp for an hour's Bible-study with the Governor.

A full year passed in work among the soldiers in General Feng's army, during which time over four thousand of the soldiers were baptized. Then Dr. Goforth received an urgent call from the old field of Changte, again to lead a campaign of tent evangelism through the field as before. Dr. Goforth hesitated. He had promised the Christian General to give the rest of his time till furlough to the soldiers, but the call of his old field was the call of his first love. He decided to lay the matter before the General, who, on hearing the whole matter, generously set my husband free to spend the winter before furlough in leading this evangel in Honan.

Dr. Goforth no longer had his wife to take care of him, as she had been forced to return to Canada in broken health. For weeks he tried eating the same food and in the same irregular way as the Chinese of the party; but, fortunately, he was able to secure our old cook as "boy" and so fared better.

In every place souls were being saved. In one place Dr. Goforth mentions seventy having taken a stand, in another over one hundred. At the close of one of his last letters, he wrote: "I am sixty-five today. . . . *Oh, how I covet, more than a miser does his gold, twenty more years of this soul-saving work.*" Immediately at the close of this long and physically testing, but blessedly fruitful tour, Dr. Goforth left China for furlough.

On the steamer crossing the Pacific were two ladies, one was Miss Rollier, a French lady and an Indo-China missionary. The other was Madam Karinski, a former prima donna of the Russian court, upon whose head a price had been set by the Soviet government. This Rus-

sian lady was in great distress. Her outlook financially
was hopeless; spiritually, the foundations of what faith
she had seemed sinking from under her.

Miss Rollier came to Dr. Goforth and begged him
to help this distracted woman. Then for several days,
passengers pacing the deck witnessed a remarkable
scene. The three sat side by side, Mr. Goforth in the
centre with his English Bible, Miss Rollier with her
French Bible, and Madam (a most striking personality) with her Russian Bible. Each difficulty of
this poor woman, each question of faith, Dr. Goforth met with a passage of Scripture, Miss Rollier acting as interpreter. Madam had a deep reverence for
the Bible. On the third day she exclaimed, "I see it
all now. Praise the Lord! I must tell the good news
to my people!" She had been urged by some theatrical
men from New York on board to sign a contract to sing
for them. At once she gave up all thought of that life
and joined the missionary party.

One of Mr. Goforth's most lovable traits of character was his simple humanness. We are told this was
very evident on this journey, as with great zest he joined
children or older ones in deck hockey and shuffle-board.
Though an opportunity to engage in outdoor sports came
his way but rarely, when it did, he entered into the
game with such joyous enthusiasm as to add to the
pleasure of others. Many were the contacts he thus
made with those who habitually avoided missionaries,
when testimony for his Master came naturally and without effort.

IV.
1926 - 1936

INDWELT

Not merely in the words you say,
Not only in your deeds confessed,
But in the most unconscious way
    Is Christ expressed!

Is it a beatific smile?
A holy light upon your brow?
Oh, no! I felt His Presence while
    You laughed just now.

For me 'twas not the truth you taught
To you so clear, to me still dim,
But when you came to me you brought
    A sense of Him.

And from your eyes He beckons me
And from your heart His love is shed,
Till I lose sight of you—and see
    The Christ instead.

—ANON

XXI.

THROUGH CLOUDS AND DARKNESS

Where'er you ripened fields behold
Waving to God their sheaves of gold,
Be sure some corn of wheat has died,
Some saintly soul been crucified:
Someone has suffered, wept, and prayed,
And fought hell's legions undismayed.
                        —A. S. Booth-Clibborn

On reaching Canada, the spring of 1924, Jonathan Goforth found the whole church in the throes of the Union crisis. Foreign Missionary Secretary, Dr. R. P. MacKay, urged all foreign missionaries home on furlough to take no part in the struggle and to this Dr. Goforth agreed. Very soon, however, he found the churches were so engaged in the question of union or non-union that it was practically impossible to carry on effective deputation work on behalf of foreign missions. He therefore decided to accept calls from conferences in the United States. Most of the summer was given to conventions in Keswick, New Jersey, Beulah Beach and other similar gatherings. Consequently, Dr. Goforth was completely out of touch with what was going on in Canada till the autumn. Up till this time he had taken it as a matter of course that he would go into the Union.

A long tour had been arranged for him through the Maritime Provinces. While on this tour he heard many things that made him uneasy and doubtful as to what stand he should finally take. He was still in this unsettled state of mind on returning to Toronto in December. The vote was to be taken in Knox Church early in January and a decision had to be made. Gladly would he have kept out of it all. He had heartfelt sympathies toward all denominations, for his life as a city missionary in connection with the Toronto Mission Union during his student days, and his later revival ministry had brought him in close touch with all sections of the Christian Church. But the vote must be given, and on January 5, 1926, he gave it to continue in the Presbyterian Church of Canada.

Later, when looking back upon that time, Dr. Goforth felt, in view of the glorious opportunity which came to him in Manchuria, God had guided him in voting as he did, for had he not done so, this story of Manchuria could never have been written. A year passed in which Dr. Goforth was kept busy, both in Canada and the United States. During this furlough his record of meetings reached considerably over four hundred.

He was now nearing his sixty-eighth year and feared, at times, the possibility of being retired by his Board. It was therefore with great joy and indeed with the hope and zeal and enthusiasm of a young man that he responded to the call of the Foreign Mission Board, commissioning him to return to China to find a field and found a new mission, the North Honan Mission having gone, as a Mission, into the Union. Thus once more, when at the age many men retire, he gladly faced the strain and responsibility of another season of pioneer life.

In view of Dr. Goforth's advancing years, it seemed
imperative that at least one young man should accompany him in the founding of a new Mission. He felt
the need of a young co-worker, but unless he could get
the right man, he was determined to go alone. We
will give in Mr. Reoch's own words, how he and
Dr. Goforth came to meet:

"I first met Dr. Goforth in 1925 at a dinner for
the Presbyterian students of Knox College, given by
Dr. Inkster in Knox church, Toronto. I was sitting
beside Dr. Goforth, and when the student on the
other side of him said that I was thinking of the
foreign field, he turned to me with the words 'Come
to China.' I had been thinking of the foreign field
ever since I was about fifteen years of age, and
particularly of India, but Dr. Goforth said, 'Come
to China,' with such a persuasive and appealing
voice, I felt China was the place for me."

Later, when Dr. Goforth had heard the story of
Mr. Reoch's spiritual experience through the ministry
of a visiting preacher in Toronto, he felt convinced
he had picked on the right man, and undoubtedly
time proved he was right.

The story immediately following we give as nearly
as possible in Dr. Goforth's own words, as he delighted to tell it.

"One day, early in February, 1926, my wife,
whose health had for some time been steadily declin-
ing, was resting on the sofa, waiting for the ambu-
lance which was to take her to the Toronto General
Hospital. Suddenly the door-bell rang, and the phone
sounded simultaneously. The latter was to say the

hospital was full and my wife would need to wait two or three days before a bed was vacant. The door call brought a cable from Marshal Feng in China, begging me to come at once. Reading the cable to my wife, I said, 'What shall I do? It is impossible for me to leave you as you are,' for we all thought she could not live many months. My wife, after covering her face for a moment, as if in prayer, looked up and said with decision, 'I'm going with you.' The Board was meeting at the time, so I laid before them Marshal Feng's cable and they heartily agreed to my going at once, but, when I said my wife would accompany me, they looked aghast and said that was impossible, for she would die on the way. I replied to this, 'You don't know that woman as well as I do. When she says she is going, she will go!' So they gave in."

A little servant girl once said to her mistress, who was weeping bitterly in face of a great need, "Dear madam, be comforted, *this is just an opportunity to see what God can do.*" So in the week that followed, before the Goforths once more left Toronto for China, those near them marvelled at what God was doing. In answer to prayer strength was given the wife to deliver a short farewell message in Knox Church. At the close of that meeting, so many promised to "hold the ropes," they felt, as it were, a veritable barrage of prayer followed them as they once more faced the future.

Through the generosity of friends, it was made possible for Mary and her husband, the Rev. Robert Moynan, and their little boy, to accompany them. Several wonderful days were spent in Los Angeles, during which

Dr. Goforth had a number of opportunities to deliver his message. The following is one of several heartening letters received on the eve of their departure from Los Angeles from the Glendale Presbyterian Church, Glendale, California:

"DEAR DR. GOFORTH,

"Permit me, in behalf of our church, to express to you our most profound gratitude for your most marvellous address of last night. You have put us under an obligation that we will never, never be able to discharge. In fact, it is only as we enter into your great program for China financially, spiritually and sacrificially that we can ever discharge it.

"It was a great awakening to our people and gave us a new vision in the whole mission program. We shall watch your work with keen interest and give ourselves unreservedly to prayer in your behalf. *Would it be too much to ask the Chinese Christians to pray for us?*"

Before leaving Toronto, there had been some consultation with the China Inland Mission in Toronto regarding the taking over of their "Anwei field," but the final decision had to be left for the leaders of that Mission in Shanghai. Early in March, Dr. Goforth and party, including Mr. Reoch, who had joined them at Los Angeles, sailed from San Francisco by a Japanese boat. Rough, stormy seas were encountered all the way to Yokohama. The following was written by Dr. Goforth to a son in Toronto:

"S.S. Korea Maru, about 1400 miles S.W. of San Francisco, March 6-26.

"Allan Reoch is not afraid to let his light shine on

board. There is a young man going to Kansu as a missionary who is a number-one musician, having for several years played the pipe-organ for one of the big Presbyterian churches of Los Angeles. While this Mr. Walton plays, Allan will sing by the hour of an evening and loud enough to let half on shipboard hear. I am more and more taken with Allan and believe he will make a splendid missionary. Keep on the lookout for more missionaries for our new China field. But make plain to all that modernist higher critics are not eligible. Men who have a story of salvation to tell and who are willing to endure any hardship for the privilege of telling it are the missionaries which China needs (and we need). The year I graduated from Knox there were thirty-three of us, all volunteers for the foreign field. Pray and agitate, and men of the right kind are sure to come."

The early morning of March 25, our boat reached the wide mouth of the great Yangtse River. All were on deck, but as the shores could scarcely be distinguished, we grouped together for a time with the *Daily Light.* How our hearts thrilled in response when the following verses were read:

"I will never leave thee, nor forsake thee." . . .

"Behold, I am with thee, and will keep thee in all places whither thou goest, and will bring thee again into this land; for I will not leave thee, until I have done that which I have spoken to thee of. . . . Be strong and of a good courage, fear not, nor be afraid of them: for the Lord thy God, he it is that doth go with thee; he will not fail thee, nor forsake thee." . . .

"All power is given unto me in heaven and in earth. Go ye, therefore, and teach all nations, baptizing them in the name of the Father, and of the Son, and of the Holy Ghost. . . . and, lo, I am with you alway, even unto the end of the world." . . .

Then, just at the last, came the very same promise which Dr. Goforth had been given thirty-six years before, when first crossing the border into North Honan: "My word . . . shall not return unto me void, but it shall accomplish that which I please."

Oh, how we needed such promises to uphold us in the months ahead! One of the greatest mercies for which we should thank God is that we cannot see what is before us.

The year on which we now entered proved to be the most prolonged period of unbroken testing in sickness, separation and repeated disappointments the Goforths ever experienced. The first disappointment came when Dr. Goforth, laid before the China Inland Mission leaders at Shanghai the matter of the "Anwei Field" being handed over to our Church; this was, however, considered by them as quite impossible. On hearing this, Dr. Goforth, being most anxious to reach Marshal Feng's army, had arrangements quickly made to leave at once by steamer for Hankow. From there, a few hours' run by train brought them to their home in Kikungshan. Here Mr. Reoch, Mr. Moynan, and Mary began intensive study of the language.

Dr. Goforth left immediately for Peking, but on arriving there, to his great disappointment, if not consternation, he found the Marshal and his army had been forced beyond Peking, northwestward, and the enemy in control of the capital. Of that terrible conflict and time, it is unwise, nay impossible, for me to write. Who can say but that even this disappointment was God's appointment, thus enabling Dr. Goforth to give his whole time and thought to the finding of a field. To this task he now bent every energy.

In the following six months, five times the door into what seemed a promising field, opened to us, but when with joy we began to plan upon entering, the door closed! All through these dark days, Dr. Goforth's faith never wavered. He was always buoyantly happy and optimistic, never giving way for a moment to down-heartedness. When doors had thus closed several times, his wife, who through all these months had been steadily going down, as it seemed, nearer the border, broke down one day, saying, "O Jonathan, has God forsaken us? Is there no place left to us in this great needy land?"

Can I ever forget the joyful hopefulness with which he replied, "No, Rose, I am perfectly certain there is some Divine purpose in it all, and that God has a field for us of His own choosing and beyond all we perhaps can imagine: No, God has not forsaken us! He has said, 'My presence shall go with thee,' and He is with us and that is all we need."

Soon he left in search of another field, little dreaming he was never again to see the dear mountain home. Shortly after he had gone, reports of Communist activities, within menacing distance of the mountain, kept all in a state of suspense. It was thought best that Mary and her husband and child should go to Hankow with a number of other missionaries. The civil strife in China was becoming increasingly acute with an ever-growing anti-foreign feeling. Then events moved rapidly. Soon there came to be a perfect exodus of missionaries from the mountain. Mr. Reoch and Miss Graham (who had joined us), and the writer, who was carried on a stretcher down the mountain, were the last to leave before the hill was isolated.

Then followed a five or six days' hard journey by boat and train before we reached Hsuchow, an important city on the railway west of Kaifengfu, Honan. Here loving care and nursing were received and here we waited till Dr. Goforth joined us, when the further journey to Peking was made. His wife was carried into the hospital.

A few days later, Dr. Goforth received a letter from the Rev. James McCammon of the Irish Presbyterian Mission, Newchwang, Manchuria, urging him to come to Manchuria. He wrote of three possible fields. Dr. Goforth was all eagerness to start for Manchuria at once, but his wife lay so low in the hospital he was obliged to wait a week before the doctors gave their consent for him to leave, for, as the future proved, the lowest ebb had been reached, and the long two years' fight back to health had begun.

XXII.

MANCHURIA

Oh, friends, have great faith. Little faith will take your souls to heaven, but great faith will bring heaven to your souls.

C. H. SPURGEON

AT LAST, early in January, 1927, came the message by telegraph, from Dr. Goforth to his wife in Peking, "Pack for Manchuria." Could it be another door had opened, and if so, was this door, too, to close as the others had done? But Manchuria! The country which we, south of the Great Wall, always thought of as "the land of ice and snow," of great sparsely populated regions—indeed, much as dwellers in Ontario think of the far North of Canada. But, a few days later, Dr. Goforth returned from Manchuria, full of such joyous optimism and plans for an immediate advance northward, the question as to the advisability of such a course, with the bitterest cold season ahead, was not considered.

So our little band gathered together and started for Manchuria by train—and what a weak band we were! The leader, an old man nearing seventy, with a semi-invalid wife; a "Salvation Army lassie"—Miss Graham, from New Zealand; a Dutch lady—Miss Annie Kok; and one young recruit—Rev. Allan Reoch, as yet struggling with the language. Little wonder, then, that a young missionary, of a certain mission in Manchuria, on hearing of the personnel composing the Presbyterian Mission from Canada, exclaimed, *"Well, that sure is some Mission!"*

But, as it seemed to us later, our very weakness was an opportunity for our Almighty Lord and Captain to reveal what He could do. There was one thing which Dr. Goforth greatly rejoiced and took courage in, and that was—we were all absolutely of one mind and heart with him in making the preaching of the simple soul-saving Gospel the supreme work of the Mission now to be founded.

Our train reached Changchun (now known as Hsinching—the new capital) in the early morning of one of the bitterest, cold, stormy days of our long experience, either in Manchuria or Canada. As we drove through wide, *clean* streets, between well-built foreign-looking houses, and over excellent roads in an open "drosky" (a Russian carriage) we simply marvelled at it all. So utterly unlike was it to the unsanitary, narrow, rough streets we had been accustomed to, except indeed in foreign settlements.

Dr. and Mrs. Gordon, old missionaries of the Scotch mission, welcomed us all into their home, but Dr. Gordon at once turned to Dr. Goforth and said sternly, as he pointed to the writer, "How could you dare risk bringing a 'sprue' patient into Manchuria at such a time as this?" To relieve the situation, for my husband looked somewhat abashed, I answered for him, "Where Dr. Goforth goes, I go."

We went to Manchuria with our future still clouded as to where we should finally locate. Of the three possible fields, one, to the far northeast, was soon considered out of count, as it would mean our Board taking over a fully established mission plant, including two high-schools, two hospitals, five foreign residences, besides many other buildings, and it was not *a pioneer field*—the only field which now appealed to Jonathan Goforth's spirit. For the carrying on of such a work we had neither the finances nor the staff, even if our Board were willing, which they were not. The second field, immediately north of Korea, with the city of Kirin as its centre, was being partly worked by the Irish missionaries, who were not willing for us to enter that region.

The third field comprised a vast territory reaching westward from the South Manchurian Railway, in shape not unlike a fan two-thirds open. About thirty miles only actually touched the railway, the field gradually increasing in width westward to the border of Mongolia, and on northwest to the Russian border, a distance of almost four hundred miles.

When we learned the following facts, we all realized that God had been leading us in a most unmistakable way to come to Manchuria and take over this great semi-virgin field at a most crucial time. The facts are these: Up to the time of the revolution, when China overthrew the Manchu dynasty, the Manchus ruled in Manchuria with a rod of iron. The whole region, of which we are now speaking, had been kept by them very largely for the raising of horses and cattle for military purposes. Part of it was then reckoned as Mongolia and the whole was a very sparsely settled semi-desert; a vast area with no railways. Certainly it was at that time a most uninviting field for any mission to enter.

Then all changed with the overthrow of the Manchus. That marvellous tide of emigrants began trekking or travelling from the congested and politically disturbed northern provinces of China, northward, past the Great Wall into the then new land of new hopes—Manchuria. In 1926, the year before we entered Manchuria, this human tide had reached into the millions. The region which we hoped was to become ours, received its full share of these newcomers, so that all through that great area villages and towns began to spring up with mushroom growth. Then came the railways. The first of these to be built had its main junction on the South Manchurian Railway at the city of Szepingkai (pronounced Sipping-guy), and ran right through our field in a semi-circular fashion, connecting with the north main line from Harbin. This railway was completed *but a few months before we entered the field.* A second railway of strategic importance was completed the following year, and a third, opening up the farthest northwest region, was commenced a little later. Then, finally, we were told missionaries had toured some but never resided in any part of that whole region. When we heard these things we could not but exclaim, "Truly the Lord's hand has been guiding us!"

The only place free for us to live in at Changchun was part of an empty Chinese girls' school-building. We had absolutely nothing with which to furnish even one room or start housekeeping, as we had been obliged to leave everything behind in our old home at Kikung-shan, South Honan, except what we could carry away in two or three trunks. But, most fortunately—rather would we say, providentially—a roomful of old furniture was at Changchun, which had belonged to a former missionary who had been murdered eight or ten years before. We were given the use of what things we might need with the option of buying. Needless to say, we were most thankful for this chance of getting together sufficient to start, without delay, at least a temporary mission home. For three months, we women waited at Changchun for an opening into Szepingkai. Our young colleague, Allan Reoch, had secured quarters in a small Japanese house at Szepingkai, where he studied the language and was ever on the lookout for a possible foothold for the rest of us. Dr. Goforth gave much of this time of waiting to holding missions in Harbin and elsewhere.

Then a time of real testing came. China to the south of us was in a state of indescribable confusion and chaos. Hundreds of missionaries were being recalled from all parts of the country and many were being sent back to the Homeland; among these latter were our daughter and her husband and child. Then a message came from our British counsel in Mukden, ordering all British subjects to be in readiness to flee at a moment's notice, so we began living with valises packed. The Nanking atrocities which had just taken place had alarmed all foreigners to such an extent, many believed that a second Boxer outbreak was at hand.

It was at this juncture a letter came from Mr. Reoch, telling of an ideal place, situated on one of the

main streets of Szepingkai, suited for all our require-
ments, both residence and preaching-hall, which could
be obtained, but the rent was excessively high and the
landlord demanded that it be paid a year in advance.
Mr. Reoch asked that word be sent back immediately
by telegraph as to whether he should rent or not, lest
we lose the chance.

It can readily be seen the problem before us was
acute. Some of us felt to go forward and rent was
much as if one were to start building a house in a city
aflame. If we gave Mr. Reoch permission to rent,
word might come at any moment from the British Consul, forcing us to flee, which meant roping our Board
into heavy expense for nothing. We were brought to our
knees, and our little band, Miss Kok, Miss Graham and
our two selves, together definitely sought for guidance,
but no light came that night. All went to bed hoping
that by morning we could see things clearly. As we met
at breakfast, Miss Graham with shining face opened her
Bible and read the following verse: "He that observeth
the wind shall not sow, and he that regardeth the clouds
shall not reap" (Eccles. 11:4).

What could we do in the face of such a message but
trust God and go forward! A telegram was sent to Mr.
Reoch to secure the property and *we never heard any
further word from the Consul.*

Then, at this time, again we saw a wonderful indi-
cation of God's guiding and *preventing* hand over us,
for *every one of the five fields I have mentioned as having opened and then closed to us, had been completely
evacuated of all missionaries and the work brought to*

a standstill, continuing so for a considerable time. On April 28, 1927, we moved into Szepingkai and took possession of our "promised land."

XXIII.

LAYING THE FOUNDATIONS

. . . as a wise master-builder I have laid the foundation . . . other foundation can no man lay than that is laid, which is Jesus Christ.

THE APOSTLE PAUL

IT IS a very human story I am about to tell. But is it not true that it is because we are human, we are interested in just those touches that make all men kin? Weeks before we actually moved down to Szepingkai, I had asked Dr. Goforth if it were possible for us to raise two hundred dollars for the furnishing of a Mission Home there; but he was quite unable to help me in the matter, and was so taken up with "more weightier things" (?) the matter did not appear to assume the importance to him that it did to me. Day by day the question ever before me was, "How can I furnish and make a home for us all at Szepingkai without money?" Then again, as so often before, I found this need was *but an opportunity to see what God could do.*

At our farewell meeting in Knox Church, Toronto, more than a year before, two hundred dollars had been given us as a personal gift. On reaching China, Dr. Goforth received from Chancellor Kok, his friend in Peking, an appeal for help for the starving soldiers of Marshal Feng's army. At once the two hundred dollars was sent to meet that need. Then, at my time of extremity in Manchuria—when I needed just that amount, a letter came from Chancellor Kok enclosing a cheque for two hundred dollars, saying, "I am returning your gift for the soldiers for the response to my appeal was so generous, I found it was not needed." With a perfectly beaming face, Dr. Goforth held out the cheque to me saying, "Now go ahead and make a fine home for us all." Indeed, he said much more which showed me he had really felt for me more than I had realized. Would that I dare give a whole chapter to the story of how that two hundred dollars made possible the making of a livable Mission Home in which there was at least one cosy homey place where we all gathered twice daily for prayer!

One of the first things we all joyously took part in on arriving at Szepingkai was the decorating of the preaching-hall, which could hold two or three hundred, and over which was the Mission Home. A large number of beautiful texts and pictures illustrating Bible stories had been secured from Shanghai through the kindness of the Milton-Stewart Evangelistic Fund. We literally covered the chapel walls with these, making the place beautiful and attractive. Mr. Reoch had had the chapel filled with fine, comfortable benches. Then, with the preacher's table, beside which was placed the literature table, and the ever-needed hymn scroll and baby organ, the preaching-hall was ready. I only wish those who pity missionaries could experience, if only for a brief spell, the pure joy we had in getting that chapel ready, and in the contemplation of what it was going to mean to multitudes in the days to come.

The following letter written by Dr. Goforth just five weeks after coming to Szepingkai, tells something of how God set His seal of blessing upon the work from the very outset:

"We moved in on the twenty-eighth of April and commenced on Sunday, May first. Since then the preaching of the Word has gone on for three hours in the forenoon, and four in the afternoon. We have never been without hearers, and if our force of workers were only larger we could add to the preaching hours. From the very first day men began to turn to the Lord, sometimes more than a dozen during the day. You can imagine our joy at seeing about *two hundred decisions during the month of May*, and yesterday, the first of June, fully a dozen yielded. Our service here for the month of May proves that the Chinese people, free from Bolshevik meddling, are as open to the message of the grace of God as ever they were. During all our years in China we have never met with greater respect and friendliness than from all classes here. Let us not be discouraged for the cause of Christ must triumph in China.

"No one can escape the fact that the harvest to be gathered in the newest mission field of the Presbyterian Church in Canada is very great. The preachers at present taking part in the preaching here day by day are Mr. Su, my very able personal evangelist; a Mr. Cheng, whom the Scotch Mission has loaned to us for a time; Miss Graham and Miss Kok, my wife and myself. But what are these among so many? We haven't the shadow of a doubt but that the results we have seen here during May might have been seen in dozens of other centres in our new field had it been possible for our little band to be in other centres at the same time. *We plan for no big schools, no big hospitals, until the converted Chinese build and equip them, but we do plan to evangelize intensively.* We are praying every day that the Lord of the harvest shall call and send us many Chinese and Canadian workers to reap this field. Our expectation is that the Home Church will measure up to this unparalleled opportunity.

"This ten-year-old city and junction is the natural base for the evangelization of the field. We succeeded in renting a range of buildings sufficient for men's and women's chapels and quarters for evangelists and servants, as well as ample room for our present missionary force of five. The buildings are all new and the location is the most strategic in the city.

"The area of our field is much larger than that of the old Honan field, with a population about as great as that of Ontario. This Northeast of China is the counterpart of the Northwest of Canada. It has vast areas for colonization. *Almost a million settlers from Honan, Chihli, and Shantung provinces poured in this spring.* In working the field we can take advantage of the railways for five hundred miles. In the western part of our field lives one of the most noted and powerful of the Mongol tribes. It will be our privilege and duty to carry the gospel to them also."

Just as soon as it had become certain the field of which I have been writing was to be given over to us, Dr. Goforth had sent a full description of it to the Board, ending his letter with an earnest appeal for recruits. In the meantime, at Szepingkai, our little band met twice daily in the "Cozy Nook" over the chapel, for prayer. The burden on each one was how to evangelize the vast unreached field for which, as a mission, we were now responsible. Dr. Goforth, in his glowing optimism, fully expected the Board, and the Church behind it, to respond generously with men and money when they came to know of the field he had secured.

But alas, when Dr. Grant's letter came, it made only too plain that we could not hope for the generous backing which Dr. Goforth had been anticipating. "No recruits for an indefinite period,"—"necessary to keep within your budget apportionment." (This was so small as to make a forward movement of aggressive evangelism with increased evangelists impossible.) Further, "the possibility of giving up the field because of political troubles,"—"impossible to say definitely whether the field could be taken over,"—"heavy deficit,"—and so on. Dr. Goforth's disappointment was crushingly great.

It seemed as if every human prop was being removed from under us. To one of Jonathan Goforth's spirit and pioneer vision, the situation was impossible— to remain at the door of the great region of untouched millions and to leave them to perish, he could not and would not stand for. One day, after a time of intense prayerful waiting on God for light, as we rose from our knees, Dr. Goforth drew himself up and with passionate earnestness exclaimed: "Our home Church has failed us; but the God of Hudson Taylor is ours. He will not fail us if we look to him. THIS FIELD MUST BE EVANGELIZED and it cannot be done with our present small force. If we cannot get Canadians as channels for the Gospel message, we must get Chinese." Thus the blow that seemed to threaten the very existence of the new mission proved to be the blow that set Jonathan Goforth free and gave him the very opportunity for which he had prayed in those days back in North Honan —the opportunity to demonstrate to the missionary body and the home Church what results would follow if the Gospel of the Grace of God were given HALF A CHANCE.

In the Province of Shantung, North China, there was a very fine college and seminary for the training of young men and women as evangelists, of which Dr. Goforth's old and honoured friend, Dr. John Hayes, was founder and principal. At once, Dr. Goforth sent a letter to Dr. Hayes, asking if he could send him some evangelists. It is strange but true that about the same time this letter was written, Dr. Hayes had written and sent a letter to Dr. Goforth, saying that contending forces had swept over their whole region seven times, all churches were closed and Christian work was at a standstill. Consequently none of his graduating class had doors open to them. He closed his letter by saying, *"Could you use any of these men?"* At once, the message was sent, "Send us all you can."

Humbly, I must record that his "little faith" of a wife, on hearing what he had written, exclaimed anxiously, "But Jonathan, they can't live on air—where is the money to come from for their support?" He replied, half sternly, half kindly, "Where is your faith? If God sends us men, He will send money for their support."

Some weeks passed before the first band of evangelists from Dr. Hayes arrived, and by that time we had received in *unsolicited* gifts sufficient to meet at least two months' salary for these men. Dr. Goforth then said, "I see we have taken the right step in the right direction. I must send for more men."

As Mrs. Goforth was unable to undertake outside work, it was thought best by all that she be appointed secretary-treasurer of the "Evangelist Trust Fund"— later named by the bank—"The Goforth Evangelistic Fund." This fund was, from the first, kept quite separate from the budget funds received from the Home Board, as no allowance was made in them for evangelists' salaries.

Szepingkai had been for years an outstation of the Irish Mission, but until we moved in, no foreigners had actually resided there. Our coming was received with distinct suspicion, especially by the Japanese. Almost daily Dr. Goforth received visits from Japanese military officers who asked all sorts of questions, the answers being carefully recorded. When these visits were repeated with the same questions asked, it certainly became irksome. Dr. Goforth, however, never lost patience. Then after this had been going on for five weeks, the Japanese suddenly, without warning, closed our preaching-hall, Dr. Goforth considered it necessary to appeal to the British Minister in Mukden, who advised our all going for a few weeks to Peitaiho, the seaside summer resort, and while we were absent, he would have the matter gone into.

We all had a delightful and helpful holiday by the sea, returning to Szepingkai in August, having received word from the British Minister that all had been arranged satisfactorily with the Japanese. From that time we had no more serious trouble, though the visits of the military continued several times a month. One little courtesy to the Japanese undoubtedly helped. There were a number of Japanese Christians in Szepingkai. They had no place in which to hold their Sunday-school and for this we offered the use of the preaching-hall. This gave us a very pleasant contact with the Japanese Christians.

It was at this early stage that a very great boon to the work came through Rev. George T. B. Davis, who was carrying on his Million Pocket Testament Campaign for China. Box after box of these beautiful pocket Testaments came from him till we had received in all ten thousand of these little books. Mr. Reoch, though still hard at the language, found a real ministry in this connection. At the close of study hours, accompanied by a trusty evangelist, he, day by day would start off with as many of these little Testaments as both could carry. Every shop was visited and the Gospel story told and a Testament given to those willing to meet the simple conditions. In the preaching-hall, a pile of these Testaments was always in evidence on the literature table. Dr. Goforth was later often heard to express his conviction that this timely influx of Testaments had much to do with the remarkably rapid change in the people's attitude towards us from suspicion to utter friendliness.

The latter part of September, Dr. Goforth, Mr. Reoch, and three evangelists made a tour of the field. The following are a few brief extracts from Dr. Goforth's account of that trip as sent to the Board:

"We all travelled third-class. It almost seemed that we were conducting an evangelistic campaign on wheels for the testimony to the grace of God was almost continuous. On the day going up to Taonan, the conductor and others of the train crew invited me to go to the first-class carriage where it would be quieter and tell them of this salvation. I took one of the evangelists along. We both talked to them and the conductor and five or six others decided to serve the Lord Jesus Christ. Through the preaching going on at Szepingkai these months, dozens of the railway men have decided to serve the Lord. This Manchurian call is as clear and insistent as was the Macedonian call to Paul and his co-workers."

"We saw the field from the car-window over about five hundred miles of rail. There is but one evangelist along three hundred and fifty miles of rail. He is stationed at Taonan, a city of perhaps one hundred thousand people. We were told six years had passed since a missionary had visited that city. Along the railway north and south from Taonan, are six other cities with populations running from ten to forty thousand and as many more cities are from ten to twenty thousand off from the railway, and all these without even one evangelist. Indeed, you might go for over one hundred miles east of Taonan and a thousand miles west and never find an evangelist. Thus in the providence of God a door is opened for us and we should heed this Manchurian call."

"If thou forbear to deliver them that are drawn unto death, and those that are ready to be slain; if thou sayest, Behold we knew it not; doth not He that pondereth the heart consider it? and He that keepeth thy soul, doth not He know it? and shall not He

render to every man according to his works."
PROVERBS 24:11, 12.

On the above trip, Dr. Goforth was taken ill. Leaving the rest to complete the tour, he hastened home arriving about five o'clock in the evening in a high fever and heavy chill. I did for him all that experience had taught me in such an emergency, but by about eight o'clock, he became delirious. Mr. Reoch returned at ten o'clock, and after consultation, we decided if Dr. Goforth was no better by eleven-thirty, Mr. Reoch would take the midnight train to Mukden and return if possible with a doctor. I then went to my husband's bedside and stood there quietly praying the Lord to undertake for us. As I prayed, his restlessness ceased, and turning on one side, he fell into a sound sleep. At eleven-thirty, he seemed quite cool, and the fever gone, and was still sleeping quietly. Mr. Reoch did not go to Mukden and the following morning after a restful night, Dr. Goforth insisted on getting up and seemed quite himself.

Dr. Goforth was a firm believer in D. L. Moody's axiom that "it is better to get ten men to work, than to do the work of ten men." Just as soon as he saw the preaching-hall work at Szepingkai was in good running shape with Miss Graham in charge, assisted by several evangelists, he decided to give two weeks to Tungliao, an important centre in the southwestern section of the field and situated on the newly built railway. The usual evangelistic meetings were carried on, at Tungliao, but of that trip I have memory only of three experiences, all of which might easily have become tragedies.

The first was what seemed little less than a miraculous escape from fire. The room we lived in had a ceiling of paper so old and dry, festoons of the broken, torn paper, hung down here and there two and three feet into the room. One day, when Dr. Goforth was preaching in the next room, my spirit lamp, resting on a bench, became ignited and set fire to the bench. A sudden, bright light made me first aware of the fire, which, in a matter of seconds, would have reached the festoons hanging from the ceiling. All was over in a few seconds, but my beating out the flames was so violent, Dr. Goforth wondered at my *swatting flies* so noisily when the meeting was going on!

We had had very little mail since leaving Szepingkai, so were not aware of the fact that the dreaded plague had broken out in a region but a few miles west of Tungliao. The first word of this came to us in a letter from Mr. Reoch informing us of the deputation from Canada having reached Korea. They requested that we all meet them there as the news of the rapid spread of the plague in Manchuria was so alarming it was thought best that they remain in Korea.

We at once packed up and started. It was a bitterly cold day and the train was not heated. We had travelled probably an hour, when suddenly the train jolted and shook so, we were thrown from side to side. Just when the train seemed about to turn over, it came to a standstill. An iron bolt had broken and the train derailed. We were told to walk half a mile to the station ahead and wait there for a train from a distant point along the line. Arriving at the station, and anxious to get warmed up, we opened the door of the waiting-room, a large one, to find it literally packed with men sitting on their bedding. Making our way as best we could to the one stove, we stayed there for several hours until we could hardly breathe. Then we went out and faced the cold till the emergency train arrived. We had wondered over one thing. Every few minutes, during those hours in the waiting-room, an official had entered and with a plague-mask on, had gone the rounds carefully scrutinizing every face. It was not until we had boarded the train that we learned the station waiting-room was being used as *a plague detention camp!* Thus, on that one trip, we had been graciously delivered, from fire, wreck, and plague! That year's plague report stated probably one-third of Tungliao's population had died of the plague.

On our return from Korea, we were right into the long, intensely cold Manchurian winter. Yet this very extreme cold helped to keep up the preaching-hall audiences. Dr. Goforth felt it was money well spent to keep a good fire going in the preaching hall downstairs. Carters passing the door half-perishing with cold, would stop, come in, and get warm and so hear the Gospel of the grace of God for the first time. One day, from my seat at the organ, I counted two hundred people pass the door in seven minutes. Dr. Goforth, though speaking usually only twice daily, spent many hours each day in the hall. The benefit of this to the work was twofold—his presence helped to attract the people, and by listening to the evangelists, he was able later, to correct or suggest as need be. Newcomer evangelists soon learned that only soul-saving messages would be favoured by the old pastor. All loved Dr. Goforth so much, none seemed to resent his quiet, gentle, guiding hand. The early half-hour for prayer and a brief message, each morning from eight to eight-thirty, was taken in turn by all the workers. Dr. Goforth always attended. It was a time of helpful fellowship.

At the early approach of spring, and with an increased staff of evangelists, Dr. Goforth felt the time had come for the opening of Taonan, the city next to Szepingkai in strategic importance. Indeed, in one respect, Taonan as a mission station was of *supreme* importance, being the centre of the vast northwestern area, though Szepingkai, because of its geographical position on the junction of the South Manchurian Railway, made it the natural head-quarters of the Mission.

It must be confessed that to take this advance step was quite contrary to the Home Board's orders, for as yet they had not even officially accepted the field. Dr. Goforth's position at this time was by no means an easy one. He fully realized his age limitations as he had already entered his seventieth year, but this fact, instead of causing him to "slow down," seemed to intensify the urge within him to press forward. Again and again, when urged by his wife to take life more easily, his reply would always come as in many past times:

> *"Slacken not pace yet at inlet or island,*
> *Straight for the haven steer,*
> *Straight for the highland!"*

So to the opening of Taonan, Jonathan Goforth gave himself in his characteristic, whole-hearted way. Miss Graham, whose years in the Salvation Army had given her a unique power in preaching to men, was put in charge of the preaching-hall work at Szepingkai, while Miss Kok gave herself to the women's work for which she was equally well-fitted. A band of fine, consecrated evangelists remained to help Miss Graham for the preaching was kept going for seven hours daily.

A mission centre had been secured at Taonan. About the middle of February, Dr. Goforth with his wife (who had just recovered from pneumonia), and Miss Annie Young, an elderly lady loaned to us by the Alliance mission, started for Taonan. Mr. Reoch was to follow a few days later. To make things doubly safe, Dr. Goforth had sent a trusty evangelist ahead three days previously with instructions to have stoves put up at once and fires kept going till we arrived, as the building we were to live in had been closed all winter. Stores, bedding, and other needy things were sent on with the evangelist.

The day we started was extremely cold, but the temperature of the car was kept excessively hot all the nine hours' ride to Taonan. On alighting from the car, we were greeted by a fierce blizzard sweeping from the great plains of Mongolia. No one was at the station to meet us. During that mile and a half ride in the open drosky facing that biting blizzard, I kept praying and trying to keep up courage by the thought of the fine, warm house we were coming to. But on reaching the Mission gate we found the evangelist who had been sent ahead, standing in open-mouthed astonishment. "Pastor!" he exclaimed, "I'm so sorry! I mistook the day you were to come. No stoves are up and the stores and baggage have not arrived!"

Undoubtedly, it was only the Lord who shielded us during the following twenty-four hours till our baggage and provisions came. We slept that night in our clothes with scarcely an inch between us and the cold bricks,

MRS. JONATHAN GOFORTH
1925

yet not one of us was physically the worse. The following day, we inspected the buildings outside which were just rooms side by side, the whole being in the shape of an "L," the lower, shorter end facing on the busy street. We were simply horrified to find that every door and window-frame and other inside woodwork had been wrenched away and carried off. This, we were told, was the custom at Taonan when property changed hands.

The whole place, except the small house we occupied, looked a hopeless wreck, but a month later, the place could scarcely have been recognized. All attention was at first concentrated on fixing up for a preaching-hall a large room facing the street. Here, as at Szepingkai, illuminated texts, pictures, hymn-scrolls, and organ transformed the place into a beautiful room for the preaching of the gospel. An order for fifty benches had been given to a local carpenter and these now filled the hall. What gave joy to us all was that many were coming day by day, listening to the soul-saving gospel. During those first two weeks after the hall was opened, four hundred had given in their names as believing. Then came the problem how to follow up and keep in touch with those who had taken this first step. One evangelist, therefore, was set apart for this follow-up ministry.

During the four months Miss Annie Young remained at Taonan, she, with the Bible-woman, daily visited in the homes. Her saintly personality, pure white hair, and winning way opened to them many doors. Though with us such a short time, we all realized she was a very real contributing factor to the early overthrow of the suspicion which invariably accompanies the opening of new work. No foreign women had ever been in that whole region before. To have such a woman as Miss Young as first representative of Western women, meant much for the future of the women's work at Taonan. When this dear lady left, she was remembered by us all as "Saint Anne."

For years a promise to visit Indo-China for revival meetings had remained unfulfilled. Dr. Goforth decided to give the summer months, which he might have claimed for his own holiday, for the making of this trip. It was indeed a wonderful experience. First came two weeks' meetings for the Alliance missionaries at their annual convention held in the home of Rev. and Mrs. D. I. Jeffrey (Ruth) at Tourane. This was followed by days of blessing with the native preachers and workers at a place near Saigon.

A call had come for Dr. Goforth to give a series of revival talks to the missionaries gathered for the summer on Cheung Chau, an island near Hong Kong. Lack of space only keeps the writer from dwelling on this latter ministry. The affection and sympathy and the hearty response given to the messages, remained as one of the most precious memories to both Dr. Goforth and his wife. The day we boarded our steamer for Shanghai, numbers of both missionaries and Chinese Christians came on board to see us off. We had not had an opportunity to see our cabin until all had gone and the vessel was well on its way. Then, when we went below, we found the cabin filled with marvellous flowers. One specially beautiful bunch had a message attached to it, from two young lady missionaries who had attended our meeting. Their message was in verse, as follows:

(A parting message to Dr. and Mrs. Goforth, from Gladys Ward and Esther Schell—Cheung Chau, Hong Kong, August, 1928.)

Our tongues are not gifted with language,
With words we should like to command;
So we "Say it with flowers" for they speak
A language that all understand.

They are perfumed with fragrance of heaven
And clothed with colors divine,
Just so to those all about you
Your lives with His love-fragrance shine.

God bless you in all your endeavors
Wherever your paths may wend,
We thank Him for bringing you our way,
Just a breath from our Heavenly Friend.

On reaching our field in Manchuria we found already rumours were afloat of the dreaded plague having again broken out and in the same region as the previous year. Day by day the news of its coming nearer and nearer was, to say the least, somewhat disturbing. The ninety-first Psalm came to mean something to us in those days. Plague-masks were generally worn and the report one day was that twenty-five had died one night in a section of Taonan. But after this the plague gradually lessened, due to the splendidly efficient plague prevention measures carried out by the Japanese.

Dr. Goforth had planned to give the whole winter to Taonan, but God ordered otherwise. We had been there only a month when a letter came from the evangelist at Szepingkai, begging Dr. Goforth to return at once and take charge as Miss Graham had gone to open work at Tungliao.

Thus, Mr. Reoch, who had little more than two very broken years at language-study, and less than eighteen months of close touch with mission work, had to take over the charge of that great field. But he did not fail us nor his Divine Master as may be seen by the following testimony written by Mr. Hanna of the China Inland Mission, less than two years after the Taonan field had been given over to this young, inexperienced missionary:

(Written for China's Millions, November, 1930.)

". . . Mention must be made of the fine work being done in Taonan, in Fengtien Province, by Rev. Allen Reoch of the Canadian Presbyterian Mission (Dr. Goforth's work). In the month of April I visited Mr. Reoch, who, with a force of some fourteen Chinese workers, is carrying on *the finest piece of aggressive evangelism I have seen anywhere.* Here one lone man, with his Chinese staff of three pastors, three Bible-women, four or five evangelists, and several colporteurs, is not only carrying on an intensive campaign in the big city of Taonan, but is also reaching out to the cities and towns in an incredible area. Both at the Mission house and at a splendidly situated street-chapel, Gospel preaching goes on daily from nine in the morning to six in the evening without intermission. The street-chapel is always filled with interested listeners, and many are being brought to Christ. . . . . ."

XXIV

TESTINGS AND TRIUMPHS

When I attempt to do what I can't do, then I do it in the power of the Spirit.

G. CAMPBELL MORGAN

THE WINTER of 1928-9 was a very severe one. In a letter to her home-folks at this time, Mrs. Goforth gives a glimpse into their living conditions at Szepingkai as they really existed.

"Where we live, above the chapel, is scarcely ideal during this cold weather. We have no shed, no storeroom, and absolutely no place where we can put things to keep from freezing *but in our bedroom!* Fortunately, it is a large room, and with careful adjusting, has been made into not only our bedroom, but also study and general sitting-room and store-room. We have packed under our bedstead, among other things, apples, eggs, oranges, canned milk, and anything and everything that might be spoiled by freezing.

"Here we learn to make the most of things and really, in spite of what I have described, we are very comfortable, and scarcely a day goes by but we praise the Lord for His great goodness in giving us this place, for had we the pick of sites and buildings, we could not have found a better place to reach the largest number with the Gospel. I have counted over two hundred heavily-laden grain carts pass the door of our preaching-hall in a single hour.

"It would be impossible to give even a tithe of the interesting and often touching incidents that occur in the chapel from day to day. The following is one of them: An old man of seventy came in with every appearance of being frightened. He no doubt had heard many evil stories about us all. Sitting some seats back he showed signs of not hearing, but as time passed, he leaned forward eagerly, trying to catch what was being said. At last, Dr. Goforth, who happened to be the speaker, concentrated all on this old man. I stepped forward, getting a seat, and put it directly in front of and near where Dr. Goforth was standing. The old man gratefully accepted my invitation to take the seat. Then as Dr. Goforth, step by step, led him into the way of salvation, the others drew nearer, listening eagerly, at first, no doubt, largely from curiosity as to what the foreigner was going to do with the old man. But as the truth took more hold of him they too listened and wondered at the old, old story. The old man, whose name was Chang, returned again and again till we believe he came to truly believe in Jesus as his Saviour. He died a few months later."

Soon after our return to Szepingkai from Taonan. Dr. Goforth was urged by the Mukden doctors to have his teeth extracted. This was done by a Japanese dentist. Returning to Szepingkai, we found our youngest child, Fred, had just arrived from Canada. It seemed to us later his coming was truly of the Lord, for Dr. Goforth had caught cold in the lower jaw and very serious complications followed. For nearly four months, he was unable to go down even to the chapel. He suffered at times intensely, but bore all with marvellous patience and fortitude. He would not remain in bed, but rose as usual every morning.

For years Dr. Goforth had been asked to write out his revival experiences, but living always a full life, he could never get time for this work, though he greatly desired it should be done. Strange as it seemed to us, this illness was the opportunity for the accomplishing of this task. Day by day, Fred would sit at his typewriter (he was a very rapid typist) and take down story after story from his father as with hand pressed to face, he paced the floor and at the same time told his son a revival story. Thus the main manuscript was written, the first and last chapters being written by Dr. Goforth later. In the spring, Fred left us for Canada with the precious manuscript. Of the many and beautiful tributes by letter which Dr. Goforth received, telling of the blessing received through the reading of *By My Spirit*, none perhaps touched him more than the following from a son:

"I have at last received a copy of your wonderful book, *By My Spirit*.* I felt like Enoch walking with God as I read it. It lifted me out of this grinding world of realism into the much more real and eternal one of the Spirit. Many of its passages recalled the days of my boyhood spent with you, Father, and my violin at Pengcheng, Tzechow, and Takwanchuang, etc., etc. I have only one criticism to make of it, and yet it is not altogether a criticism. Let me explain. Very, very few of the people in the materialistic, lucre-seeking Western world know anything of the world of the Spirit or have ever given it a thought. These (and they are the ones who need to be reached

*By My Spirit, Harper and Brothers, New York; Marshall, London.

most) will never read, or if they do read, will never understand the world of the Spirit, of which you have so ably written. They are so immersed in the world of the Flesh and so self-satisfied with it that they just cannot realize there is any other.

"If there is one thing that I regret, it is that your book might have started out with a reasoned appeal to this other, baser world, to leave their muck-rakes for a moment and look up—to appeal to their sense of the eternal things that they know—the stars—the everlasting hills—the vast sweep of the universe. Then it is not a long step to lead them on to the Great Omnipresent Spirit whose guiding hand has brought order out of chaos, whose undying love has made all things work together for good for those who follow the trail that He has blazed.

"When I tell my friends about you—about your courage and fortitude, your patience and perseverance, your loyalty to ideals, to friends, even to enemies—your hardships so lightly borne—and your achievements so modestly taken—they say, 'Goforth, they belong to another world, to another and greater age than ours, but if all of us could practise the rule of life as they do, then and then only would we be living in Utopia.' "

Throughout the winter of 1929, while confined to those "upper rooms," Dr. Goforth directed the work of the Szepingkai field through the evangelists. The work throughout the entire field was growing rapidly. How to keep pace with it became the real problem. "Aggressive Evangelism" was the key-note of the work everywhere. Tent evangelistic campaigns during the warmer months were held at theatres or fairs or any-where crowds could be reached. Shops, schools, prisons and homes were visited, tracts were given away and portions of Scriptures sold—this all outside the regular preaching-hall work.

Outstanding among the evangelists was Pastor Su, whose conversion at Changtefu in 1913 has been given in an earlier part of this record. Through all the years he had been Dr. Goforth's most constant companion and friend. (Dr. Goforth never would allow the word "helper" applied to him.) Pastor Su was Dr. Goforth's "right hand" in the work. They were indeed just brothers.

For some time the matter of expense in getting evan-gelists from long distances, as Shantung, Honan, or even Shansi, had been greatly troubling Dr. Goforth and his co-workers. At the beginning of the work, when he had no Christian constituency to draw from, it was necessary. But now, some of our own Christians were coming forward, offering themselves for the work. There had been much prayer in this connection, but we had neither the staff nor the money to start a Bible-training school of our own.

It was, therefore, with great joy and relief Dr. Goforth heard from his good friend, the Rev. James McCammon, of the Irish Mission at Newchwang, a port on the southern coast of Manchuria, telling of a Bible Training School being started there. It was a step of faith on the part of the founders and the seal of God was upon the school from the beginning. Men and women from many missions in Manchuria and North China have already passed through the school and are proclaiming the Gospel in far distant regions. This Bible School proved to be a timely and valuable adjunct or auxiliary to our Mission. Our young workers, after a time of testing on our own field, were sent for the three half-years' training, six months each year being given to the school work and six months to practical evangelism on the field. Dr. Goforth had the utmost confidence in Mr. McCammon, he being absolutely true to the fundamentals of the Christian faith, and eminently fitted for the founding of such a work.

Thus far, little has been said concerning the support of our evangelists. Well over three years had now passed since Dr. Goforth took the step of faith for the supply of workers and money to support them. The workers had, during this time, increased from three to thirty, and as the staff of workers increased, so did the donations for their support. *There was absolutely no soliciting of funds.* As secretary-treasurer of this faith phase of the work, I simply acknowledged promptly each donation as it came, giving a numbered receipt and as much information regarding the work as possible.

It had been decided by the Mission that we should return to Canada for furlough early in 1930, one reason for this being the writer was fast losing her sight from double cataract and at least one eye needed to be operated upon. Some weeks before leaving for furlough, the following illuminating "parry" between Dr. Goforth and his wife occurred. The evangelist fund was very low and the end of the month near. Going to my husband, I said, "Do you realize how low the funds are? I am beginning to feel very anxious. The end of the month is near and there is not nearly enough money on hand to meet the evangelists' salaries." He replied almost sternly: "Rose, you speak as if you supported the evangelists. You do not. Neither do I. Your part is simply to be a faithful steward of the funds and leave the Lord to do His part in sending them. Trust and pray more and all will be well."

"But," I persisted, "it is you who have taken the responsibility of this faith work. In less than a month we are to leave for Canada and we should have enough in the bank for at least three months' salaries for Mr. Reoch to draw from, allowing one month for travel to Canada, one month for return mail, and one month for donations to reach us."

"What of that?" Dr. Goforth replied. "Is the Lord not able for this also? Wait and see. He is not going to fail us!"

How gladly, yet humbly, do I record that before the end of the month came, when we were about to leave for Canada, ample funds had come to meet not only all salaries for that month, but several large donations came in, one for five hundred dollars from an unknown woman in California. These unusually large donations enabled us to leave a balance in the bank sufficient for *three months' salaries* before we left for furlough.

Little wonder, with such repeated evidences of the Lord's faithfulness, even the weak faith of the writer grew stronger and less like a *barometer*.

A very beautiful and outstanding evidence of God's overruling hand came at the outset of our furlough. Our mission staff had been increased by three recruits, a married couple and one single woman, but these were

at the language school in Peking, and possibly three
years must needs pass before they could be expected
to take over important responsibilities in connection with
the work. Added to this, Mr. Reoch, who had been
working under great strain, greatly needed furlough, but
this was impossible until our return, as he was the only
man now able to shoulder the burden of the field.

Dr. Goforth and I had been greatly pressed in spirit
to pray for a missionary who could give *immediate* help,
a man of experience, with a knowledge of the language,
tried and proved as a lover of the Chinese, and a winner
of souls, and above all, true to the Word. One day on
shipboard as we were talking over this matter, I said
to my husband, "If you could pick and choose from
all the missionaries you have met in China, who would
you wish to join us at this time to meet this crisis?"

After a few moments' reflection he replied, "Apart
from one of our former colleagues in Honan, whom I
know I couldn't get, there is a man who stands out
above all others whom I would wish to have."

"Who is he?" I asked.

"Rev. William Davis of the Christian and Missionary Alliance in Central China," he replied.

"Why, Jonathan, that is the very man I had in my
mind!" I exclaimed.

We did not know till weeks later that *at that very
time,* Mr. and Mrs. Davis, who had been evacuated with
many others from their China field, were in Toronto and
were praying the Lord to open up their way to join us in
Manchuria, if only temporarily. Many difficulties were
in the way of Mr. and Mrs. Davis' joining us, which
seemed, at one time, insurmountable, but prayer over-

came all, and early that autumn, Mr. and Mrs. Davis, with their two children, sailed for our field in Manchuria. To Dr. Goforth, who had come more and more to realize his age limitations, the addition to our staff, of such outstandingly successful missionaries, was a tremendous relief. Mr. and Mrs. Davis remained with us and have proved themselves to be all and more than we had hoped of them.

The 1930-31 furlough was indeed a strange one. Trouble, disappointment, even tragedy, on the one hand, but on the other hand repeated mercies, joy of friendships renewed, and evidence of God's presence in being used as channels of blessing. The first cause for rejoicing we have already related. Then came the testing with the cable from Manchuria that our valued and honoured co-worker, Miss Graham, had left the Mission for independent work in China. This was indeed a great blow to us both. Then came an unforgettable tour, taking in among other places, Boston, New York, and Philadelphia, to contact with supporters of evangelists in Manchuria. The "Boston Circle" alone supported several evangelists. This tour was followed by a very great mercy — the operation for cataract on Mrs. Goforth's left eye which proved a complete success.

A few weeks later came the staggering word by cable that Miss Annie Kok had resigned and left Manchuria for Peking. This was indeed serious news, seeing that our staff was so pitifully small. But all through that time of testing, Dr. Goforth's faith and courage never wavered. Little did we then realize that a still greater time of testing was at hand.

It had been decided, owing to Mr. Reoch's urgent

need for furlough, that we should hasten our return to Manchuria. Our family reunion took place on Christmas day. Two days later we left Toronto for Vancouver. Dr. Goforth had felt a slight irritation in his right eye for some days, but it was not till Winnipeg was reached, where he was to hold meetings, that anything serious was suspected. Specialists, on examination of the eye, insisted on our immediate return to Toronto. During the following four months, Dr. Goforth went through operation after operation for dislodged retina of the right eye. The operations were nerveracking in the extreme, but doctors and nurses alike testified to Dr. Goforth's marvellous calmness, patience, and fortitude during the ordeal. Not till the latter part of April was all hope of restoring sight to that eye abandoned.

Again, God used a time of illness in Jonathan Goforth's life for the writing of a book. Miss Margaret Gay, an experienced nurse, and a former worker in Honan, on hearing of Dr. Goforth's condition, cancelled all her cases and gave herself to act as his night nurse. For months, with eyes bandaged, when able, Dr. Goforth recounted to Miss Gay, story after story as they later appeared in *Miracle Lives of China*. These stories, Miss Gay took down in shorthand and later handed them to Mrs. Goforth in a form that she could get ready for publication. The book was actually in print before Dr. Goforth even saw the manuscript.

In the latter part of May, for the second time, Dr. Goforth and his wife, accompanied by their son, Paul, left for Manchuria. We cannot resist sharing the following extract from a dear son's farewell letter, written

May, 1931, as we were facing, once more, service for Christ on the foreign field:

"... The ages of sixty-seven and seventy-two seem so dear and mellow and sweet—like the red and russet and gold of autumn leaves. Do you remember the Indian legend about the autumn leaves? They had just fallen from the trees and were lying on the bosom of Mother Earth, when the Great Spirit passed by. He could not bear to have them die and disappear, so to each leaf he gave a pair of wings—from the red leaf there rose a robin—from the brown, the swallow—from the golden leaf, the wild canary,—and so the leaves lived again in the birds and rose into the clear blue sky to give thanks to the Great Spirit, their Maker. Thus will your dear lives endure forever in the winged thoughts of gentleness and goodness and kindness that you have planted in the minds and hearts of all those who have known and therefore have loved you. . . ."

XXV

RESULTS OF AGGRESSIVE EVANGELISM

How can we save a dying world?
That problem has been solved above:
The key is found in Calvary,
The only way is love!

MRS. BOOTH-CLIBBORN

TWO REQUESTS have reached me. One is that I give some "Pictorial background of conditions in China, political and otherwise." The other request urges that I "carefully avoid touching on things political." To the writer, the latter is the wiser course to take. Nevertheless we give the following:

During one of China's chronic national typhoons, events happen with such kaleidoscopic rapidity, a statement made one day might the next be quite misleading. Dr. Arthur H. Smith, one of the most brilliant men in China, during one of those chaotic periods received a cable from a leading New York paper which said, "Send us bottom facts *re* situation." To this Dr. Smith replied, "There is no bottom and there are no facts." At another time when asked, "What do you think will be the outcome of it all?" Dr. Smith replied, "I don't know — you don't know — nobody knows. If anyone says he knows, he knows nothing about China!"

In the midst of another long period of political unrest, a letter reached us from an old missionary residing at a port city. He said: "Since the establishment of 'glorious republic' in China, revolution has followed revolution. Carlyle in his *French Revolution* wrote, 'Revolution is like jelly sufficiently boiled; it needs only to be poured into shapes of constitution and consolidated, *could it only contrive to cool.*' The trouble with poor China is, the jelly is not only over-boiled, but *kept* at boiling point, and the moulds of constitution, if China ever had any, have been lost."

In view of the great changes now taking place in China, and the brave efforts her leaders are making to consolidate reforms, the above quotations seem somewhat hard and cynical, nevertheless they picture only too truly China's periodic, if not chronic, chaotic condition for as long as missionaries now living can remember.

While it is thought best that comments on the political struggle going on, in and around our field, should be avoided, it may be permissible to let a few facts speak for themselves as to conditions under which we lived and worked in Manchuria almost continuously.

From our windows over the preaching-hall at Szepingkai could be seen a sort of miniature Eiffel Tower, from the top of which a brilliant electric light shone at night and searchlights were continuously covering the town—this to guard against attacks by the threatening hordes of bandits, sometimes over one thousand strong. Barbed wire entanglements surrounded a large part of the town, electrically charged at night. Wrecking of the railways to the north, south, and west, was not uncommon. These are but a few indications of the perils and disturbed conditions which continued for years throughout the field. When the clouds became very threatening, we lived for days with valises packed, though none of us ever did have to leave. Yet through it all, the work went on. Not one of the ten preaching-halls throughout the field had to be closed. New centres were being opened and promising young converts were offering themselves as evangelists.

The following letter written by our own son, Paul, September 8, 1932, gives a picture of the conditions at that time, and indeed not only that time, but we are sorry to say, is probably true even now.

"On the way home from Tungliao, that hotbed of banditry and cholera, I was forced to stay here over-night because there seems to be another bandit block-ade on the main line.

"When Pastor Chang wrote this week to say he could not come to Szepingkai on account of sickness in his home, I decided to take the rent money to Tungliao. Telling none of the Chinese about my financial plans, I left Szepingkai at 8 A.M. on the 6th with seven hundred dollars in ten dollar notes pinned into the pockets of a waistcoat which I wore under a khaki shirt. I travelled third-class, with a ticket to Chengchiatun, only; then from here I bought another third-class ticket to Tungliao.

"Thirteen hours before, I learned a lively battle was raging along the road between the chapel and the railway station; bandits broke through the lines. Man-chukuo troops engaged them, but Japanese soldiers had to finish the job.

"I was shown the new electrically charged fence surrounding Tungliao to keep the bandits out. The

DR. AND MRS. GOFORTH AT KESWICK, ONTARIO,
AUGUST, 1930

main effect apparently has been to *keep them in*; and the victims have been numerous dogs and pigs. Little brick forts throughout the city indicate that street battles with the bandits are part of the regular program. Pastor Chang says that all Tungliao was governed by bandits from October, 1931, to January, 1932. In the magnificent railway station and its outbuildings, I looked in vain for a single door or window which the vandals had not smashed—glass, woodwork, and all. The station safe, a bulky one, is still lying where they left it in the open—upside down, door ripped off its hinges, and empty.

"Cholera has claimed over four thousand victims in Tungliao this year. The epidemic is abating, but stringent precautions are still taken; every passenger was sprayed with disinfectant when landing today at Chengchiatun. Pastor Chang says seventy per cent of the Tungliao victims were buried without coffins. Seven of our Christians lost their lives.

"Dust in blinding clouds greets the traveller at this time in Chengchiatun and Tungliao. This morning in the "drosky," Pastor Chang remarked that he had swallowed at least one "chin" (1¼ lbs.) of dust, and that it wasn't all clean either. It strikes me that people who have to live in Tungliao deserve a vacation more often than those who live in Szepingkai."

A little homely touch comes in the following extract from a letter of Dr. Goforth's to a daughter in the home land:

"Mother has a kitten two months old and very progressive. He exercises enough to do two kittens. I call him Pompey. He delights to rustle chunks of coal around the coalhod, so you can imagine how dirty a yellow kitten can get. Mother undertook to give him a bath this morning with the temperature at ten above zero. The little beast, to escape the ordeal, clawed furiously and finally bit your mother. I have reminded her that it was safer to bathe her babies."

From the starting of the Manchurian Mission, the attitude of the Home Board was for "retrench," owing to the Church's financial condition, while Dr. Goforth and his co-workers were ever for "advance." At last, early in January of 1932, Dr. Goforth felt he must make his position, once for all, clear to the Board. This he does, as will be seen, in the following letter to Dr. Grant, our foreign mission secretary:

"... *Our estimates for 1932-3 are cut to the lowest possible amounts to maintain any kind of efficiency and you will notice that not one dollar is down in the estimates for evangelists' salaries. ... You express a fear that we may extend the work in Manchuria beyond the resources of the Board to carry it. As we on the field in intimate touch with the need see it, the Lord of the Harvest has entrusted our church with a work He wants done. If we will not do this work for Him, it remains undone, and these millions perish. I for one cannot assume such responsibility; therefore, as long as the Lord of the Harvest gives me strength I dare not stand still, but must extend the work. It may be questioned whether any other portion of God's earth so strongly invites to a forward evangelistic effort as does this Manchurian field. No matter how the work expands on present lines, the Home Church is not responsible for a single school,*

*a single hospital, a single house, or a foot of land. All
the buildings are rented, and the year we cease to pay
the rent they revert to the owners. Up to the present
all evangelists used are paid by funds not raised by the
Home Church, and they are clearly told that when the
funds fail they return home. Even we missionaries can
be recalled when the Home Church considers her obli
gation to evangelize this great perishing multitude o'
Chinese and Mongols has ceased. But we think better
of the Home Church than this. At present there is a
spiritual depression in the Home Church as well as a
financial. Consequently there is a temporary inclination
to walk by sight. We do sympathize with the Board on
account of the deficit. . . ."*

Shortly after writing the above letter, Dr. Goforth
entered his seventy-fourth year, but with increasing age
came a greater urge to make his life tell to the utmost
for the winning of souls and the leading of believers
into a fuller vision of their heritage in Christ. The first
six months of 1932 were given to continuous and strenuous revival missions in the main centres throughout the
whole field. Then came for Dr. Goforth and his wife the
most delightfully quiet, refreshing holiday of their life,
by the sea at Peitaiho, the most beautiful summer resort
of the Far East. Each evening towards sundown, chairs
were drawn together on the west veranda and here we
sat drinking in the marvellous beauty of the scene before us. The wide, deep valley, reaching far westward to
the mountain ranges beyond. Then as the sun came near
setting, the indescribable colouring and changing glory
of those sunsets! Later, Dr. Goforth recalled with deepest gratitude to God that he had been given such a rich

feast of vision to remember when physical darkness came.

Dr. Goforth had a very wonderful escape from taking what might easily have been a fatal step. We had taken passage on a Japanese boat from Darien to Tangku on the mainland of China. We had often been on boats where a narrow passageway led from one side of the boat to the other, connecting the two decks. It was evening when we boarded the vessel. Dr. Goforth opened a door, leading as it seemed to him, across the passage to the other deck. He had taken one step and had actually raised a foot for the next, when a hand seemed laid upon him, pressing him back against the door, which had sprung to. At first he thought that he had met somebody, but on looking closely, he discovered that it was not a through passage, but steep steps leading down to the lower deck. The walls on either side were straight, with no banisters, and had he taken that step, he would undoubtedly have been thrown headlong to the foot of the stairs. When he came to me, his face was quite white, and he said, "Rose, the Lord has delivered me again!" Then there came to me those words in the thirty-fourth Psalm—"The angel of the Lord encampeth round about them that fear him and delivereth them."

Those who have followed this story through the early years at Changte, North Honan, will be able to enter somewhat into the joy experienced by both Dr. and Mrs. Goforth when the way opened for them to accept the warm invitation from the missionaries and Christians of their old Changte field to visit them and to hold a week's meetings. It was indeed a glorious week for all. It

THE ABOVE PICTURE REPRESENTS BUT A PORTION OF THE CHRISTIANS ATTENDING THE SERIES OF MEETINGS ON DR. COFORTH'S LAST VISIT TO THE OLD STATION OF CHANGTE IN 1932.

seemed to Dr. Goforth and his wife, later, one of the Lord's "exceeding abundants" that they should have been permitted once again to visit the old scene and meet with many of their beloved children in Christ. But time had wrought great changes—many loved faces were missing. The little treed-in corner of the compound, the sacred spot, was fast filling. Beyond our own three precious mounds, among others, was that marking the resting-place of our beloved co-worker of many years, Dr. Jean Dow, thought of by us and others as "our beloved, beautiful doctor."

A tent which had been erected for the meetings and which held from eight hundred to a thousand people, was filled several times a day. The warmth of affection shown by Christians and missionaries alike touched Dr. Goforth and his wife beyond words to express. Many times later, we both praised God for allowing us to have that last visit to the dear old station with many unforgettable memories.

As I write, there rests on the desk before me Dr. Goforth's Chinese New Testament, printed in 1926. On the fly-leaf is written in almost indecipherable writing, owing to the breakage of a bone in his right hand, the following note: "Oct. 18-32—Have read this Chinese N. T. (New Testament) sixty times."

Dr. Goforth's habit was to have his English Scofield Bible beside the Chinese one, constantly comparing the two. The above simple brief record meant much time, spent in reading the Word. The question often asked was, "How did he, living the full life he did, manage to get so much time for Bible-study?" The answer to this is—by always rising early, having his Bible at hand

and using the extra minutes of opportunity as they came. What a story might have been told could we record all those led to Christ on train or steamer just through his habit of having his sharpened sword at hand. Jonathan Goforth LOVED the Word. To him the simple reading of it was a delight. It was sacred, divine. How often have I seen him, when taking up his Bible to read, first uncover his head and in an attitude of deepest reverence remain so a few moments before beginning his reading. In this simple act we see the secret of his life. Before he crossed the Borderland he stated that he had read the Bible seventy-three times from cover to cover!

XXVI

TRIUMPHING OVER TRAGEDY

Most of the grand truths of God have to be learned by trouble; they must be burned into us by the hot iron of affliction, otherwise we shall not truly receive them.
C. H. SPURGEON

NEVER HAD the progress of the work throughout the whole field given greater cause for rejoicing than in those early months of 1933. The adult baptisms for 1932 had numbered four hundred and seventy-two, and the givings of the Christians reached over four thousand, three hundred dollars. At each centre visited, Dr. Goforth was cheered to note signs also of higher spiritual life.

Returning home from the outside touring, the latter part of March, he began a series of meetings at Kungchuling, an important centre on the South Manchurian Railway, two hours' run north of Szepingkai. Early each morning he left by train, returning late in the evening.

One evening, March 30, he walked in gropingly to where I was sitting and stood before me for a moment. I wondered, for he was very pale. Then he said quietly, almost in a whisper, "I fear the retina of my left eye has become dislodged." So it was. But from that moment he was never heard to question or complain because of his loss of sight. At once arrangements were

315

made for the carrying on of the work and then the long journey to Peking was made, where for four months he went through, almost daily, the same terrible ordeal as he had suffered in Toronto two years before, but to no avail.

It was reported that a Japanese doctor in the great hospital at Dairen, South Manchuria, had had remarkable success in replacing dislodged retinas. Dr. Goforth, therefore, rented a missionary home close to the hospital for July and August. Here our daughter Ruth and her husband, the Rev. D. I. Jeffrey, with their three children, joined us, en route for their field in Indo-China. We will here let Ruth give a glimpse of that time:

". . . . . When with you at Dairen, Ivory (Mr. Jeffrey), accompanied father to the hospital three times a week for those painful injections in the eyeball. Ivory said, 'Father never flinched during those excruciatingly painful treatments'; and as you know, we never heard from him one word of complaint. There were several British warships in the harbour that summer and a number of the sailors visited our home. Father took every opportunity to press lovingly the question of personal salvation and allegiance to Christ. He was never preoccupied with his own affliction, but always alert and eager to draw each one out into conversation that invariably led up to the supreme question of personal salvation, or opened the way for him to witness to the great things God had done in China and other places in answer to prevailing prayer."

When recalling the facts of which I am about to

write, it seemed very wonderful indeed to Dr. Goforth and his wife to trace God's hand working through it all and turning the very factors which seemed about to wreck our Mission into the agencies which brought about that which we were all working and praying for, namely, SELF SUPPORT.

We had not been long in Peking when letters from the field began to cause Dr. Goforth great uneasiness. About the beginning of July, we went to Dairen, on the southern coast of Manchuria. It was here that word reached us of the Home Board's drastic cut in allowance for general Mission expenses: these included travel expenses of missionaries and evangelists, rent of living quarters for evangelists in over twenty centres throughout the field, also mission gatekeepers' salaries and other minor expenses. How drastic was the cut may be seen when only twenty-four dollars, Mexican (about eight dollars, Canadian currency), was to be allowed per month for all general mission expenses for Szepingkai, and its fourteen outstations, and the same amount for the whole Taonan field. It simply meant the work could not be carried on.

The missionaries in charge of the work "were dumbfounded by the severe cut in the budget and distressed over the situation it brought about." But when Dr. Goforth heard of evangelists being dismissed, this to him was the most serious part of the situation. A letter had been sent by the Council to all the church centres of the field, telling them they could no longer expect any help from the Home Board.

It was probably the most serious situation Dr. Goforth had ever faced, yet those who were with him at this time and knew what he was going through in facing his loss of sight and the possibility, as some had suggested, that he might be recalled home, and now this threatening break-up of the work, marvelled at the calmness and patience with which he bore it all. One day he exclaimed, "The devil is trying his best to wreck our mission, but God is with us and he will bring us through!"

The events of that period brought Kipling's lines vividly to mind:

If you can watch the things you gave your life to, broken
And stoop and build 'em up with worn-out tools . . .

Preparations were at once made for the break-up of our party. Our dear ones left us for their distant southern field, while Dr. Goforth and I started northward to Szepingkai. But before breaking up, the following which is a brief extract from a letter dictated by Dr. Goforth, was dispatched to the Home Board:

". . . We have just received word of the outcome of the Council recently held at Szepingkai. One item will give you some idea of the dismay caused by what has been decided at this Council. Twenty-four dollars per month, *Mexican*, is all that is being allowed for Szepingkai main centre and its fourteen outstations. To save money it is even being suggested that we dismiss our good trustworthy gatekeeper, a man who has been with us for four years and does not only the hundred and one things required of one in his position, but often takes charge of the street-chapel and preaches to those who come. He is, as it

A GROUP OF EVANGELISTS WORKING IN THE SZEPINGKAI REGION. MOST OF THESE ARE SUPPORTED BY THE GOFORTH EVANGELISTIC FUND. MR. SU SITS NEXT BUT ONE ON DR. GOFORTH'S LEFT. BEHIND HIM IS THE REV. ALLAN REOCH.

seems to us both, an absolutely necessary man to have and for this reason rather than risk his being sent away in our absence we are writing to Mr. Reoch to put his next three months' wages to our account and at next Council we will know better how you as a Board will be able to meet our needs. But even the saving of this fifteen dollars a month—how could the twenty-four dollars allowed be sufficient? I could not go to our farthest out-station and back without spending forty dollars on travel expenses! It simply means that we cannot carry on the work unless we use our own depleted salary to meet the extra expenses. *We are determined that if we have to spend our last dollar, the Lord's work must go on.*

"You as a Board should feel greatly encouraged at the results of the work done here in Manchuria. The tide of self-support is rising in a most gratifying way. Several centres are giving either buildings or support in money in a way that surprises other missions in Manchuria and elsewhere. Szepingkai main station has just called Mr. Wang Yuan-teh, one of our most spiritual evangelists, as their pastor at a salary of thirty-five dollars per month (Mexican) to be met by the native church. They are now also taking steps to build their own church as soon as funds sufficient are in hand to begin. Several hundred dollars have already been promised. This is also true of Taonan and also two smaller centres."

On reaching Szepingkai, a general meeting of missionaries, Chinese workers and leaders, was called for conference to face the crisis. The result was, some of the evangelists who had been dismissed were restored, but others who had not proved satisfactory were not taken back. Our evangelists now numbered well on to seventy. Then reports began to arrive from all sections of the field indicating that a wave, or rather the spirit of self-support, seemed to have settled down upon the Christians everywhere. With hardly an exception, *the reaction of the Christian centres to the withdrawal of support was definitely towards self-support!* Even small groups began to vie with one another in getting up their own church buildings and undertaking all running expenses of their centre.

The definite advance made at this time may be seen from the following brief comparative statistics:

Adult baptisms, 1932, 472: Givings of Christians, $ 4,312.12
Adult baptisms, 1933, 778: Givings of Christians,   8,285.05
Adult baptisms, 1934, 966: Givings of Christians, 14,065.98

When Dr. Goforth's letter reached the Home Board, an extra one thousand dollars was at once cabled to our Mission. None of this, however, was used for the re-subsidizing of the native churches. Thus the Lord brought us as a Mission victoriously through that time of crisis.

To return to Dr. Goforth. Of the many loving messages expressing sympathy at his loss of sight, none, perhaps, touched him more than the one from a son-in-law, from which we give a few extracts.

". . . Our hearts ache for you, dear father, and yearn to be of some comfort and help. We know that you will use it as a stepping-stone to even greater usefulness and glory in Christ. We have always been inspired by your work for the Master, father, and have loved you for it, but this recent tragedy makes us love you all the more. How we wish that a realization of our love may come to you and comfort and cheer your heart. . . . You are held very precious, so that I rejoice in your triumphs and grieve with you in your sorrows. . . . You will go on living deeper and deeper in Christ, fighting the good fight and being more precious not only in His sight, but in the sight of your own children as well. We shall pray for you, father, that this physical handicap may be turned into a rich blessing, and may Christ lead you very gently through these trying days and give you bountifully of his loving spirit and power, that you may be able to rejoice in your affliction for His sake. . . . We, your children in the homeland, are holding you tenderly in our thoughts, wishing we might make the load easier to bear, and thanking God for your noble life, which we pray will shine brighter and brighter until the perfect day."

The first imperative need as Dr. Goforth faced blindness, was for a Chinese companion. It was indeed a problem how to find just the right man for such a position. We prayed much about it. The chief qualifications we had in mind were — he must be a Christian and of high character, young, alert, of good education, and one who could meet and hold his own with the highest, and also one who would undertake the position, partly at least, as a Christian service.

Before leaving Dairen, we decided the companion should not be paid from the evangelists' fund, so we would need to pray for a donation so ear-marked that it could be put to this man's support. On reaching Szepingkai, a letter awaited us from a gentleman in New York enclosing a cheque just sufficient for one year's salary. The letter said, "This is for Dr. Goforth, to help in any way because of his loss of sight." So we had the year's salary in hand one week before Mr. Kao came, a young man filling every requirement that we have mentioned.

When Dr. Goforth faced inevitable blindness, for a very brief season, he feared his ministry for the Lord had come to an end, but soon it became evident to all that his blindness was not a handicap in his ministry, although his public preaching to heathen audiences had largely to be given up, but not personal interviews. His wonderful knowledge of the text of Scripture enabled him to deal with a seeker, for he could tell such where to find a passage needed, and the reading of it, himself, made it all the more impressive.

One of Mr. Kao's chief duties was to read the Chinese Bible aloud to Dr. Goforth. Sometimes, as he read very quickly, a character would be overlooked or miscalled. To his astonishment, Dr. Goforth never failed to detect the error and quietly check him up, so familiar had the Chinese text become. It seemed to some of us that Dr. Goforth's blindness helped, rather than hindered, because of the influence it had on the church as a whole. Yet his loss of sight was a sorrow, a tragedy, felt by all. There seemed to come over the Christians a new friendliness and sympathy not perhaps sensed before, at least not in the same way.

The following little incident, though it be "but a straw," still we give it: At the first series of meetings led by Dr. Goforth at Szepingkai after he became blind, a little boy, five years of age, tried twice to pray, but the praying of the grown-ups drowned his voice. At the close of the meeting, the wee tot came up to Dr. Goforth and looking up into his face, he grasped him by both hands, and said, "I can pray." "I know you can, for I heard you," replied Dr. Goforth. "Are your eyes better?" said the child. "Not yet," was the reply, "you must pray for them." "Oh, I do pray for them!" said the little one, still holding fast on Dr. Goforth's hands, till called away.

How we wish it were possible to give several chapters to the personal stories of some of the men and women who have been led out of darkness "into His marvellous light"! The following are but brief outlines of a few Dr. Goforth most delighted recounting later when in Canada:

The poorest Christian in the Tungliao church, a swineherd, on hearing Pastor Chang's plea for funds to purchase a plot of ground on which to build their own church, came forward saying, "Pastor, I want to help, but I have only my pigs. The Lord Jesus has done so much for me, I must do my part. Tell me, what can I do?" The Pastor knew the desperate poverty of the poor fellow. The most he could get to live on probably would not exceed two or three dollars a month. All he could say was, "Ask the Lord to show you." As the man turned away, he thought, *"I cannot give the Lord anything but my best."* Going to where his pigs were, he picked out the fattest and finest and drove it to the market where he sold it for thirteen dollars and thirty-five cents; perhaps he never had seen so many silver dollars at one time. But as he counted out the thirty-five cents, he said to himself, *"I can't give the*

Lord a broken dollar!" Somehow he made up the amount to fourteen dollars and brought them to the Pastor as his share in getting their own church. Is it any wonder, with such an example, that within a year not only the land was secured, but a simple and suitable church erected free of debt? Better still, before another year had passed, the church had to be enlarged and since that time has been enlarged a second time.

Our second story is that of a Christian woman living in one of the far northern centres. She and her husband some three years before had been saved as "brands plucked from the burning," and *gloriously* saved they were! This woman had a silver dollar which had been given her and which she kept and treasured "as an emergency fund." Then came the word that the Presbyterian Church in Canada was failing to send sufficient funds to the Mission Board and consequently the Board was getting deeper and deeper into debt. This woman thought over with great concern the sad news and no doubt, not without a struggle, she wrapped up her precious dollar carefully and sent it to the missionary at Szepingkai as her share in "filling up the Home Board's hole (or debt)." It may be here added when it became generally known that the Home Board was facing a heavy deficit, over *three hundred dollars were raised by the Christians of our field and forwarded to the Board in Toronto to help meet the deficit!*

A true miracle of grace was Mr. Tung of Fanchiatun, an important centre up the line from Szepingkai. He was an old Manchurian Christian, baptized thirty years before, but for many years a backslider, living deep in sin; drink, opium, gambling, etc., all had gained a strangle-hold upon him. Through one of our Christians, he was persuaded to attend revival meetings at Szepingkai, where he and his family were billetted in the Goforth's guest-room. He became awakened, convicted, and before leaving, was literally "a new man in Christ Jesus." Returning home, he at once set himself to win others to Christ and became the leader in one of the most remarkable Christian movements we have yet seen. When visiting his centre six months later, it took almost two hours for the members of the forty families he had won as believers, to pass before us in single file, they each one being introduced to us by Mr. Tung. A street on which all the houses had been owned by Mr. Tung, was named "Harlot Alley." After these houses had been cleaned out and only Christians allowed to live in them, the street was re-named, "Heaven's Grace Alley." In 1935, that centre contributed five hundred and thirty-four dollars for the starting of a self-supporting church, Mr. Tung himself donating the building, and also an organ for services.

Many a Sunday-school in the homeland has been thrilled with the story of the two Sun girls. When the alarm came that bandits were at the front gate, all the family managed to escape, but two girls of about twelve and fourteen. The younger hid in an inner room, but the elder stood in the centre of the main room, quietly praying as the bandits rushed in. While many of them began looting, the leader seized the girl by the throat, threatening to choke her if she did not tell where her father had hidden. "I don't know," she said. He then tightened his grip so that she was indeed nearly choked, saying, "You lie!" She replied, "I am a Christian," and then with a sudden inspiration, she said, "I think you would like me to sing." At this the men stopped looting and shouted for her to sing to them. Calmly she sang a verse of "Jesus Loves Me." They were all so delighted that they called for more. She said, "My cousin sings better than I do, I'll call her." When the child who had hidden appeared, the two sang together the second verse of "Jesus Loves Me." Then the bandit leader called to the others to stop looting and to bring back everything that had been taken away. Putting into the children's hands two dollars, he shouted to the men to leave. They made off without doing any further harm. When this story was told me by one of the girls, I asked her, "Did you not feel greatly terrified when the bandits were all about you?" "Oh, no!" she replied, "I knew the Lord was with me."

For four years we had as gatekeeper, one who was perhaps the most outstanding example of the transforming power of the grace of God we had ever known in all our years of service. So tragic, so terrible had this man's life been, we cannot give the facts. Suffice it to say that he who had once been a terror to all, when Christ came into his heart, became the gentlest, humblest, and most beloved of all our converts. When sickness or sorrow or bereavement had entered a home, this man was the one sought for to comfort and help. It seemed to some of us that it was with him as with the woman of Scripture,—"He loved much because he had been forgiven much." Shortly before we left Manchuria, Dr. Goforth received an urgent request from a new centre in a bandit-ridden region that this man be sent to them as their leader, "for he loves us and understands us."

XXVII.

CLOUDS BEFORE SUNSET

The Gardener is never so near as when He is pruning. ANON

EARLY IN January, 1934, the Mission Council met at Szepingkai and all were cheered by the reports received from every section of the field and this in spite of ever present political menace for most of our field was in the very centre of the troubled area.

Some wonderful stories were told indicating God's over-shadowing care of us all. One instance of this may be given. Two of our missionaries planned to start from Szepingkai for Taonan on a certain day but without apparently any reason, they changed their plan and left a day earlier. The train they originally planned to travel by was wrecked by bandits tearing up the track, and while wholesale looting was in progress, a freight train going at full speed ran into the wreck and over two hundred were killed or injured.

Immediately after Council, Dr. Goforth started for a full campaign of revival missions throughout the field. The first centre visited was Tungliao. Reader, try to visualize what the following combination might inevitably result in: zero weather, packed audiences, every inch of windows and doors zealously guarded from permitting a breath of air from entering and an epidemic of flu raging! Dr. Goforth's voice was often drowned by the coughing. As to the *air*, or rather lack of it, by the close of a meeting—well, it can be imagined better than described. Thus the inevitable came: Dr. Goforth contracted the flu, or whatever the epidemic was. How I begged him to give in and be nursed, and even let me take his meetings, for I could see he was really ill! But no, he never missed a meeting. He was very quiet but very pale and seemed all through these days— indeed, through the next three months, like a man gropingly taking one step at a time, and doubtless he was, going on, trusting for the needed strength which the Lord never failed to give him.

I simply cannot give the details of that winter. Sufficient to say, that for many weeks, what I have just described was repeated at other centres. Then came Taonan. Little did we know it was to be our last visit! The bitterest of winter blizzards was in full force when we arrived and continued throughout the twelve days of our stay. The Davis' home was a considerable distance from the meeting-hall. Twice, sometimes three times daily, Dr. Goforth was led through the deep snow and storm to address the audiences of Christians which packed the chapel, the original opening of which we have already described when opening Taonan. But since then, this building had been enlarged four times. Dr. Goforth and I were simply thrilled again and again when we heard how the Lord had been working in the city of Taonan and many, many centres throughout that great northern region. Truly few missionaries are spared to see such days of harvesting!

But God's servant was paying a price. Racked with coughing, sometimes he would stand holding to the desk till the attack passed, and then go on with his message. This went on all through the winter till April when we returned home to Szepingkai. Then the collapse which all had been fearing for months came. One morning, he arose intending to go for a day's preaching up the line, but he became so deathly faint, he yielded to my urging that he return to bed. I give the following that you might know what kind of a man I had to deal with. I bent over and said, "Have you any pain?" "Yes," he replied, "very severe under my left shoulder." "How long have you had it?" "Three days." "Why didn't you tell me before?" "Because I was afraid if you knew, you would keep me from my work!" was his reply.

Not an instant of time was lost. Fomentations, inhalations, and everything I could possibly think of to do, I did. A Japanese doctor was sent for. It was four hours before he came and then his diagnosis was—"aborted pneumonia." So the acuteness of the attack was checked, but in the days that followed, Mr. Reoch and I were in despair for Dr. Goforth insisted on the Chinese being allowed to see him. In they flocked, and between his violent attacks of coughing, he entertained with a cheerful, smiling face, the Christians who would not be kept from him nor he from them. So to save him from himself, it was decided I should take him at once to the seaside. Pastor Su was also in very poor health, so with the two invalids, and Mr. Kao, the companion, and one servant, we started for the seaside. Mr. Reoch wanted to go with us, but the work needed him and I insisted on managing alone.

For weeks Dr. Goforth rested by the sea. His great weakness and incessant coughing with slight hemorrhages, gave great concern. At the beginning of June, a doctor who had arrived, pronounced one lung affected. A month later, Dr. Struthers from North Honan, after careful examination, said the other lung was also affected. I had sent to many friends word of Dr. Goforth's condition, asking for prayer. About the middle of July, or perhaps a little later, I noticed a very marked change coming over my husband. His temperature became normal, his old strength and vigour returned, so much so, he insisted on accepting an invitation to become guests at the conference being held about two miles distant. He attended all of Dr. Turner's and Dr. Barnhouse's meetings. On returning to our cottage, I determined to have Dr. Goforth examined again, for he seemed wonderfully better. Dr. Struthers came, accompanied by his brother, the doctor from Chinan, Shantung hospital. The examination was very thorough. Then one of the doctors with a very happy smile, turned to me and said, "Well, Mrs. Goforth, we are able to give the good Doctor a clean bill of health. We can find nothing wrong!"

Three days later we were en route for Szepingkai! Among the many letters awaiting us on our arrival "home" was one from a prominent Presbyterian minister in Toronto. It said in part:

". . . I have a growing conviction, and I believe it is of the Lord, that you ought to return home and spend a few years in the homeland before your call comes for higher service. I very well understand that you will feel that you ought to stay at the post of duty up to the very end—but have you ever thought that God may be demanding the greater sacrifice of coming home and out of your ripe experience, re-

kindle the fires of missionary zeal that are, I assure
you, on the decline in the Home Church. . . . I believe
we need you, the Church needs you to arouse it."

Not long after, the above letter was followed by
another, also from a leading minister in Canada. The
gist of it was much the same in thought—Dr. Goforth
should return, he was needed to awaken the Church
in the homeland. To these, Dr. Goforth at first gave
little attention, but went on as before—working to the
limit of his strength. Then Mrs. Goforth's steady decline in health led them both to pray that the Lord might
make it unmistakably clear as to whether they should
remain or return home.

When possible, I accompanied my husband on his
tours for his recent illness had made me afraid to allow him to go out alone with just Mr. Kao. The following last record in my diary, when on that last trip
to the most northern of our stations, is here given just
as it was written at the time. It will perhaps be read
with interest as the veil is lifted a little on the conditions outside.

"Tuesday, Nov. 6, 1934: I suppose we are getting
too old to stand roughness easily. I am so glad I
brought my camp chair. It is quite comfortable and
such an improvement on the hard high stools. When
we are both in, Jonathan and I take turns in sitting
in the camp chair to get a rest. But, oh, this kind
of work PAYS! We will soon forget the hardness and
discomforts. The meetings are going well.

"Wednesday, Nov. 7, 1934: Chapel filled to capacity — the women and some of the outside men
were standing at the back during my meeting this

morning apparently taking deep interest in my illustrated talk.

"Thursday, Nov. 8, 1934: I wonder how Jonathan can stand the strain of these days. He always attends the early seven o'clock prayer-meeting. At nine, or a little after, Mr. Kao reads the Scriptures over to him. At 10:30 he takes his first meeting. On his return, we have dinner. We try to take a little rest after dinner, but almost every day, something disturbs or hinders. Visitors come in and Jonathan is kept constantly engaged till Mr. Davis' meeting at 3:30 which he attends. On his return, I try to get him to relax some, but it is not always possible. At 5:30 he goes for his evening meeting and at seven or after, we have supper, and after that, visitors. This goes on day by day.

"Neither of us is sleeping well. Unfortunately, we did not bring our camp cots, thinking the straw on the k'ang would make our beds sufficiently soft, but alas! we made a mistake! The kind of straw obtained here seems to pack down in hard lumps. Last night, when unable to get into a comfortable position, I said, rather complainingly, 'Oh, but it is hard!' Jonathan replied quietly, 'Yes, I know it is, but let us endure it for the work's sake—it will be but for a few days.'

"It is marvellous to see how, in spite of his blindness, Jonathan is able to hold his own as if he could see, when talking with the evangelists and Christians."

A few weeks later, the writer's sudden and serious collapse resulted in the question as to whether or not we should return to Canada, being quite laid aside. The question, now, was "how speedily arrangements could be made to get the Goforths home." Paul was appointed to accompany us. Everything took place too rapidly, it seemed, for thought.

A sidelight on Dr. Goforth's character may be seen in the matter of the disposal of our household goods. It will be remembered how the furnishing of the Mission Home at Szepingkai had been made possible through the returned donation from Chancellor Kok of Peking. Dr. Goforth therefore insisted that a nominal price should be put on everything (except a few personal gifts to our fellow-missionaries) and the proceeds, (which totalled less than one hundred dollars) should be left in charge of Mr. Reoch to help meet the evangelists' children's school-fees. Our other worldly possessions (what remained of them after several lootings), were in the old home, at least two thousand miles distant, at Kikungshan, and nothing could be done regarding either house or contents.

Of the many farewell messages which reached us we give but one—an extract from a farewell message from the Reformed Presbyterian Mission, Manchuria:

"Our acquaintance with Dr. Goforth goes back to the days of fellowship and blessing through the Holy Spirit's presence and power in the far South. The outstanding impression we got of him then was this: 'In quietness and confidence shall be your strength' and 'the work of righteousness shall be peace, and the effect of righteousness, quietness and confidence forever,' and the firm foundation of it all was he KNEW Jesus Christ and also he TRUSTED his righteousness and he lived in the Holy Spirit's presence so that no power on earth could shake his confidence.

"In the meetings he seemed like a man who was clearing the track for a powerful locomotive that was waiting only for a clear track and that would not come until the track was clear. He was as sure of the Spirit as of tomorrow's sun, and just as sure that only clouds of sin could obscure His glory."

In the midst of the home-going preparations, annual reports from all parts of the field were received. When these were made up, they revealed that in the year 1934, almost one thousand had been received into the Church by baptism. To be exact, nine hundred and sixty-six adults were baptized and the givings of the Chinese Christians were fourteen thousand, six hundred and sixty-five dollars and ninety-eight cents. These cheering facts helped to lessen the "sadness of farewell."

For days before we were to leave, Christians were coming in with most mysterious hints, but none would reveal what was going on. Then came the farewell service. Though Dr. Goforth could not see, many were eager to tell him of the beautiful banners, silk, satin and velvet, which covered the entire walls of both men's and women's sections of the chapel. Then on a long table in front of the preacher's desk, were tastefully arranged twelve beautiul silver shields, each engraved with a message such as: "Faithful Servant of Jesus Christ," "A True Pastor Leaves Love Behind," etc. But that which called forth the greatest admiration from Chinese and missionaries alike, was a framed character or Chinese hieroglyphic for "love" worked in delicate colours on white satin in Shanghai embroidery and framed. This came as a personal gift to Dr. Goforth from a prominent Szepingkai merchant whom God had used Dr. Goforth to lead out from a very evil life into a life of fellowship with Christ. There were other gifts, that from Pastor Su being especially touching. He had come to us alone with two gold rings. He said, "I want you always to keep these on your bodies to remind you of my devotion to you."

Some who spoke at that farewell meeting broke down. One said, "Elijah is leaving us—we must all be Elishas." Three days later, the Szepingkai station platform was crowded with heartbroken Christians. I placed Dr. Goforth carefully in front of a large window and before this the crowd pressed together. Dr. Goforth, though unable to see them, kept gently bowing his head that they might know his heart was with them, his face turned upward at times, indicating the blessed hope of reunion. Mr. Kao was closest to the window and was the first to break down weeping. The others followed quickly and as the train began to move, that great crowd kept following, straining through tear-dimmed eyes to catch a last glimpse of their beloved Pastor.

What was to the Goforths a sweet little incident occurred just before their boat, "The Empress of Japan," was about to sail from Kobe. They had been several days there and had had dinner with a missionary family. There were several beautiful children in the home who flocked about Dr. Goforth in spite of his blindness and drew him into their hearts. Our boat was to leave the wharf at five o'clock Sunday afternoon. About four-thirty, to our great surprise and delight, this missionary, with several of the children appeared. As the little ones crowded about Dr. Goforth, he drew me to one side and whispered, "The children insisted on my bringing them to see you off. Coming down, I asked them, 'Why do you want to see the Goforths off? You have never wanted to see others away?' They all exclaimed at once, 'Why, Daddy, because we have taken them into the family!' "

We cannot but speak of the very great kindness shown to us by all on board that boat. Dr. Goforth's seventy-sixth birthday, the tenth of February, was reached on board. Quite a ripple of excitement occurred in the dining-room that evening when the chef marched slowly in, bearing a truly magnificent layer-cake topped by many lighted candles. All eyes watched as it was placed before Dr. Goforth, and later such a laugh went up when with one blow he extinguished every candle! One by one, the passengers came around and shook hands warmly with the old, blind veteran of many spiritual wars, whose calm, saintly countenance bore silent, but powerful witness for his Master.

There was one on board whom, many times then, and later, we thanked God for—Miss Henderson, our stewardess. Her ministries were unremitting and it was no doubt due to her that we both reached Vancouver in such good physical condition. Only so few months later, the following exquisite message was received from this dear lady:

"As 'ships that pass in the night'—my memory takes me back. As I sit here today and look upon the picture in our daily pages of one whose dynamic personality shall live on in the hearts and minds of all those who touched the hem of his garment, I can only offer this note of affectionate understanding. 'What glorious memories you have to live on with.' You can look back on the harvest of labour in life's vineyard and again inhale those reinvigorating vibrations of 'Christ-likeness' which tones you up in life—and what greater comfort could one ask for in death than to have tasted of life's noblest gift—the companionship joy of understanding.

"Rough places, not smooth ones, have made great men and great women. God sent you to the highways and the byways and He made your reverses your stepping-stones—then He brought you back to your native land and He gave you both His 'Victoria Cross' as He did to Paul—a cross which hid you entirely in the carrying of its illumination, 'I have kept the faith.'

"Your garden must be very fragrant. You have crossed many deep gorges, many deep valleys, and have climbed many Alpine peaks—and just to look back and remember *you did it together*. Shining behind like a rainbow, I know there is an evening glow, the perfect symbol that there is no separation in the perfect love of Christ. No time, no death!—all one in Christ Jesus. 'As ships that pass in the night' we greet each other on passing to our heavenly home."

The "Empress of Japan" had scarcely touched dock when Dr. Goforth was claimed for numerous meetings in Vancouver and his word was barely given for these when a telegram came from Dr. Grant, our Foreign Mission Secretary, saying, "Come on by first train." To this Dr. Goforth replied, "Delayed by meetings." Then he set himself to face a full schedule for Vancouver and Victoria.

On reaching Toronto, two weeks later, he fully expected a stern rebuke from Dr. Grant for his disobedience, but the old secretary simply smiled as he warmly welcomed back the Church's missionary pioneer. Then it came out that Dr. Grant had been receiving such glowing reports of the Vancouver meetings, he was more than glad Dr. Goforth had not obeyed his summons.

Dr. Goforth was greatly cheered on receiving the following welcoming letter from his old friend, Rev. Dr. A. J. Vining, Secretary of the Baptist Convention of Ontario and Quebec:

". . . How lovely it will be to see you again, dear old friend.. Do not think, Jonathan, that you escape my thoughts. Never a day passes, no matter how busy I am, that I do not think of you . . . and always with gratitude to the Lord for your friendship and for your magnificent record in the Lord's work. My love for you deepens as does my admiration with the passing years. God bless you, and give you peace."

No time was lost by the Board in preparing a heavy itinerary for Dr. Goforth to include the most strategic centres throughout Ontario and Quebec. The travelling was to be chiefly by motor. The schedule, outside of travel, arranged on an average of from eight to ten meetings a week. Some, on hearing of this proposed itinerary, said "It is simply suicidal for one of his age to attempt such a strain!" But not for a moment did Dr. Goforth hesitate. He rejoiced only that doors were open to him. It was for him to enter them and go on through each day as it came, quietly, trustfully, in the strength given him. Eighteen months later, the little address book he carried always with him, when laid down for the last time, was found to contain four hundred and eighty-one records of addresses.

The lowest ebb, in all his itineraries was reached one Sunday morning, when the rain was falling heavily, and Dr. Goforth was motored out to a country church for the service. Less than an hour later, he returned, looking far from his usual optimistic, cheerful self. Then he told the reason for his early return. On reaching the church they had found it empty, the minister and two summer visitors only awaiting his arrival. As these latter intended going to the evening service, the meeting was given up. On their way home, when passing the Roman Catholic Church in a country centre, they found so many motors surrounding the church, it was with great difficulty they were able to get through. What a contrast! Needless to say, Dr. Goforth did not fail, later, to press home this story, and with effect.

All through the journeyings up and down the country in Ontario and elsewhere, Dr. Goforth never failed to meet a scheduled appointment. There were times when others could see he was all but exhausted after a long journey and had to step from the car to the church, but no word was uttered by him as to how he felt. I knew as no other that he simply went forward by Divine empowering.

How many hundreds, nay thousands, will still remember his striking appearance, as with Bible always in hand, he gave forth his messages fearlessly with much of the old fire of fifty years before. It is doubtless true that many of his clerical brethren did not see eye to eye with him and "some were offended at the words which he spake." Yes, some—not many—received him not into their pulpits. Only one whole Presbytery actually closed their doors to him. Many times as he went throughout the churches he remarked on the blessed and powerful influence of the Women's Missionary Society. When inclined to be depressed at the general deadness of the church, cheer and comfort would often come from the warmth of receptions given by the women.

The last family Christmas Day reunion was a very broken one. Of the six living children, only two, Mary and Fred, were present. Towards the end of the evening, a niece with her husband joined the party. The husband, somewhat of a stranger, sat apart. He had at one time been an earnest Christian, but had backslidden. Months later, after Dr. Goforth had gone, the niece told Mrs. Goforth the following: "My husband took little interest in what was going on that evening, but kept watching Dr. Goforth and what he saw in his face and actions brought him back to his Lord. Since that evening he has been a new man."

XXVIII

SUNSET

We have all eternity to tell of victories won for Christ, but we have only a few hours before sunset to win them.

ANON

THE EARLY months of 1936 were spent in strenuous itineraries through Ontario. Then, as the time for the General Assembly in June drew near, a great burden seemed to come upon Dr. Goforth that he might be given a message which would awaken the Church from its terrible lethargy. It was his last Assembly address and it was listened to by that great body of Church dignitaries and leaders with marked attention, but as far as one could tell, with no special signs of spiritual awakening.

A short rest in a cottage by the lake followed the Assembly and as no calls had come for summer conferences in Canada, Dr. Goforth accepted invitations to conventions in the United States. The first of these was held at Keswick, New Jersey, and a most blessed ten days was spent there. We give a brief paragraph which appeared in *The Sunday School Times* some months later:

"It was Dr. Jonathan Goforth's last conference at Keswick as a missionary speaker, although none of us realized that this radiant, energetic saint of God was within just a few days of being called into the

341

presence of the One for whom he had been a veritable bondslave. He had become totally blind, but we seemed to forget that fact as he poured out the message of his heart and spoke of his vision of a lost world. Holding up his precious Bible one morning in the missionary hour, he said: 'It was lost in our journey—I've just got it back. I can't see it, but I love to hold it!' "

From Keswick, New Jersey, we motored down to the beautiful Southland, farther south than we had ever been, to Asheville, North Carolina. For more than a day we had been passing through most charming scenery and, as it seemed, steadily on the ascent. Then toward evening, after winding around sharp, steep turns for some time, we came suddenly upon "Ben Lippen," the site of the Convention, and what a welcome awaited us! It was our first experience of what we had so often heard, the warm-heartedness of the Southern people.

As I attempt to recall that month spent among those dear people on Ben Lippen, words simply fail me. Dr. Goforth repeatedly spoke of it as "the crowning Conference of my life," though in saying this, he did not know it was to be his last. Dr. McQuilkin, the beloved leader, gave over to Dr. Goforth, as part of his work for the three conferences that were to follow, the early morning prayer-meeting from seven to eight. The attendance at these morning meetings was exceptionally large—probably four-fifths of the entire Conference.

One morning, I was rather late, and overtaking a lady, I said, "Do you manage to get out to these early meetings?" She replied, "Oh, I never miss! It is at these meetings I get such a blessing. I'm too nervous to pray aloud, so when the meeting is left open for prayer, I lean forward and raise my head, keeping my eyes on Dr. Goforth's face. It is from what I see there that my blessing comes. He stands so still and is so calm and quiet and seems to just radiate peace and joy and faith and hope—everything my heart craves for!"

It was remarkable how the young people flocked about him. One day I laughingly told them, "You never give me a chance to get near my husband!" There were always two or more contending for the honour and favour of leading him. The main hostel building at "Ben Lippen" was not complete. Cardboard walls, rough ceilings, etc., were everywhere in evidence. Ultimately each room was to be finished at the cost of one hundred dollars and designated as a memorial to some missionary.

One day, Dr. Goforth said to me, "I have a bright idea and I want you to fall in with it. Let us take one of these rooms as a memorial to William C. Burns of China. We don't want to keep more than our travel expenses." Of course, it was not for me to say "No," so we had the joy of taking over "our" Memorial room with its two windows in full view of valleys and mountains and upon the walls of the room will hang a photo of Dr. Goforth, standing beside the grave of that most saintly missionary, William C. Burns.

All too soon, as it seemed, the time came for farewells. A number escorted us down the mountain to the railway station at Asheville. One of those who came with us wrote later:

". . . In recalling those precious days here at Ben Lippen, it comes to me that the very gates of heaven must have been opening for him and the glory light we saw upon him was that light, for as those of us who took you to the train, stood outside and looked up into Dr. Goforth's face, there was a shaft of sunshine that opened up in a most phenomenal way, shining upon his face, which illuminated it with a heavenly glory. We were moved with a holy awe at the wonder and glory of the scene." (How near the unseen *living* world is to us, who can tell?)

A stop was made on the return journey at the cottage by the lake, and here a few days only of partial rest was obtained, for Dr. Goforth felt time was too precious to allow even one Sunday to pass without some ministry for his Master. Then on to Toronto.

On that first Sunday, a brief record was kept of how that day was spent, which I give here as it is at least revealing of one day in a missionary's life. At the time, the story we heard in England came to mind, of a business man, who on hearing how a missionary was being worked when in the homeland, said, "I think you people are inclined to say when missionaries return home—'Here's a missionary. Come, let us kill him!'"

"Sunday morning, at nine o'clock, Mr. and Mrs. A. arrived in their motor. We drove with them thirty miles to . . . ., where we were taken into the home of Mr. and Mrs. B. The A's left at once and for some time I endeavoured to entertain our host and hostess as Jonathan was to have a heavy day. By ten forty-five we were driven over to the church and handed over to the Rev. Mr. C., who had Jonathan address the Sunday-school and, later, the morning service, at the close of which Mr. C. drove us to the house of Mr. and Mrs. D. Dinner was late, so to be on time for the afternoon service we had to leave before we could finish. We were driven some miles to . . . . . . and handed over to the minister, Rev. Mr. E., who after the service, put us in charge of the F's, who took us to . . . ., where we had supper with Mr. and Mrs. G., after which we motored to . . . . . . for the evening service, after which we were given over to Mrs. H., with whom we were told we were to spend the night, though we had hoped to return to Toronto that evening. The following day, Mrs. I. arrived some time after noon and motored us back to Toronto. Needless to say, we were glad to get home! I may say that the above is but a sample of what we not infrequently met with, an illustration of being 'killed by kindness!' "

I think it was the next Sunday, Dr. Goforth was to speak but once, and that an evening service. On rising he said, "Instead of going out this morning, let us have a feast of the Word. Read me that precious book, the Gospel of John." So that day, as he reclined, I read to him chapter after chapter, sixteen in all. We hoped to have finished the Gospel, but supper-time came, and he returned too late from the evening service to read more that night. Sometimes when I was reading to him, a slight slip was made, but quickly the correction would come from him! What a feast it was to him could be seen by the intentness with which he listened and the glow of understanding which constantly lit up his countenance at certain passages.

How full those last days in Toronto were may be realized by the fact that from September 7th to 24th, there were twenty-two records of addresses made in his note-book. We say comparisons are odious, and as a rule they are, but surely Dr. Goforth will be pardoned in making the following comparison since only so could he make clear the greatest, yes, the very greatest victory of his whole life. Long years he had contended for the putting of aggressive evangelism FIRST and in overwhelming proportion to all other phases of mission work. Jonathan Goforth went even further, urging that any line of mission work, whether medical, educational, or any other kind, could only be justified when made means to the one great end — the propagation of the Gospel of the grace of God in Jesus Christ.

It may be remembered that years back in Honan, Dr. Goforth had said how he wished that before he passed on he might have the opportunity to demonstrate what broadcasting the Gospel by every possible means — in other words, by just GIVING GOD A CHANCE — would result in. One day in that last week in Toronto, he had been reclining on the sofa, as usual, apparently thinking very keenly, when he called me to him. He rose, drew me down beside him and said, "I have been doing some mental figuring and the result is beyond what I expected. My dear, I HAVE DEMONSTRATED BEYOND ANY QUESTION OF A DOUBT WHAT JUST GIVING THE GOSPEL A CHANCE WILL RESULT IN! If all the missionaries in China in 1934, our last year in Manchuria, had had an equal number of converts per head, as our six missionaries, namely, one hundred and sixty-one per missionary, or a total of nine hundred and sixty-six, the total converts in China would have numbered well-nigh a million souls, whereas the actual baptisms for that year in China numbered only thirty-eight thousand, seven hundred and twenty-four."

The last Sabbath spent in Toronto was an extremely strenuous one for Dr. Goforth. Four times he spoke for the Rev. R. McPherson at Riverdale Presbyterian Church, at both morning and evening services, to the Catechumen class, and to the Sunday-school. Weeks later, came testimonies from some of those attending the evening service. All of these referred to the "radiancy" of Dr. Goforth's face as he gave his last message in Toronto. We give but one of these. Miss Bertha Hodge, a beloved co-worker of the Honan Mission, wrote:

"As Mr. McPherson led Dr. Goforth into the pulpit he walked with firm step, head erect, and face aglow with the joy of Christ, the sightless eyes were turned upward as if he could see. The congregation listened with marked attention and stillness as with radiant joy, as seeing the Lord he loved, he delivered his address in the power of the spirit."

On September 26, we left Toronto for the home of our son, Frederic, a Presbyterian minister at Wallaceburg, Ontario. A full schedule of meetings had been arranged. Dr. Goforth was to be driven to his appointments, returning each evening. On Wednesday, October 7, the appointment was forty miles distant. Dr. Goforth's address that evening was on "How the Spirit's Fire Swept Korea," one of the longest and most testing of his addresses. Refreshments were served at the close of the service, but Dr. Goforth declined to partake, saying he had "a little indigestion." It was very late when he finally got to rest that night. About seven o'clock the following morning, I rose and dressed, thinking my husband was still sleeping, but as he remained strangely quiet, I looked more closely and saw that my husband's earthly casket was there, but that HE had passed the Borderland into "the land that is fairer than day." His attitude was one of complete rest, his face resting on one hand, relaxed and open, while the other, also relaxed, lay beside it. The doctor said he had passed just about the time I had risen and *had not known death*. He simply slept one moment on earth; the next, he was awake and *seeing once more* in the Gloryland. He had said but a few weeks before when at "Ben Lippen," that he rejoiced to know the next face he would see would be his Saviour's. Now, he had met "his Pilot face to face." *"I shall be* SATISFIED *when I awake with Thy likeness"* (Psalm 17:15).

Those who were present at the funeral service held in Knox Church, Toronto, October 10, 1936, when a great company gathered to pay their last honours to the memory of Jonathan Goforth, can never forget the triumphant note which sounded all through the service. Our thoughts were not centred on what lay beyond that great bank of flowers; rather did we all feel Jonathan Goforth's radiant, joyous spirit present with us. One later wrote, "We seemed to be taken up to the very gates. . . . There seemed no place for sorrow, only joy and hope and praise."

The address of Dr. Wilson (Chairman of the Board of Missions), based on the passage "And David, after he had served his day and generation according to the will of God, fell on sleep," was very beautiful. Then, when Dr. Armstrong (Secretary for Foreign Missions, United Church) said, "I think of today as being Jonathan Goforth's *Coronation*!" a distinct thrill of response was felt. Rev. James MacKay, who had recently visited Manchuria said, in part:

"Love begets love, and I can testify that wherever we went in Manchuria we saw evidence of the love of the Manchurian people for the Goforths. In fact, so great did we find that love to be, that we regarded it as coming perilously near to worship. They loved him, however, because he first loved them, and showed that love by giving them his all. He greatly loved and he was greatly beloved."

Rev. Dr. John Gibson Inkster, Pastor, Knox Presbyterian Church, Toronto, spoke as follows:

". . . Jonathan Goforth was a man like the Apostle Paul. The qualities of his mind and his heart and his spirit resembled those of Paul. He had a master mind. He had undaunted courage and perseverance; he had unflagging zeal and earnestness; and he had a heart which believed unto righteousness. He was a God-intoxicated man—fully surrendered and consecrated. Above all, he was humble. He was baptized with the Holy Ghost and with fire. He was filled with the Spirit because he was emptied of self— therefore he had power which prevailed with God and man. He knew what it was to pray the prayer of faith in the Holy Ghost.

"He resembled Paul more than he resembled any other man in the Bible. In missionary zeal, for example, I never met a man so like Paul. I have *read* about such men, Livingstone, Judson, Taylor, and such like. He burned himself out preaching the Gospel of salvation and everlasting life to perishing men. His life shames us and stirs us into action and zeal for the cause of Christ. It is in Paul's writings that I find the text which best fits Jonathan Goforth. Here it is: 'This one thing I do, forgetting those things which are behind, and reaching forth unto those things which are before, I press toward the mark for the prize of the high calling of God in Christ Jesus.' . . .

"Those things so highly prized by the natural man, Paul forgot—left them behind and counted them 'but dung'. These were the things which were dear to Jonathan Goforth by nature; but he left them behind. He forgot them. What an example! What an inspiration to us!

"What were the things before—the prize? Here they are: 'That I may win Christ, and be found in him' . . . 'that I may know him, and the power of his resurrection, and the fellowship of his sufferings.' Paul wanted to know experimentally the person of Christ, the resurrection of Christ, and the atonement of Christ.

"That was the goal which Jonathan Goforth set before himself; that was the prize; those were the things 'before' to which he looked forward. His song was, 'Christ for me, and Christ for the world.' He saw and knew Christ, and he saw and knew dying men. The *one* thing he did was to bring dying men to the living Christ. And, thanks be to God, he brought them together."

Rev. Canon Howitt, a greatly honored and beloved friend of Dr. Goforth's closed with the following:

"It is with a deep sense of loss that I rise to add my tribute of loving respect and sincere appreciation to the memory of dear Dr. Goforth. Few men, that

it has been my privilege to know, have impressed me
as he did. To be with him was to realize the presence
of the Lord Jesus Christ, Whose he was and Whom
he so long and faithfully served. I remember having
the same blessed realization when in the presence of
Dr. Hudson Taylor and Dr. A. J. Gordon and one or
two besides. He, like them, was one who walked with
God and whose every word and act radiated a sense
of the Divine Presence.

"What can I say by way of comfort to those whom
he has left behind? I feel that I can not do better
than to pass on to them the Divine Prescription for
an hour like this. You will find it in Paul's First
Epistle to the Thessalonians, beginning at Chap.
4:13, where the Apostle, speaking in the Spirit,
says: *"I would not have you ignorant, brethren,
concerning them which are asleep, that ye sorrow not even as others which have no hope. For
if we believe that Jesus died and rose again, even
so them also which sleep in Jesus will God bring with
Him. For this we say unto you by the Word of the
Lord, that we which are alive and remain unto the
coming of the Lord shall not prevent them which are
asleep. For the Lord Himself shall descend from
heaven with a shout, with the voice of the archangel,
and with the trump of God: and the dead in Christ
shall rise first: Then we which are alive and remain
shall be caught up together with them in the clouds,
to meet the Lord in the air: and so shall we ever be
with the Lord. Wherefore comfort one another with
these words."*

APPENDIX

THE FOLLOWING letter from REV. GILLIES EADIE, Changtefu, North Honan, dated October 31, 1936, though seemingly long, is given in full for the valuable pictures it contains of a certain period of Dr. Goforth's life. Mr. Eadie was Dr. Goforth's co-worker for years.

"Dear Mrs. Goforth:

"It was with much sorrow, and yet with joy, that we heard by cable that our esteemed friend, Dr. Goforth, had entered into the presence of the King, and had his sight restored to him again. Now he sees the King in His beauty, and has received the 'Well done, good and faithful servant.' That is a thought which brings joy even in the midst of the sorrow of his loss. . . .

"On receipt of the cable from our office in Toronto, it was arranged that a Memorial service be held on the following Sunday by those of us in our compound here in Changte. Dr. Grant was in charge of the service. He asked me, as one of Dr. Goforth's oldest friends, to take part in the service. Dr. Grant first spoke of his early acquaintance with your husband, when they were both students in Knox College. He told us of his conversion and the life of consecration which followed it. His great passion was to win men to Christ, and he went out to his work in Toronto even at the expense of his studies, his recreations and his ordinary social life. He won a great place for himself, however, in the lives of the many in high and low places who were influenced by his life and preaching.

"Dr. Grant also spoke of his splendid knowledge of the Bible, which he had read through many times, and which was evident by the familiarity with which he used it. This was true not only of the English Bible, but also of the Chinese Bible. . . . . .

"I was then called on to speak. 'Before I came to China,' I said, 'Dr. Goforth's name was a household word in our home, as my father and mother were both very much interested in foreign missions. On my arrival in Changte, Dr. Goforth was one of those who met us at the station and escorted us to the compound. Ever since then we have been the best of friends. . . If I were to speak from a text, I could not take a more fitting one than, 'Wist ye not that I must must be about my Father's business?' I well remember an incident illustrating this on the very evening of our arrival in Changte. Dr. Goforth had been appointed in charge of new language students. Before leaving us that first evening he said, 'Well, your language teacher will be here first thing in the morning to start your lessons.' 'Why, Mr. Goforth,' I said, 'we have not our things unpacked yet,—we have just arrived.' 'Well, then, the next day,' he said, and sure enough, on the following day our teacher arrived and we set to work at the study of the language.

"Again, this characteristic is well illustrated by another series of incidents. Dr. Goforth, while not an athlete, was a great walker, and when on tour covered great distances on foot. I remember the first tour I made with him. It was from Pengcheng, a large town in the foothills, to the northwest of Changte, and it took us over the hills and mountains to the neighboring county of She Hsien and then on to the next county of Wuan. We would start at daybreak and cover five or six miles before breakfast. Visiting Christians as we went along, we would walk along till noon, then on again until evening. What impressed me was that everywhere on the road, to those who happened to be going the same way with us, on the street of the village where we had dinner, and in the inn which we reached at night, it was always Mr. Goforth who took the lead in telling the Gospel message to those ready to listen. We would arrive, footsore and weary, at the end of a day's travel, at an inn, and the crowds would gather around. While the Chinese helpers would be drinking hot water or taking a rest, Mr. Goforth was on his feet, bringing the Gospel message to the crowd. After a half an hour or so, he gave way for one of the Chinese to speak and he would rest. That is one of my earliest impressions of him, always at it and first at it.

"He had a great faculty for seeking out and putting to work men who might become good evangelists. The most of the evangelists in the northern field were men whom he had called. I saw an instance of this on the first visit I paid to the country. In the evening some educated people had come in to see the Doctor. They were discussing religion and he called on a young man there to reply to some of these men. Dr. Goforth had seen in this young graduate much promise and had invited him to come along with him for a couple of

weeks. He gave him the task of presenting the arguments for
the Christian religion to the group who had come in and thus
led to his definitely allying himself with Christ. This young
man, who is now one of our brightest workers among young
people, told me recently that he had no idea of becoming a
Christian, much less a preacher, when Dr. Goforth invited him
to go along with him, but he felt he could not well refuse
the kind invitation given him. In the end, however, he yielded
himself to Christ and became one of the brightest of evangelists, at first in our Mission, and later in Y. M. C. A. work
in China.

"Dr. Goforth believed firmly in the Divine guidance
through the agency of God's Holy Spirit. He made this the
basis of his preaching and he sought to live thereby. When
the invitations came to him to carry on special evangelistic
meetings in other parts of China many members of the Honan
Mission urged upon him that his first duty was to Honan.
He had been instrumental in founding the Mission—the work
was great—the laborers few—he should remain and consolidate the work he had begun. The reasons seemed weighty,
but Dr. Goforth was convinced that it was the Spirit's guidance and he remained firm in his purpose, although he came
back at intervals to carry on work in his own field.

"Above all, one must mention his optimism, due to faith
in God and in the power of prayer to accomplish the impossible. He did not seem to get discouraged as so many of us
do. He acted on the belief that God's cause must prevail and
He would prove faithful if we only trusted him. The success
of the work in Manchuria was but another proof of this. Dr.
and Mrs. Goforth won the affection of the Chinese people as
very few of us have done and it was always a great joy to
them when they were able to return to Changte and meet with
the people who mourn with us his loss and rejoice in his victory over death and the grave through our Lord and Saviour,
Jesus Christ."

REV. ALLAN REOCH: "It seems a fitting time to consider
what qualities made him so outstanding and so marvellously
used in his work for the Saviour. While recalling to mind
some of the qualities that explain the secret of his spiritual
power, I came across the following seven rules for daily living
made by Dr. Goforth in 1894 and written on the fly-leaf of
his Bible:

" '1. Seek to give much—expect nothing. 2. Put the very best construction on the actions of others. 3. Never let a day pass without at least a quarter of an hour spent in the study of the Bible. 4. Never omit daily morning and evening private prayer and devotion. 5. In all things seek to know God's Will and when known obey at any cost. 6. Seek to cultivate a quiet prayerful spirit. 7. Seek each day to do or say something to further Christianity among the heathen.'

"That Dr. Goforth lived up to these rules there is not the least doubt. He surpassed them. His love for the Bible is well known. His Bible was always open and he took every opportunity to read it. Even after becoming blind, he had a Chinese read to him at least twelve chapters a day. His loyalty to the Bible as the Word of God and his defense of the fundamentals of the Faith have been outstanding in his career.

"He was a man of prayer and through prayer and Bible study has sought to know God's Will. It was this love for Bible reading and communion with God that gave him the power to move audiences to a conviction of sin and repentance. At all times he kept 'self' in the background and relied wholly on the power of the Holy Spirit to take of the things of Jesus and reveal them unto his hearers. 'Not by might nor by power, but by my Spirit'—'But ye shall receive power after that the Holy Ghost is come upon you'—have ever been his battle-cry. Though Dr. Goforth's preaching contained a stern denunciation of sin and would in no case tolerate compromise with sin, he has always been very tender in dealing with sinners.'

The following is but the closing part of a resolution sent to Mrs. Goforth by the Mission Council of the North Honan Mission,—the first part covering much that is included in these Memoirs, being omitted.

"Dr. Goforth was one who from early youth was devoted to the Master's service. He felt it his duty in season and out of season, in the house and by the way, to preach the Gospel. He had a great familiarity with the whole Bible, which he had read over many times in both English and Chinese. He had unbounded optimism and it took a great deal to discourage him. He was fearless in the expression of his convictions, and in condemnation of all kinds of evil. His relations with the Chinese were very intimate and he held a very deep place in their affections. He had a great faculty for

APPENDIX 357

choosing and putting to work young Christians, and he always
had a number of these accompanying him in his work among
the villages. Many of the evangelists who have labored long
in the northern field were of his choosing and training. His
faith in God and in the value of prayer was very strong. He
believed in and constantly preached the power of the Spirit
of God to convict of sin and to cleanse, and the necessity of
being filled with the Spirit for effective service. His labors
were great and effective, and now he rests from his labor, but
his works do follow him. 'He being dead, yet speaketh.'

"On behalf of the members of Mission Council, I wish to
extend to you and to your family our sympathy and love.

"Sincerely yours,
G. K. KING,
Mission Secretary."

REV. DR. W. M. ROCHESTER, Editor, *The Presbyterian Record*,
makes the following tribute: "Dr. Goforth's last day found
him in St. Andrew's Church, Wyoming, Ontario, addressing
a large congregation combining the four churches there. So
clear was his voice and with such vigor and passion did he
speak that when bidding him farewell the minister of the
church expressed to him his confidence that he was yet cap-
able of many years of service. His son, Rev. J. Fred Goforth,
confirmed this when he said he never spoke with greater
power and the congregation was deeply moved . . . and thus
peacefully ended a great missionary career, a life of exalted
aim, boldest adventure, passionate devotion, self-sacrifice, and
incessant labor. . . . He was courageous, buoyant, alert, ardent,
aggressive, humble, mirthful, and resolute. His convictions
were definite and strongly held, and the substance of these
beliefs being the need of man and the efficacy of the Gospel
to meet that need, it was no wonder that he went forth in
the power of the Most High. His surrender to God was full
and was made more and more complete as he discovered lack
in himself and was confronted by open doors of opportunity.
His one desire was to be the 'slave of Jesus Christ' at whatever cost. His energy seemed inexhaustible. He labored in
season and out of season, obeying the law of the harvest that
to reap bountifully one must sow bountifully. . . . His consecration was marked by concentration intense and steady. Above
all however was his passionate fervor and this was born
of God. He held that all things are possible to him that

believeth. His enthusiasm was quenchless. Throughout a period of impaired vision and three years of total blindness and with age creeping on, his buoyancy and zeal were wonderfully sustained as seen in his sprightly step and radiant countenance, and he did not cease from his labors. . . . Jonathan Goforth has not run in vain, nor labored in vain. Thousands in Honan and Manchuria rise up to call him blessed. Posterity will place his name high on our Church's honour roll and accord him eminence among the world's missionaries. Our Church should regard with pride his devotion and achievement and give thanks to God for such a son."

Extracts from MRS. DAVIS' notes of the Memorial Service to Dr. Goforth held in Taonan, Manchuria, November the 3rd, 1936.
. . ."There was a Memorial service held in the Taonan Church, November the 3rd, 1936. It seemed fitting that it should be so for the revival meetings were to begin the following day, and how oft in years past, has Dr. Goforth been with us in blessed revival seasons.

"PASTOR YUNG spoke of Dr. Goforth's 'victorious ministry'. He referred to the many churches established throughout this great field as the results of his efforts. Each member of these churches, he said, should with deep gratitude cherish the memory of the founder and seek to follow his example. Mr. Davis in his message referred to the remark made by one of the Chinese brethren at the time of ·Dr. Goforth's farewell service nearly two years ago,—'Elijah is leaving us, we must be Elishas and carry on his work.' We must more than ever have this as our purpose. His mantle will fall on such as like Elisha are willing to follow all the way—theirs will be the vision that sees what others miss and upon them will fall the mantle of spiritual power which clothed the founder and leader of our work.

"PASTOR CHIANG told the story of the establishing of the work in Manchuria. He spoke of his first meeting with Dr. Goforth and of the deep and lasting impression made upon him by this first contact. He said, 'I had heard of Dr. Goforth's great spiritual power. The first glance showed me a great benevolence beaming from his countenance. Dr. Goforth showed great love in his treatment of others. Coming into his presence, one always received comfort. . . As to doctrine, Dr. Goforth guarded against heresy on the one hand and against all kinds of extravagances in worship on the other. He preached the pure truth. . . . Now though he is gone to glory it seems as though we could still see his face and hear his voice in our midst. Let us not depart from his example in the work. Let us not depart from his mission policy, but let us follow on in his steps till we all come into the presence of the Lord even as he has.'

"Pastor Liu spoke of Dr. Goforth's great love both of reading and preaching the Word of God. He read the Word as though he were finding great spoil. The familiar promises and passages were precious treasure to him. He had read the Bible through seventy-three times and was still reading it. In preaching the Word, Dr. Goforth used great energy, the energy of the Sower and the Reaper. He wanted all the native preachers to give forth the message of Life in such a manner that the hearers would be impressed with its vital importance. Whether to a large or small audience he wanted the message proclaimed with a convincing force.

"Pastor Su told of an incident which was characteristic of Dr. Goforth. Once when they were travelling together by boat, Pastor Su being very tired, laid down on the little deck and went to sleep. It was cold and the following morning he woke up with a fright lest he had taken cold, but to his amazement he was quite warm and then he found that Dr. Goforth had taken off his own overcoat the evening before and placed it gently and carefully about him.

"It was a thrilling moment in the service when Mr. Davis passed the news on of how Dr. Goforth was translated and the people learned that there had been no time of illness at all. Surely his was an abundant entrance into the Kingdom of our Lord and Saviour!"

The Writer of these *Memoirs* feels that many of Dr. Goforth's friends would wish her to share some of the tributes received by her. The following are but a few culled from the hundreds received. To God alone be the glory.

Dr. J. Lovell Murray, Director, *The Canadian School of Missions:* ". . . He was greatly admired and loved by many in the School family who were personally acquainted with him, and to all the members and missionaries of the Canadian

Mission Boards he stood out as a shining example of missionary devotion, leadership, and achievement. His name will forever shine in the annals of the world missionary enterprise, both for his striking accomplishments in the planting and spreading of Christianity in China and for the inspiration which he gave to the missionary life of the home churches."

REV. DR. A. J. VINING, his old school-friend: . . . "Oh how sorry I am that we have all been so busy that we have not had time for fellowship together! Dear, noble, faithful, well-beloved friend, Jonathan. I shall be lonesome for him the rest of my days. But thank God for the Christian's hope! Whatever would we do in an hour like this if it were not for Jesus Christ—the conqueror of Death! His victory is our victory and His glory is our glory. We shall meet again very soon. . . . He is one of Canada's greatest and noblest sons. How proud I have been for more than half a century to boast of our friendship. How I loved him! Daily I have thought of him from the time he went away to China and daily I have rejoiced in his devotion and his gifts of head and heart. . . . And I shall still think of him daily and always with sincere thanksgiving to God for your dear one's beautiful, unselfish, fearless life. And my feeling towards him is shared by hundreds of thousands of Canadians and by as many more beyond the seas."

REV. A. C. SNEAD, *The Christian and Missionary Alliance:* ". . . . Oh, that the Spirit of Christ which was so fully in and upon Dr. Goforth may be manifestly in absolute control and in gracious enabling in my life and the lives of God's people everywhere!"

A FRIEND IN ENGLAND: ". . . Praise God, that when bereft of sight, he did not lose the vision of the ever-surrounding love of God. That no shadow was cast upon his witness for Christ by repining or by faith staggering. 'He looked unto Him and was radiant.' By thus triumphing through Christ, 'He being dead yet speaketh.' In that great day of His glorious appearing, how many the jewels Dr. Goforth will have to lay at Christ's feet! How the Chinese brethren will sorrow — how deep their love for their leader. How we praise God for this long, useful, wonderful life."

DR. ROBERT C. MCQUILKIN, *President, Columbia Bible College, South Carolina:* ". . . This was certainly of the Lord that he should broadcast that message of revival through the Southland. I can hear him now saying, 'your Southland.' We have never had anyone at 'Ben Lippen' who gripped the hearts of the people more than Dr. Goforth did. God surely sent Dr. Goforth and you to 'Ben Lippen' and the South. His message is bearing fruit and we shall continue to plead for revival here, to which he so faithfully called us. One of the greatest privileges of my life was the fellowship with you two at 'Ben Lippen' and on the journey to Buffalo. If I could write all my heart feels about Dr. Goforth, it would be a high tribute."

A FRIEND: ". . . I cannot be sad though I have always hoped to see him again and to feel what he always gave—a sense of the Presence of the Lord coming to us through him."

EXTRACT FROM A LETTER TO A SON: ". . . The peace and inspiration of your father's service yesterday made for me a sanctuary. The sunlight seemed to fall on everything like His benediction. Your father's life was consistently "focussed" and so consecrated that one felt to be near him, was to be near the Lord he loved intensely. There seemed to be more of triumph in the service than grief, for one felt it wrong to grieve because of what must be his joy. It was a mighty testimony of love and will leave a lasting impression and mean re-dedicated lives. . . . The grief in the faces of the Chinese men there yesterday was so poignant and there must be thousands sorrowing in China. I was wishing they could have had the comfort of that service yesterday."

FROM HIS SON PAUL: "Inexhaustible energy was characteristic of father to the last. My memories of him are as motion pictures of a man in action: defending a boy knocked down by a tough; 'taking it' from the Boxers, with blood streaming from his head to his waist, while he appealed to them to spare our lives; cutting himself on the Peitaiho rocks, to save me from drowning; climbing a mountain to get the view; going through his regular running exercises at 6 A.M. on those winter mornings in Manchuria when the water was frozen in the pitcher on the washstand; humbling the pride of Chinese scholars with his astronomical charts; preaching, without sight, to a small gathering on a Wednesday afternoon in a large church auditorium—and directing some of his most earnest words to empty pews! To me my father was a great man."

REV. DR. ROBERT A. MITCHELL, *a former colleague of North Honan:* ". . . We shall just remember Dr. Goforth as we knew him in past years, ever with the upright head and the far-away gaze. Optimism and faith showed in his very carriage. One could not wish for a better passing home than Dr. Goforth had. He did a long hard day's work and then fell asleep. For the awakening he, and we, had no doubts. . . . You have often been separated from your husband. He has gone to distant quarters about his work. Frequently he sent for you and you went to him. Now he has gone off on another journey at the Master's call. Shortly will come the word that you are to follow."

THE MOODY MONTHLY: "Mingled emotions stirred the hearts of a multitude of the Lord's children, a few weeks ago, as they read of the sudden home-going of this widely honored and beloved servant of the King, whose testimony has sounded with the clearness and sweetness of a silver bell for a full half century. . . . The hand of God was upon Goforth in a mighty way, and his ministry was almost like that of Charles G. Finney and Evan Roberts combined. . . . With characteristic sweetness and gentleness, his daily life constituted a testimony to unfailing divine grace, ripened by long years of walking with Christ in joyous fellowship. . . . What a company of redeemed ones in the Glory Land would welcome his coming up there! Our sense of loss melts away as we think of the faithful, humble warrior, worn out by long strenuous service, entering into the joy of his Lord."

DR. GEORGE W. VAN GORDER *(a son-in-law):* ". . . Father was one of my true heroes and his memory will always remain a great inspiration to me. I would have loved to have seen his face again and stood by in deep reverence and affection at his grave. He has left to us all the highest and most beautiful ideal that man can give to his loved ones and now that he has finished his course, it can truly be said of him, "Well done, good and faithful servant.' When I think of the glorious life he led, it makes me feel very unworthy and insignificant."

MR. JAMES DUTTON, *Peterborough, Ontario:* ". . . I cannot help feeling that I should express a sense of triumphant rejoicing in the life that was lived, the testimony given, and the service rendered by him. It was one of the great privileges of my life to have had the honour of knowing your husband . . . and to have been privileged to have such happy fellowship and a real benediction when he visited our home. I feel that the whole world is poorer today because of Dr. Goforth's homegoing, but at the same time I realize the rich heritage which he has left to all who profess and call themselves Christians. He knew his Lord intimately and had proved to a remarkable degree that Jesus Christ was a living, reigning, triumphant Saviour. Not only this, but he had been used of God in a remarkable manner to transmit that knowledge to thousands of others."

OUR LITTLE WAITRESS AT 'BEN LIPPEN' BIBLE CONFERENCE *(a college girl):* "Just a few days ago I learned that Dr. Goforth had gone to be with the Lord. How precious to know that he is with his Lord and Master Whose life was so manifest through him on earth. . . . It was a joy even to look at him for his radiant face was a true witness of the words 'To me to live is Christ.'"

MR. JOHN DOUGALL of *The Montreal Witness:* "What a picture Dr. Goforth presented as day by day he stood in the pulpit during the meetings in Montreal! The veteran missionary standing there before his audience with his beloved Bible in his hands, turning (approximately) to places where were the passages he was reciting from memory, as he expounded the Scriptures. It was hard to realize those open eyes were sightless, so naturally and confidently, out of long practice did he handle his Bible, so earnestly did he seem to scan the congregation or lesser and more intimate fellowship gathered about him. But in truth he saw much that was hid from multitudes that have physical sight, for he saw deeper into the Truth of God and into the hearts of men and their needs. . . . Jonathan Goforth was a great man for great was his love for God and for man, and great was his obedience to the leading of the Holy Spirit. And he was everywhere greatly beloved. When we heard of Dr. Goforth's translation only a few hours after addressing a congregation, we could only think of the joy of the meeting between the great Teacher and the disciple."

A COLLEAGUE OF EARLY YEARS IN NORTH HONAN: "I never saw Jonathan Goforth depressed as so many missionaries are occasionally. He always had such a buoyant hope, joy, and expectancy in connection with the work. Whenever one met him, one was impressed with his overflowing joy and the serenity of his life."

REV. DR. W. D. REID, *Westmount:* "And yet it was a most wonderful way to go. Just to go to sleep in this world after a great day's work and waken up in the presence of the King. It was wonderful! Just the kind of home-going Dr. Goforth would have chosen if he had had the choice. I remember him telling me that was the way he wanted to go."

REV. DR. W. HARVEY GRANT, *Changte, Honan, China:* ". . . The devotion of Dr. Goforth in North Honan shall always be remembered with thanksgiving to God that He used him to lead so many to Christ of whom scores rise up today to call him 'blessed,' for no other has surpassed him in his devotion to the evangelization of North Honan. Dr. Goforth's tireless devotion in preaching the Gospel, his loyalty to God's word, his constant optimism, his steadfast faith and his habitual fishing for men, were all emphasized as being an inspiration to us who remain in service here."

HIS DAUGHTER RUTH, *(Mrs. D. I. Jeffrey, Saigon, Indo-China):* . . . "After the first shock of receiving your cable, I can only think of the glory part of Father's going. He was *always* steadfast, unmovable, and *always* abounding in the work of the Lord. God has simply promoted him to higher service. His Board down here had just retired him, he had finished his course, at last the glorious moment had come to which father had looked forward with such expectation, he has been ushered into the Presence of the King of kings, whom he loved so supremely and served so faithfully. There is nothing but glory then, in the thought of father's abundant entrance into the home above."